Canine Practice

THE BARONY COLLEGE

The *In Practice* Handbooks Series

Series Editor: Edward Boden

Past and present members of *In Practice* Editorial Board

Professor J. Armour, Chairman 1979–1989,
Dean, Veterinary Faculty, University of Glasgow

P.B. Clarke
Professor L.B. Jeffcott
J. Richardson
S.A. Hall
Professor M.J. Clarkson
Dr W.M. Allen
B. Martin
K. Urquhart
Dr P.G. Darke
S.D. Gunn
I. Baker
A. Duncan
Professor G.B. Edwards

Titles in print:
Feline Practice
Canine Practice
Equine Practice

Forthcoming titles:
Bovine Practice
Sheep and Goat Practice
Swine Practice

The *In Practice* Handbooks

Canine Practice

Edited by E. Boden
Executive Editor, *In Practice*

Baillière Tindall

LONDON   PHILADELPHIA   TORONTO   SYDNEY   TOKYO

Baillière Tindall   24–28 Oval Road
W.B. Saunders   London NW1 7DX

The Curtis Center
Independence Square West
Philadelphia, PA 19106–3399, USA

55 Horner Avenue
Toronto, Ontario M8Z 4X6, Canada

Harcourt Brace Jovanovich Group
(Australia) Pty Ltd
30–52 Smidmore Street
Marrickville
NSW 2204, Australia

Harcourt Brace Jovanovich Japan Inc
Ichibancho Central Building,
22–1 Ichibancho
Chiyoda-ku, Tokyo 102, Japan

© 1991 Baillière Tindall

Typeset by Photo·graphics, Honiton, Devon
Printed and bound in Hong Kong by Dah Hua Printing Press Co., Ltd.

A catalogue record for this book is available from the British Library

ISBN 0–7020–1522–9

Contents

Contributors

W.E. Allen, Senior Lecturer in Animal Reproduction, Department of Veterinary Surgery and Obstetrics, Royal Veterinary College, University of London, London, UK.

P.G.C. Bedford, Reader in Veterinary Ophthalmology, Department of Veterinary Surgery and Obstetrics, Royal Veterinary College, University of London, London, UK.

D. Bennett, Senior Lecturer, Faculty of Veterinary Clinical Science, Small Animal Studies Division, University of Liverpool, Liverpool, UK.

A. Blunden, Pathology Unit, Animal Health Trust, Newmarket, Suffolk, UK.

S. Crispin, Lecturer in Veterinary Surgery, School of Veterinary Science, University of Bristol, Bristol, UK.

G.C.W. England, Department of Surgery and Obstetrics, Royal Veterinary College, University of London, London, UK.

D. Grant, RSPCA, Sir Harold Harmsworth Memorial Animal Hospital, London, UK.

M. Herrtage, Department of Clinical Veterinary Medicine, University of Cambridge, Cambridge, UK.

P. Holt, Lecturer in Veterinary Surgery, School of Veterinary Science, University of Bristol, Bristol, UK.

D. Jacobs, Professor of Veterinary Parasitology, Department of Veterinary Pathology, Royal Veterinary College, University of London, London, UK.

G.C. Skerritt, Lecturer in Veterinary Anatomy, Department of Veterinary Preclinical Sciences, Division of Veterinary Anatomy, University of Liverpool, Liverpool, UK.

M. Stockman, Riversdale, Stour Provost, Gillingham, Dorset, UK.

M. Sullivan, Department of Veterinary Surgery, Glasgow University Veterinary School, Glasgow, UK.

S. Wheeler, Assistant Professor of Neurology, Department of Companion Animal and Special Species Medicine, College of Veterinary Medicine, North Carolina State University, USA.

E. Williams (née Carr), Department of Clinical Veterinary Medicine, University of Cambridge, Cambridge, UK.

J.A. Wright, Safety of Medicines Department, ICI Plc, Pharmaceuticals Division, Macclesfield, Cheshire, UK.

Foreword

In Practice was started in 1979 as a clinical supplement to *The Veterinary Record*. Its carefully chosen, highly illustrated articles specially commissioned from leaders in their field were aimed specifically at the practitioner. They have proved extremely popular with experienced veterinarians and students alike. The editorial board, chaired for the first 10 years by Professor James Armour, was particularly concerned to emphasize differential diagnosis.

In response to consistent demand, articles from *In Practice*, updated and revised by the authors, are now published in convenient handbook form. Each book deals with a particular species or group of related animals.

E. Boden

CHAPTER 1

Canine Epilepsy

GEOFF SKERRITT

INTRODUCTION

Although it is not possible to put an accurate figure on the incidence of fits in dogs, it is well recognized that it is a frequent reason for seeking veterinary attention. The condition is often diagnosed as epilepsy and anticonvulsant therapy is commenced with dosages determined largely by trial and error.

The term epilepsy refers to a condition of recurrent fits which arise from non-progressive intracranial disease and should not be reserved for idiopathic (true, primary or inherited) epilepsy. A fit (seizure or ictus) is a paroxysmal disorder of the central nervous system appearing suddenly out of normality and disappearing with equal speed. There are four typical phases:

(1)   A period of mild behavioural change lasting for hours or days just before a fit, known as the *prodromal phase*.
(2)   The aura which is very short, usually lasting a few seconds, is characterized by a more pronounced behavioural change immediately preceding the onset of a seizure.
(3)   The actual *fit* which in most cases lasts only for 30 s to two min, although it may seem longer to an anxious owner.

(4)   The *post-ictal phase* which is usually a period of hours in which the animal seems disorientated and may appear blind, hungry, thirsty, affectionate or restless.

THE PATHOGENESIS OF SEIZURES

The nervous system functions by the production and propagation of electrical charges. The actual release of these electrical discharges by neurons is carefully controlled through an interaction between excitatory and inhibitory neurotransmitters, and normally occurs only at a frequency and amplitude to mediate normal sensory and motor activity (Fig. 1.1).

The potential for seizure activity exists when the excitability of a group of neurons is increased. Although the precise mechanism of epileptogenesis is not known, it is possible that factors such as an increase in excitatory neurotransmitter, a decrease in inhibitory neurotransmitter or a disturbance of cellular metabolism may all be involved.

Often the onset of seizure activity can be correlated with the occurrence of an identifiable trigger, e.g. specific sounds, flashing lights, television or drugs, although the actual manner in which they disorganize the control mechanisms is not understood.

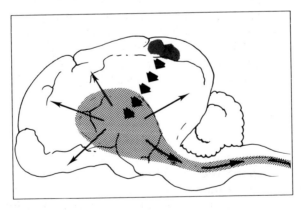

Fig. 1.1
Electrical discharge from a primary epileptogenic focus in a cerebral hemisphere.

CLASSIFICATION OF SEIZURES

The seizures occurring in canine epilepsy can be classified as either generalized or partial. The distinction is important as the two types have different aetiologies, clinical signs, electroencephalographic recordings, prognosis and, sometimes, treatment, quite apart from a different significance for breeding. The essential difference between these two types is that generalized seizures involve symmetrical activity of the whole body, whereas partial seizures are characterized by localized signs restricted to one region of the body. In dogs partial onset seizures often undergo secondary generalization as the electrical discharge is propagated through the brain.

GENERALIZED SEIZURES

GRAND MAL

The classical picture of the sudden onset of extensive convulsive motor activity is well known and referred to as a grand mal seizure. In dogs the seizure usually lasts for 30 s to 2 min and manifests itself as tonic/clonic (paddling) movements of the limbs, muscle tremors, jaw movements, salivation, urination, and defecation. This type of seizure may occur as a result of metabolic, toxic or inflammatory conditions. In fact there are many possible extracranial causes of grand mal seizures in dogs, e.g. hepatoencephalopathy, hypoglycaemia and lead poisoning. The intracranial causes of grand mal seizures in dogs include encephalitis, hydrocephalus and storage diseases, although the most common reason for their occurrence is idiopathic (true, or inherited) epilepsy.

PETIT MAL

A second type of generalized seizure is occasionally seen in dogs. This is the petit mal, or absence, seizure seen much more commonly in human beings. Petit mal seizures are characterized by a very brief loss of consciousness, often so short that the dog does not actually collapse. Usually a 30–60 s period of head nodding during the aura is a feature of petit mal seizures in dogs. This type of seizure gives a very characteristic spike and wave pattern on the electroencephalogram.

PARTIAL SEIZURES

Focal lesions within the cerebrum often result in episodic clinical signs that are related to the specific region of the brain involved. The partial seizure may consist of abnormal activity in an isolated group of muscles or an episode of abnormal behaviour. The focal lesion consists of cells which have become susceptible to exciting stimuli or triggers. Partial seizures, therefore, are an acquired condition and may be due to brain trauma at birth, neonatal hypoxia, post natal intracranial trauma, encephalitis, neoplasia, etc. The seizures may not appear until weeks, months, or even up to 2 years after the epileptogenic focus was acquired.

PSYCHOMOTOR SEIZURE

If the focus is in the portion of the brain belonging to the limbic system, e.g. the temporal lobe of the cerebral cortex, the seizure will consist of a period of altered behaviour accompanied by complex motor activity. This type of seizure is called a psychomotor seizure and may appear as recurrent episodes of bizarre behaviour such as hysteria, fly biting, tail chasing, flank-sucking, licking or aggression. Often the localizing sign of partial epilepsy is just a precursor to rapid secondary generalization, although the behavioural signs of psychomotor epilepsy tend to be of longer duration than motor signs.

JACKSONIAN EPILEPSY

This is very rare in animals. It is characterized by a slowly moving tonic spasm that spreads proximally up an appendage and may gradually extend to other limbs. The focus in Jacksonian epilepsy is in the very specific primary motor cortex and may be removable surgically.

DIFFERENTIAL DIAGNOSIS OF SEIZURES

HISTORY

Typical short duration seizures are rarely witnessed by the veterinarian and reliance for an accurate description of the clinical picture must be placed on the owner. In particular it is important to try and establish whether there are any localizing signs to indicate that the condition is acquired. Owners should be questioned carefully about possible head trauma up to 2 years previously, the earlier occurrence of any febrile illness, possible exposure to toxins and the diet.

PHYSICAL EXAMINATION

A physical examination may reveal evidence of extracranial diseases which are secondarily affecting the brain. A neurological examination may reveal neurological deficits suggestive of an intracranial lesion. It would be unusual for seizure activity to be the first clinical sign of a tumour in the central nervous system.

LABORATORY TESTS

Tests should be carried out in all cases of canine epilepsy not only to assist in diagnosis but also to give a baseline for serum liver enzymes in anticipation of chronic anticonvulsant therapy. Routine haematology and estimations of serum calcium, blood glucose and blood urea may help to exclude extracranial causes of epilepsy.

CSF TAP

An evaluation of cerebrospinal fluid may be helpful where an intracranial disturbance is suspected. An increase in CSF pressure beyond 170 mg H_2O in dogs is suggestive of neoplasia or cerebral oedema. Increases in numbers of blood cells and protein in CSF are indicative of lesions in the central nervous system.

RADIOGRAPHY

Except when the lesion involves the skull, e.g. hydrocephalus, trauma or neoplasia, radiography is of limited value in differential diagnosis.

ELECTROENCEPHALOGRAPHY

This should be considered as an additional diagnostic aid in a small proportion of cases. It should not be regarded as an essential procedure since the results are often disappointing, abnormal recordings rarely being obtained except in the presence of gross structural lesions.

IDIOPATHIC (INHERITED) EPILEPSY

If the results of physical, neurological, haematological and blood biochemical examinations are normal, a diagnosis of idiopathic epilepsy should be considered.

There is good evidence that generalized epilepsy can be inherited in dogs. Surveys, trial matings and pedigree studies have indicated inheritance of epilepsy in the German shepherd, keeshond and beagle. In addition there are a number of other breeds, e.g. golden retrievers, miniature poodles, cocker spaniels and Saint Bernards, in which inheritance of epilepsy is strongly suggested.

During the interictal period, affected dogs seem perfectly normal and there is no haematological or blood biochemical abnormality in these cases; at post-mortem examination no histopathological lesions are detected and the abnormality is thought rather to be a biochemical defect. The seizures of idiopathic epilepsy commence at 1–3 years of age, although occasional cases have their first seizure as early as 6 months old or as late as 6 years.

The seizures of idiopathic epilepsy are typical generalized seizures lasting from 30 s to 2 min. Usually they occur when the dog is asleep or resting and so commonly this is at night. Many owners recognize a prodromal phase when the dog is particularly affectionate or restless; this may be only minutes in duration or as long as 24–48 h. During the post-ictal phase most dogs are disorientated and ataxic for a period of minutes to hours. Owners often report that a voracious appetite, sleep and excitement follow a seizure.

ANTICONVULSANT THERAPY

LOOK FOR AN EXTRACRANIAL CAUSE

If an underlying cause of epilepsy has been identified, therapy should be directed towards that disorder rather than routine use of anticonvulsant drugs. The indications for commencement of anticonvulsant therapy should be as follows:

(1) Any dog having seizures at a greater frequency than once every 6 weeks.
(2) Any dog having clusters of seizures more than once every 8 weeks.
(3) Any dog having recurrent seizures which are accompanied by aggression.
(4) Any dog in which the seizures, although infrequent, are severe, generalized and concern the owner.

Anticonvulsant therapy should not be started in a dog that has experienced an isolated seizure.

TRY TO AVOID SIDE EFFECTS

Anticonvulsant therapy should achieve control of the seizures while avoiding any systemic or neurologic toxicity. Control may not necessarily mean complete elimination of seizures; a 100% increase in the interictal period or a lessened severity of the seizures may be regarded as successful therapy.

TRY TO KEEP TO ONE DRUG

Control is ideally achieved by monotherapy since it is now recognized that polytherapy increases the likelihood of adverse drug interactions, while not necessarily giving an additive therapeutic effect.

AVOID PHENOTHIAZINES

Phenothiazine tranquillizers, such as acetylpromazine should not be given to epileptics as they can actually stimulate seizures. When changing from one anticonvulsant drug to another it may be necessary to have a period of overlap in therapy as the abrupt cessation of any anticonvulsant may result in seizure activity. During the changeover it is best to withdraw the drug gradually, reducing the dose by no more than 50% every 7 days.

TRY PHENOBARBITONE, PRIMIDONE OR PHENYTOIN

The choice of anticonvulsant drug must take account of efficacy, side effects, cost, ease of administration and possible toxicity. Currently the anticonvulsants most used in dogs are phenobarbitone, primidone and phenytoin (diphenyl-hydantoin). Recent evidence suggests that phenobarbitone is as effective as any other agent, much less expensive, but variably absorbed. Carbamazepine and sodium valproate are anticonvulsant drugs that are used in human beings but not yet properly evaluated in dogs. Diazepam is not very effective as an oral anticonvulsant drug in dogs because its absorption from the gastrointestinal tract is rather irregular and its half-life is only 3.2 min. Table 1.1 compares the three most commonly used anticonvulsant drugs in dogs.

The effectiveness of any oral anticonvulsant drug is related to its half-life, time taken to reach peak concentration after administration and the period required to reach a steady serum level. Liver enzyme systems are developed over the first few weeks of therapy to metabolize the anticonvulsant drug. The serum level of the drug therefore gradually decreases during the initial period, and changes in the dosage regime required may be necessary. The half-life of the drug determines the frequency of administration required. The only real guide

Table 1.1 Comparison of most commonly used anticonvulsant drugs.

Anti-convulsant drug	Recommended dosage	Effective serum level	Toxicity and side effects	Comments
Phenobarbitone	1–5 mg/kg daily in one or two doses	10–40 μg/ml	Sedation. Polydypsia. Elevated serum liver enzymes. Behavioural changes.	An effective and inexpensive anticonvulsant. Some suggestion that it aggravates psychomotor seizures
Primidone	50 mg/kg daily in three divided doses	15–40 μg/ml (of phenobarbitone)	Sedation. Paradoxical hyperactivity. Polydypsia. Elevated serum liver enzymes. Behavioural changes (e.g. aggression)	Phenobarbitone is one of three metabolites and is probably responsible for 80% of anticonvulsant activity. Effective but more expensive and more toxic than phenobarbitone
Phenytoin	35 mg/kg every 8 h	10–20 μg/ml	No real side effects. Toxicity does occur when chloramphenicol given concurrently	The short half-life of this drug in the dog makes it difficult to obtain therapeutic serum levels

to dosage in an individual animal is provided by assessment of serum levels of the drug.

REASONS FOR FAILURE OF ANTICONVULSANT THERAPY

The usual reasons for the apparent failure of anticonvulsant therapy are:

(1)   The owner does not fully comply with instructions on regular administration of drug.
(2)   The dose of anticonvulsant is inadequate either in daily total or in frequency of administration.
(3)   Tolerance to a drug may be developed.
(4)   Concurrent systemic disease may affect the absorption of the drug if there is vomiting or diarrhoea.
(5)   The underlying cause of epilepsy may not have been correctly diagnosed.
(6)   Some individual dogs, especially some German shepherds, keeshonds and Irish setters, do not respond whatever therapy is used.

PROGNOSIS IN CANINE EPILEPSY

Except in cases of progressive intracranial disease, the prognosis for acquired epilepsy is better than for idiopathic epilepsy. In about 60–70% of all cases of epilepsy a reasonable measure of control of the seizures should be achieved by proper, monitored anticonvulsant therapy. In a significant proportion of cases, once control has been maintained for 4–6 months, the dose of drug can be gradually reduced and may even be eventually stopped altogether.

CHAPTER 2

Primary Lens Luxation

PETER G. C. BEDFORD

INTRODUCTION

A combination of sudden onset pain, marked episcleral and, or, conjunctival congestion and corneal oedema should dictate a diagnosis of secondary glaucoma due to primary lens luxation in the young to middle-aged terrier patient. Should the clinician not see the luxated lens or its associated features, then he should look again and again before considering the alternative diagnoses of conjunctivitis, keratitis or uveitis. Unfortunately the condition is often misdiagnosed and the institution of medical therapy in the face of a surgical emergency in which sight is at risk can be of no value. The condition is known, the aetiology is understood and the surgery is very successful. As such the prognosis for each and every patient should be good, but diagnosis and speed of treatment are essential if that prognosis is to be realized.

THE CONDITION

The lens is normally held in position against the posterior surface of the iris on the visual axis by a suspensory ligament or zonule and by attachment of its posterior capsule to the vitreous body. The posterior convexity of the lens is seated into a shallow concave depression in the anterior face of the vitreous called the patella fossa, and the fibres of the suspensory ligament radiate in an almost sheet-like fashion from the zonular lamella at the lens equator to the ciliary processes. Actual insertion of the fibres is at the level of the basement membrane material of the non-pigmented epithelium covering these processes.

Lens luxation is the displacement of the lens from the patella fossa, movement only being possible as a result of total breakdown of the suspensory ligament. The term "subluxation" is used to denote the early part of the luxation process, when partial displacement is caused by incomplete breakdown of the suspensory ligament. A subluxated lens is seen behind the pupil, but a luxated lens may occupy one of three positions (Fig. 2.1). It might remain behind the iris in the vitreous cavity (A), move into the pupil (B) or be displaced into the anterior chamber (C).

Lens luxation may occur as an unusual congenital defect in the dog, as a primary condition in several breeds or secondary to glaucoma, cataract formation and ocular trauma. It is as a primary condition that it is seen most frequently in the United Kingdom, there being a marked predisposition in the terrier types of dog. It is the Jack Russell terrier which is currently most commonly involved, but lens luxation also occurs in the wirehaired and smoothhaired fox terriers, the Sealyham terrier, the Lakeland terrier, the Welsh terrier and the miniature bull terrier. There is also a marked incidence in the Tibetan terrier (despite its name, not a true terrier) (Willis *et al.*, 1979; Curtis, 1983), and the Border collie has recently been added to the list of affected breeds (Foster *et al.*, 1986). Primary lens luxation occurs in young and middle aged dogs (age range 3–7 years). There is no sex differential and the inherent defect is believed to be a structural deficiency of the suspensory ligament (Curtis, 1983; Curtis *et al.*, 1983). There may be an abnormal arrangement of the zonular fibres overlying the ciliary processes. Individual fibres break down along their length rather than at their points of origin or insertion, a process that usually starts in the dorsolateral quadrant of the ligament. Work with the Tibetan terrier breed has indicated most strongly that the zonular defect is inherited as a recessive trait

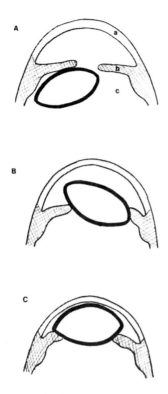

Fig. 2.1 The luxated lens may occupy one of three positions. A, remain behind the vitreous cavity; B, move into the pupil, or C, be displaced into the anterior chamber. (a, cornea; b, iris; c, vitreous).

(Willis *et al.*, 1979) and it is assumed that this mode of inheritance applies to the other breeds. The fluctuant nature of intraocular pressure in the true terrier breeds may also be involved in the aetiology of the condition, the stretching and relaxing effect upon a deficient suspensory ligament possibly enhancing the process of breakdown (Bedford, 1980).

Approximately 90% of primary luxated lenses dislocate forwards through the pupil into the anterior chamber. The lens may occasionally lodge in the pupil, and the rest remain behind the iris. Invariably there is vitreous attachment to the displaced lens and, with an anterior luxation, this material may help block the forward flow of aqueous through the pupil, or impair aqueous drainage through the iridocorneal angle. Pupillary block results in forward displacement of the iris, a physiological iris bombé, and closure of the drainage angle. The net result of the block and closure of the drainage angle is acute secondary glaucoma. Emergency lens extraction is necessary to reduce the intraocular pressure and prevent optic nerve and retinal damage.

Displacement of the lens will also be seen with other diseases. It may accompany an established glaucoma (Fig. 2.2), the suspensory ligament being broken down totally or in part as a function of the induced globe enlargement. Whereas lens extraction is the essential treatment for glaucoma caused by primary lens luxation, it is of no value in patients with precursory glaucoma. Lens luxation may accompany cataract formation particularly in patients in which the cataract is a secondary feature to progressive retinal atrophy, and displacement of the lens might accompany gross traumatic ocular damage (Fig. 2.3).

DIAGNOSIS

Primary lens luxation occurs spontaneously without any evidence of antecedent ocular disease. It has been postulated that terrier life style and local trauma go hand in hand, but rather than cause the luxation, local trauma might accelerate the process of deficient suspensory ligament breakdown. The condition is bilateral, but the time lag between luxation in the first and second eyes ranges from a few hours to many months. Owners must be warned about likely involvement of the second eye, for speed in diagnosis is essential for effective treatment. Breed and age are important factors, but primary angle closure glaucoma also occasionally occurs in the terrier group and gonioscopy of the normotensive eye might prove essential in differential diagnosis. Examination in a darkened room, using a bright light source should reveal several clinical signs and both eyes should always be examined.

The two early features of lens subluxation are the presence of vitreous material in the pupil and iridodonesis. At this stage the eye would be normotensive and features of secondary glaucoma would not be present. As the zonular fibres break down, vitreous can escape through the defects in the suspensory ligament and this material is seen as white wisps lying

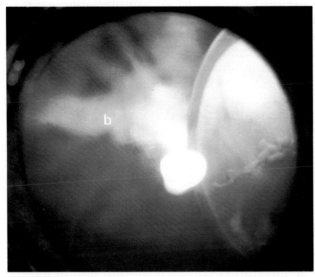

Fig. 2.2 Lens luxation secondary to glaucoma in the right eye of a 9-year-old Samoyed. The lens has luxated medially. a, Lens, b, Fundus viewed through the vitreous.

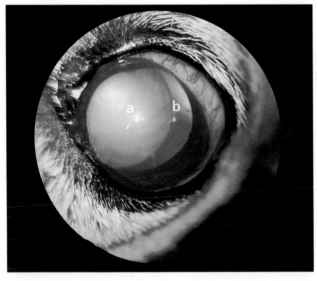

Fig. 2.3 Subluxation of a cataractous lens in the left eye of a 12-year-old crossbred. The cataract has subluxated medially. a, Lens, b, An aphakic crescent.

on the anterior lens capsule, at the pupillary margin (Fig. 2.4).
A mydriatic should always be used to expose more of the
prolapsed vitreous material and, occasionally, the zonular
defects themselves may be seen. Iridodonesis is the term used
to describe the trembling movement of the iris as it loses its
support from contact with the subluxating lens. This movement
is pathognomonic for the condition and is best seen where
the eye moves rapidly or the patient's muzzle is gently tapped.

As the degree of subluxation increases, other features may
be seen. The pupil may become irregular and that part of the
iris which has lost the support of the lens may flatten or fall
back against the vitreous to increase the depth of the anterior
chamber in that area. Conversely, where there is increased
iris/lens contact in the path of the luxation, the iris segment
may bulge forwards to reduce the associated anterior chamber
depth. These features are perhaps best appreciated by looking
across the plane of the iris surface from the side and above.
Where the dislocation will be posterior, part of the equator of
the subluxating lens may appear within the pupillary aperture.
The space between the edge of the pupil and the lens equator

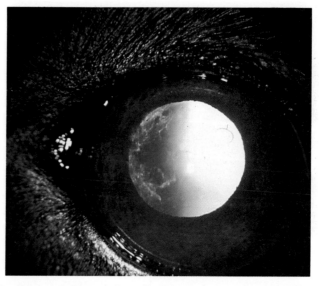

Fig. 2.4 Early subluxation in the left eye of a 5-year-old crossbred terrier. Loose vitreous material is seen within the medial margin of the pupil.

is crescentic, and this feature is referred to as an aphakic crescent (Fig. 2.5).

In a minority of patients there is evidence of increased intraocular pressure during the subluxation process. This is probably caused by the presence of vitreous within the pupil blocking aqueous movement, or occlusion of the entrance to the drainage angle and the ciliary cleft by vitreous. Undoubtedly there is hydration of the vitreous body once its anterior face has been damaged, the swollen vitreous expanding forwards into the pupil and anterior chamber.

The lens can remain lying against the anterior face of the vitreous for a variable period of time, but eventually it will either displace anteriorly into or through the pupil or remain in the vitreous cavity. When posterior luxation occurs, the whole iris plane falls backwards. The anterior chamber thus deepens throughout and, because the eye usually stays normotensive, the pupil usually remains responsive to light. The luxated lens occupies the anterior and ventral parts of the vitreous cavity and ultimately may become cataractous. Glaucoma can occur if the lens subsequently displaces forwards

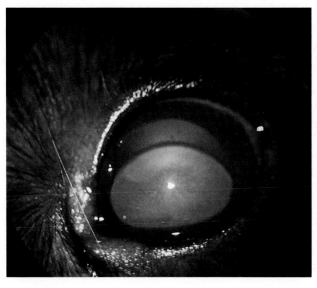

Fig. 2.5 Aphakic crescent in the right eye of a 4½-year-old crossbred terrier. A crescentic dark green space is seen between the upper lens equator and the margin of the dorsal pupil.

or vitreous movement blocks the pupil to forward aqueous flow.

Occasionally a luxated lens will lodge in the pupil, the whole lens/iris diaphragm being displaced forwards by the increasing aqueous volume behind it. The anterior chamber becomes shallow as the result of the physiological iris bombé, and the drainage angle and ciliary cleft close to produce a secondary glaucoma.

A lens which passes into the anterior chamber usually takes a variable amount of vitreous attachment with it. In the vast majority of patients there is a pupillary block, with closure of the drainage angle and ciliary cleft producing an acute glaucoma. The presence of loose vitreous material in the anterior chamber may physically occlude the entrance to the ciliary cleft and contribute to overall impaired aqueous drainage from the anterior chamber. The usual features of the glaucoma are pain, as witnessed by excessive lacrimation, blepharospasm and apparent photophobia, loss of sight, episcleral venous congestion and diffuse corneal oedema. In the absence of oedema or where the eye remains normotensive, the luxated lens can be seen clearly in the anterior chamber (Fig. 2.6). The equator shines as the result of the internal reflection of light and the iris is depressed posteriorly to accommodate the posterior convexity of the lens (Fig. 2.7). Contact of the lens with the corneal endothelium produces a diffuse, subcentral opacity, a lesion which usually persists even after lens extraction.

The companion eye is usually normotensive, but it must always be examined carefully for the early signs of lens subluxation. The existence of displacing vitreous material may require dilation of the pupil, and iridodonesis is variable, being obvious one day and inapparent the next. Gonioscopy is an important part of the examination, the presence of a narrowed drainage angle with or without apparent pectinate ligament anomaly being the essential differential feature between primary glaucoma with secondary lens luxation and primary lens luxation.

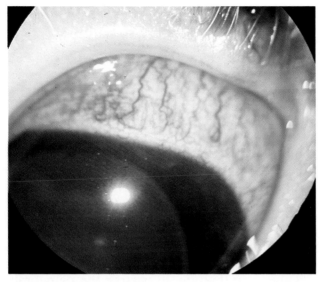

Fig. 2.6 Secondary glaucoma caused by anterior lens luxation in the left eye of a 4-year-old Sealyham terrier. There is marked episcleral congestion and the lens is seen in the anterior chamber. The anterior surface of the iris is dished backwards by the posterior lens capsule.

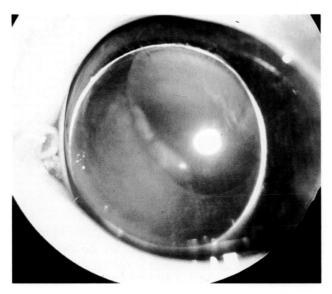

Fig. 2.7 Anterior lens luxation in the left eye of a 4-year-old Jack Russell terrier with no glaucoma. The lens equator is seen reflecting light internally and the anterior face of the iris is dished backwards.

TREATMENT

Awareness of primary lens luxation is essential if therapy is
to be effective in terms of relieving the effect of the secondary
glaucoma. The diagnosis must always be considered in any
young or middle-aged terrier presenting with bulbar conjunctival and, or, episcleral congestion, corneal oedema and pain.
The glaucoma must be relieved by emergency lens extraction
surgery, and time must not be wasted by using the traditional
medical therapies. Intravenous mannitol (1 g/kg bodyweight),
an hyperosmotic agent, will effectively reduce intraocular
pressure and is a useful adjunct to surgery in that venous
congestion is partially relieved and the hydrated, enlarged
vitreous body will be reduced in size.

The displaced lens may be removed through a clear corneal
section or a corneoscleral (limbal) section beneath a conjunctival flap. Lateral canthotomy to enlarge the palpebral fissure
and the use of a wire eyelid speculum allow good exposure
of the dorsal limbus, and the globe is fixed in position using
conjunctival stay sutures or haemostats applied to the limbal
conjunctiva (Fig. 2.8). For a corneal section the globe is
manipulated by holding the bulbar conjunctiva with forceps
and a number 64 Beaver blade is used to create a non-
penetrating groove through the corneal epithelium and
anterior stroma just anterior to the limbus from the 9 o'clock
to the 3 o'clock positions. Two sutures can be preplaced
towards the ends of this incision and the anterior chamber is
then opened at one end of the groove using a keratome or a
number 11 scalpel blade. Aqueous is always lost, and as the
section is completed using curved corneal scissors, care is
required to avoid damaging the anterior iris. Vitreous material
may appear through the keratomy wound to complicate the
completion of the section.

Alternatively the anterior chamber may be entered by a
corneoscleral section (Fig. 2.9). The bulbar conjunctiva is
incised 3 mm behind the limbus, the length of the incision
stretching from the 9 o'clock to the 3 o'clock position. The
conjunctiva is then undermined to its scleral attachment at
the limbus, incisions at right angles to the limbus at the ends
of the conjunctival wound allowing the conjunctival strip
produced to be raised as a limbal based flap and laid over the

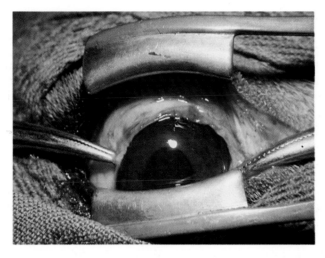

Fig. 2.8 A lateral canthotomy has been completed, the globe is stabilized with haemostats placed on the bulbar conjunctiva, the palpebral fissure is held using an eyelid speculum and the bulbar conjunctiva has been sectioned.

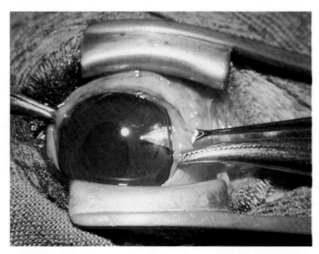

Fig. 2.9 The anterior chamber has been entered using a keratome placed through corneoscleral tissue, beneath the conjunctival flap.

cornea. This exposes the sclera at the limbus, and the anterior chamber is entered using a keratome or a number 11 scalpel blade. The corneoscleral section is then completed with curved corneal scissors (Fig. 2.10), the length of the incision stretching

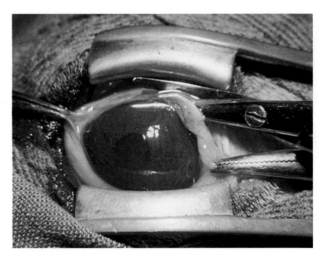

Fig. 2.10 The corneoscleral section is being completed using curved corneal scissors.

from the 9 o'clock to the 3 o'clock positions (Fig. 2.11). Again, care is essential to avoid damaging the anterior iris, and potential vitreous herniation through the wound will similarly complicate the completion of the section. The lens is dislocated from the anterior chamber by applying vectus loop pressure to the ventral limbus, and invariably vitreous material attached to the lens must be dissected free (Fig. 2.12). Very occasionally the lens is not attached to vitreous material, and vitreous loss will be minimal. Infrequently the anteriorly luxated lens will slip backwards through the pupil complicating the extraction procedure. It is important that the vitreous loss is kept to a minimum for vitreous material is never reformed and its bulk is essential in maintaining retinal attachment. Postoperative retinal detachment occasionally occurs following successful surgery, but it is more likely to be a complication of removal of a considerable amount of vitreous in those eyes where it was necessary to allow closure of the corneal or corneoscleral sections. Both types of section are closed with several interrupted 8×0 to 10×0 absorbable or nylon sutures, the conjunctival wound being similarly repaired where a corneoscleral section has been used. The suture material should not enter the anterior chamber, but be placed between Descemet's membrane and mid corneal stroma. It is essential that a suaged-on spatulate needle is used, the tissue being entered

Fig. 2.11 The anterior chamber has been entered from 9 o'clock to 3 o'clock, and the section is being held open using rat toothed forceps applied to the conjunctival flap.

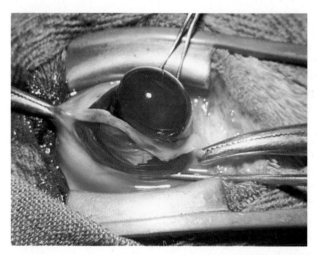

Fig. 2.12 The displaced lens is removed using vectus pressure against the lower cornea. A second vectus is being used to guide the lens over the iris surface.

1 mm away from the edge of the wound. The anterior chamber should be reformed before the final corneal or corneoscleral suture is tied, and Balanced Salt Solution (Alcon Laboratories), physiological saline or a bubble of air can be used. The lateral

canthotomy is closed and a depot corticosteroid preparation may be injected subconjunctivally to help to control any post operative uveitis. Topical antibiotics and corticosteroids are used routinely, and systemic corticosteroid together with topical atropine or tropicamide may be used if there is a marked uveitic response to the surgery.

Early lens extraction is successful in relieving the secondary glaucoma in most patients (Fig. 2.13), but in those in which time lapse has allowed extensive peripheral anterior and ciliary synechiae to form other treatment for glaucoma may be necessary. Uveitis, corneal oedema, endothelial scarring, hyphaemia, infection and wound breakdown are all possible post operative complications.

In lens luxation the presence of secondary glaucoma is a clear indication for surgery but opinions vary as to the correct therapeutic approach for subluxation and posteriorly luxated

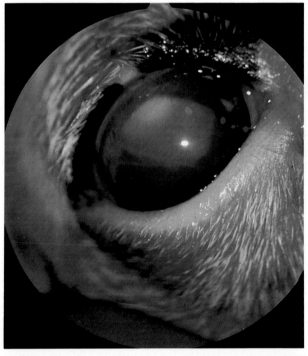

Fig. 2.13 Three weeks after lens extraction from the right eye of a Jack Russell terrier. Details of the fundus can be seen through a regular mobile pupil.

lenses in a normotensive eye. Removal is advocated by those who consider that secondary glaucoma is inevitable, and that the eye will benefit more completely from surgery completed before there is any induced optic nerve and retinal damage. Attempted medical therapy relies upon an ability to induce and maintain miosis such that the lens luxates "safely" into the vitreous cavity. Such treatment also necessitates a guarantee that once in the vitreous cavity the lens will remain there indefinitely, and considerable reliance is placed upon the owner's ability to detect subsequent movement of the lens. Of course, medical therapy avoids the practical difficulties of surgery but, on balance, the surgical approach offers the better prognosis.

Where lens luxation is secondary to glaucoma, appropriate glaucoma therapy should be instituted. This may require angle bypass surgery in the potentially sighted eye, or medical hypotensive therapy to render the irreversibly blind eye comfortable and to prevent further globe enlargement. Patients with displacement of the lens associated with gross ocular trauma or cataract formation may only require lens extraction if an attendant glaucoma is to be controlled.

REFERENCES

Bedford, P. G. C. (1980) *Veterinary Record* **107**, 76.
Curtis, R. (1983) *Journal of Comparative Pathology* **93**, 151.
Curtis, R., Barnett, K. C. & Lewis, S. J. (1983) *Veterinary Record* **112**, 238.
Foster, S. J., Curtis, R. & Barnett, K. C. (1986) *Journal of Small Animal Practice* **27**, 1.
Willis, M. B., Curtis, R., Barnett, K. C. & Tempest, W. M. (1979) *Veterinary Record* **104**, 409.

CHAPTER 3

Nasolacrimal Cannulation

SHEILA CRISPIN

INTRODUCTION

The nasolacrimal drainage apparatus can be delineated by dacryocystorhinography. It consists of an upper and lower lacrimal punctum located near the lid margin close to the medial canthus. Tears pass from the puncta via upper and lower canaliculi to the nasolacrimal duct which terminates, usually within the nose, at the nasal ostium. The canaliculi join in the fossa of the lacrimal bone and there is no distinct lacrimal sac. The nasolacrimal duct passes through the lacrimal canal of the lacrimal bone and maxilla and, in a proportion of dogs, it is incomplete medially at the level of the canine tooth. The duct terminates at the nasal ostium which, in mesocephalic and dolichocephalic dogs, is usually located on the ventrolateral floor of the nasal vestibule below the alar fold. In some animals there is a cul-de-sac in the duct beyond the nasal ostium.

In brachycephalic dogs the duct system is shorter and wider and the location of the distal ostium is more variable, for example, within the posterior nasal cavity, or even within the oral cavity (similar variation is found in cats). In all breeds of dog it is difficult, often impossible, to visualize the nasal ostium, so that investigations of the drainage apparatus commence at the lacrimal puncta.

CANNULATION

Cannulation is but one aspect of investigation of the nasolacrimal drainage apparatus. The technique is preceded by an accurate history, detailed examination, instillation of fluorescein dye within the conjunctival sac to assess patency and, possibly, probing the proximal part of the system with a Liebreich's or Bowman's lacrimal probe. Cannulation may also be required before surgery in the region of the lacrimal puncta, so as to avoid inadvertent damage (Fig. 3.1).

In many patients cannulation can be achieved in the conscious, non-sedated, animal following instillation of adequate quantities of a suitable topical analgesic such as proxymetacaine hydrochloride (Ophthaine; Squibb). However, the technique should be performed under general anaesthesia if investigations are likely to be protracted or painful and if the animal is temperamentally unsuited to delicate manipulations about the eye. In both conscious and unconscious animals the nose should be lowered slightly when irrigation is performed to prevent retrograde flow into the nasal turbinates and nasopharynx. When general anaesthesia is employed, the pharynx should be packed, using

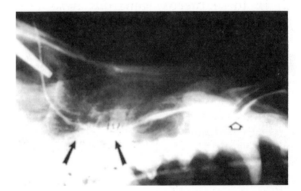

Fig. 3.1 Lateral dacryocystorhinogram of an adult labrador. The upper punctum has been cannulated, the lower punctum occluded. Contrast medium (Meglumine iothalamate. "Conray 280", M & B) delineates the nasolacrimal drainage apparatus. The position of the nasal ostium is indicated by the open arrow and closed arrows denote a region of abnormality. Part of a barley awn had been removed from the lower punctum 4 months previously and the remainder had become impacted in the region shown, resulting in stenosis as a consequence of chronic inflammation.

dampened gauze bandage, so that inadvertent aspiration into the lower respiratory tract does not occur.

A close fitting endotracheal tube, whether cuffed or uncuffed, does not provide sufficient protection for the airway and the practice of overinflating the cuff is not recommended as aspiration can still occur and, in addition, the tracheal wall may suffer pressure necrosis.

A number of different types of lacrimal cannulae, both metal and plastic, are commercially available and those with blunt or rounded ends are most suitable, so as to prevent inadvertent trauma (Fig. 3.2). For irrigation a suitable cannula, 5 ml syringe and 0.9% saline solution are required and all should be sterile. In addition, sterile sampling pots should be available if the material flushed through the duct system is to be collected for culture, and sterile water should be used for the flush instead of saline so that the growth of potential pathogens is not compromised.

The upper punctum is most commonly cannulated (Fig. 3.3) and the syringe filled with sterile saline solution is attached to the cannula. Gentle, sustained, pressure is usually sufficient to inject the saline which should emerge from the lower punctum. If digital pressure is then applied in the region of the lower canaliculus and its punctum, saline should emerge at the external nares in most animals (Figs 3.4 and 3.5). Exceptions such as brachycephalic dogs have been discussed above, and, in these breeds, generous head down tilt is

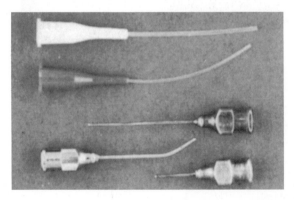

Fig. 3.2 Lacrimal cannulae. The metal cannulae (Dixey Instruments) are malleable and both metal and plastic cannulae (Arnolds Veterinary Products) are manufactured in a range of sizes.

required in anaesthetized patients and swallowing, or gagging, should be noted in conscious patients. On occasions fluorescein dye viewed directly (Fig. 3.6), or using a Wood's lamp or cobalt blue filter, may assist in deciding the patency of the drainage system, although dacryocystorhinography is probably a simpler alternative. Because brachycephalic animals have short wide ducts (Fig. 3.7), obstruction within the drainage system is uncommon.

Excess force should not be used when irrigation is attempted and it is always sensible to reposition the cannula before assuming that an obstruction is present. If desired, the procedure can be repeated after cannulating the lower punctum although, in practice, this is rarely necessary as patency of the whole system can be demonstrated via the upper punctum alone.

If saline cannot be flushed through with this technique, the next logical step is to cannulate the entire system with monofilament nylon (0 – 00) or to catheterize using polyethylene tubing (PE50–90) or a suitably sized urinary catheter

Fig. 3.3
Adult crossbred dog. Probes have been placed in the upper and lower lacrimal puncta.

Fig. 3.4
Irrigation of the nasolacrimal drainage apparatus via the upper punctum in a conscious border collie. The head is tilted down slightly and the lower punctum is occluded by digital pressure. Water can be seen at the external nares.

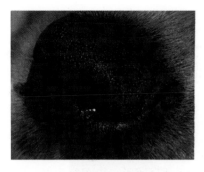

Fig. 3.5
Water appearing at the external nares following
irrigation in a young golden retriever. A sterile pot may
be used to collect the irrigate for subsequent culture.

Fig. 3.6
Fluorescein dye appearing at the external nares in a
border collie.

Fig. 3.7
Chronic
dacryocystitis in the
labrador illustrated in
the
dacryocystorhinogram
in Fig. 3.1.

(FG3–6). Cannulation or catheterization of the system in this
way is much less likely to cause damage than forced irrigation
and, if obstruction is present, it can usually be appreciated
quite readily with this technique.

When nylon is used, the end is blunted by flaming and the

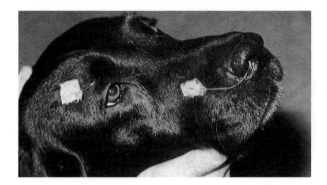

Fig. 3.8 A fine catheter has been passed through the nasolacrimal drainage apparatus of the labrador illustrated in Fig. 3.7. The catheter has been sutured to the skin by means of sticking plaster butterflies and passes subpalpebrally via the dorsomedial conjunctival fornix into the upper punctum. The catheter was inserted 23 days previously and is about to be removed. There is no longer any ocular discharge and there was no recurrence of the problem in succeeding months.

nylon is passed via the upper lacrimal punctum through the drainage system to emerge at the external nares. Slight difficulty can be encountered approximately three quarters of the way along if an accessory opening is present, or near the distal exit at the nasal ostium. Gentle manipulation of the nylon is usually sufficient to allow free passage and force should not be used.

Monofilament nylon is useful for probing the drainage system and it may be possible to re-establish patency with this technique when an obstruction is located. It is, however, easier to retain patency by means of malleable plastic tubing which can be sutured in place if required and this method is of particular value in the treatment of chronic dacryocystitis (Fig. 3.8). The tubing can either be manipulated through the system using previously placed monofilament nylon, which acts as a guide, or it can be passed directly.

ACKNOWLEDGEMENTS

I am grateful to Dr C. Gibbs for allowing me to publish the dacryocystorhinogram which is illustrated. Some of the photographic material was kindly supplied by Mr J. Conibear and Mr M. Parsons. My thanks to Mrs V. Beswetherick, Mrs C. Francis and Mrs M. Hughes for typing the manuscript.

CHAPTER 4

Treating the Everted Membrana Nictitans

SHEILA CRISPIN

Eversion of the membrana nictitans is not uncommon in certain large breeds of dog, such as the great dane, Saint Bernard, weimaraner, Newfoundland, German shepherd dog and German shorthaired pointer (Fig. 4.1). The kinked lid is unsightly and may result in slight epiphora, an ocular discharge or even a low grade conjunctivitis. It is usual to correct the defect surgically so that a normal appearance results. However, complications may arise if surgery is not performed properly and the important principles of the most useful corrective procedure are reiterated here.

The membrana nictitans is the most important of the dog's lids; it spreads the tear film and protects the cornea. The nictitans gland contributes to the precorneal tear film and there is an investing layer of conjunctiva rich in lymphoid tissue on both inner and outer surfaces. The only indication for the removal of the membrana nictitans is extensive neoplasia where local resection is impossible. Similarly, any surgical procedure should seek to conserve, or restore, the normal anatomical relationship between the membrana nictitans and the cornea; it is therefore particularly important to avoid removal of the free border at its leading edge.

Removal of the whole membrana nictitans results in dead space at the medial canthus and chronic conjunctivitis can occur. In addition, corneal ulceration can result, with a risk

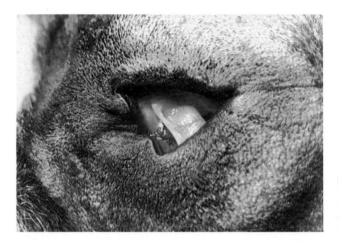

Fig. 4.1
Everted membrana
nictitans and poor
eyelid conformation
in a Saint Bernard.

of corneal perforation caused by secondary entropion from the upper and lower lids (Fig. 4.2). Such cases frequently require transposition of buccal mucosa in order to mitigate the untoward results of inadvertent removal.

Partial removal of the border of the membrana nictitans is also no solution for eversion; the kinked piece of cartilage often remains *in situ* so that the problem is still present and the exposed edge may undergo a chronic granulomatous reaction (Fig. 4.3).

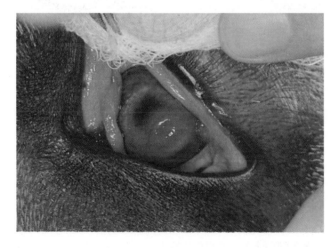

Fig. 4.2
Corneal ulcer as a
consequence of
secondary entropion
following removal of
membrana nictitans
in a great dane.

The most satisfactory treatment for eversion of the membrana nictitans is excision of the kinked piece of cartilage, utilizing an approach from the inner (bulbar) surface. In most affected animals the kinked piece of cartilage is part of the

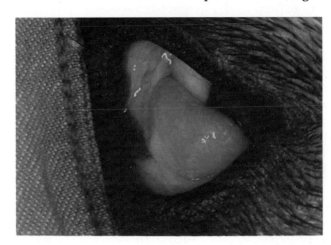

Fig. 4.3
Granuloma formation in a great dane following removal of free border of membrana nictitans. The kinked piece of cartilage is still present so that eversion of the membrana nictitans remains.

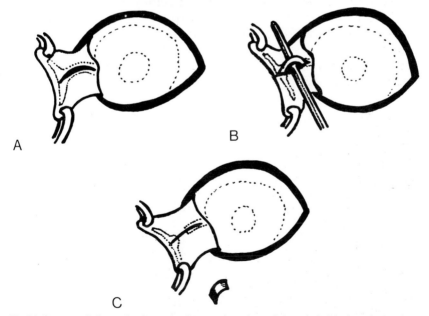

Fig. 4.4 Correct surgical procedure for treating the everted membrana nictitans. An incision is made over the kinked cartilage on the inner aspect of the membrana nictitans (A). The kinked piece of cartilage is then undermined by the mosquito forceps (B) and removed (C).

long arm of the T-shaped cartilage, whereas in others it is the junction of long and short arms and, less frequently, the short arm only is kinked.

Excision of affected cartilage is carried out in an aseptic manner with the patient under general anaesthesia. The inner surface of the membrana nictitans is exposed and fixed with tissue forceps which are placed so as to avoid the free border. An incision is made through the conjunctiva overlying the kinked cartilage (Fig. 4.4A). Tenotomy scissors are used to dissect out the affected portion of cartilage so that it may be undermined with fine mosquito forceps (Fig. 4.4B). Dissection should not involve the outer surface of the membrana nictitans and some care is needed to avoid perforating the outer surface inadvertently. The kinked piece of cartilage is excised (Fig. 4.4C) and the membrana nictitans allowed to take up its normal position; no suturing is necessary. A topical antibiotic–steroid ophthalmic ointment is all that is required for several days after surgery.

CHAPTER 5

Differential Diagnosis of Chronic Nasal Disease

MARTIN SULLIVAN

INTRODUCTION

A number of conditions must be considered when a dog is presented with chronic nasal discharge. The variety of conditions which can cause chronic nasal discharge is shown in Table 5.1.

As well as considering primary nasal disease there are diseases which mainly affect other organs (e.g. mega-oesophagus) and several systemic illnesses (e.g. distemper)

Table 5.1 Diagnosis of 100 consecutive cases of chronic nasal discharge.

Common	Neoplasia	38
	Chronic hyperplastic rhinitis	20
	Aspergillosis	18
Uncommon	Rhinarial ulceration	9
	Foreign body	5
Rare	Destructive rhinitis	3
	Oronasal fistula	2
	Idiopathic epistaxis	2
	Macroglobulinaemia	2
	Polyp	1

which can also give rise to nasal discharge. These will not be considered further as they ought to be diagnosed by a competent clinician. The diseases which primarily affect the nasal cavity cause sneezing and generally produce a non-specific discharge. To differentiate these diseases it is essential to follow a routine of investigation. This includes careful questioning of the owner and clinical examination, before undertaking radiography, endoscopy, serology, haematology or biochemical evaluation.

SUSCEPTIBILITY

Dolichocephalic and mesaticephalic breeds are prone to intra-nasal disease but brachycephalic breeds, by and large, are spared. This may be because brachycephalic breeds mouth-breathe and have less nasal tissue. Knowledge of the age range of the three most frequently encountered diseases, nasal neoplasia, aspergillosis and chronic hyperplastic rhinitis, is helpful (Fig. 5.1). The majority of nasal tumours occur in older dogs, while aspergillosis and chronic hyperplastic rhinitis are found in younger dogs, but there is considerable overlap. It is essential, therefore, to integrate history, clinical examination and information gained from ancillary aids so that an accurate diagnosis can be reached.

INVESTIGATION OF NASAL DISCHARGE

HISTORY

The terrain over which the dog is exercised, the speed of onset, the side affected and the type of discharge should be ascertained. The reported presence or absence of sneezing, epistaxis (as opposed to mucohaemorrhagic or sanguinopurul-ent discharge), coughing, gagging, facial pain or mouth breathing give much useful information. Further, changes in these signs over a period of time are important. For example, a discharge which was unilateral but has become bilateral

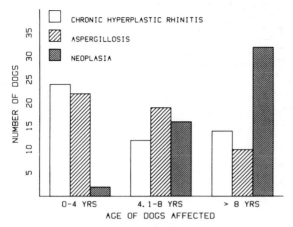

Fig. 5.1 Comparison between ages at the onset of clinical signs in the three main intranasal diseases in dogs. Tumours are seen in middle-aged to older dogs, but occasionally occur in the young dog. Chronic hyperplastic rhinitis is seen most frequently in younger animals. Aspergillosis occurs mainly in young dogs, but, a significant number occur in older dogs. Consequently, age should be taken into consideration in the differential diagnosis of chronic nasal discharge, but emphasis must also be placed on other findings.

indicates in many cases that the continuity of the nasal septum has been lost.

CLINICAL EXAMINATION

The nature of the discharge and side(s) involved can be assessed (Fig. 5.2). Unfortunately, in many dogs the discharge is intermittent and therefore may be absent at the time of examination. Ulceration and depigmentation of the rhinarium, ocular discharge (Fig. 5.3), alteration in the nasal contour (particularly at the medial canthus of the eye) and convexity of the hard palate are significant features. The presence of facial pain can be tested for by moving a hand quickly towards the animal's face or by tapping the nasal cavity and frontal sinuses on each side. A dog with facial pain will shy away and may cringe. Checking the patency of the nasal airway is very important. This can be determined easily by using a thread or wisp of cotton wool and suspending this in front of each nostril, then noting the force with which the thread is sucked towards, and blown from each nostril during

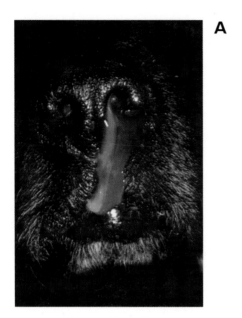

A

B

Fig. 5.2
(A) Spectacular unilateral sanguinopurulent nasal discharge from a dog with chronic nasal disease. In this case a tumour was found. (B) Typical mucopurulent nasal discharge. Although the discharge is bilateral, it is predominantly right-sided.

Fig. 5.3
A nasal tumour originating in the ethmoturbinates has destroyed the frontal bone, producing a painless soft tissue swelling above the left eye. There is some obstruction to tear flow evidenced by the ocular discharge.

inspiration and expiration. In this way an undisclosed bilateral lesion may be detected (Fig. 5.4).

ANCILLARY AIDS

RHINOSCOPY

A number of instruments such as arthroscopes and broncho-scopes can be used, but the cheapest and comparatively effective instrument is an otoscope with a long speculum. Examination is quick and allows identification of foreign bodies and fungal plaques, with removal of the former and sampling of the latter for mycological investigation. Results of rhinoscopy may be negative or inconclusive because of the

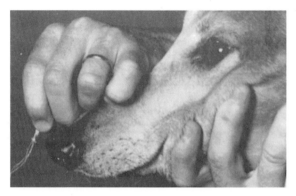

Fig. 5.4
Air-flow test. This simple
procedure permits a crude
and qualitative assessment of
nasal obstruction to air flow. A
reduction or absence of air
flow is highly suggestive of
neoplasia.

volume of discharge present or the lack of gross change in
some conditions.

MICROBIOLOGY

Bacteriology from nasal swabs is of little value as the bacteria
recovered are usually normal commensals or opportunistic
invaders. For fungal isolation, direct biopsy by endoscopy is
recommended, as nasal washings often give false negative
results.

RADIOGRAPHY/RADIOLOGY

Radiology is the most useful aid to diagnosis currently
available, but quality radiographs with good definition and
accurate positioning are essential (Fig. 5.5). General anaesthesia is therefore mandatory. The dorsoventral intraoral view
is the most informative as this allows comparison of both
sides of the nasal cavity (Fig. 5.6). Cassettes are too bulky to
reach far enough into the mouth to assess the caudal parts of
the nasal cavity. This view is best achieved with non-screen
film, which gives very good definition because of the fine
grain. Alternatively, screen film cut and wrapped in black
plastic may be used. Both these films require exposure factors
significantly increased over those used for screened film to
achieve satisfactory imaging. The lateral and dorsoventral

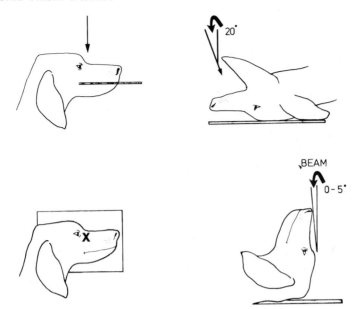

Fig. 5.5 Radiographic examination of the nasal cavity. (a) The dorsoventral, intraoral view of the nasal cavity allows the two sides of the nasal cavity to be examined and compared. This is best obtained with non-screen film which, because of the fine grain, gives excellent contrast. Poor radiographic technique can give rise to erroneous interpretation. (b) The ventrodorsal oblique, open-mouth view of the nasal cavity. This view allows the use of cassettes but requires the beam to be angled to project the lower jaw on to the cranium. Note that the hard palate should be parallel to the cassette. (c) The lateral view gives information regarding the frontal sinuses and the state of the maxilla and frontal bones. Unfortunately, the affected side cannot be distinguished from the normal side. (d) The rostrocaudal view of the skull has the effect of skylining the frontal sinuses. This allows both sinuses and frontal bones to be compared. This view is of most value in the evaluation of cases of aspergillosis. However, it is not an easy view to achieve because of the variations in skull formation between breeds.

views of the skull and the rostrocaudal view of the frontal sinuses are optional and need only be used in selected cases, e.g. to examine the frontal sinuses in suspected cases of aspergillosis.

SEROLOGY

A 5 – 10 ml clotted blood sample, preferably spun to remove serum, is all that is required by competent laboratories to test for antibodies to particular fungi, specifically *Aspergillus fumigatus*. The tests used are the agar gel double diffusion test, counter-immunoelectrophoresis and the ELISA test. The particular test used depends on the laboratory to which the

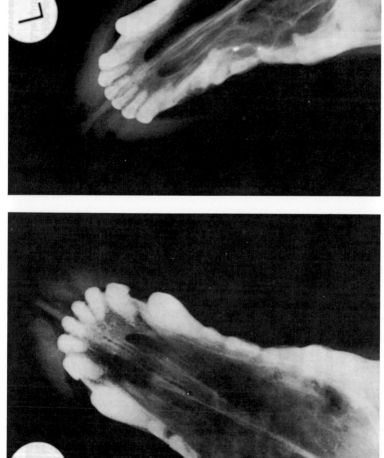

Fig. 5.6 (A) Dorsoventral, intraoral view of the nasal cavity in a case of nasal tumour. There is a turbinate destruction on both sides of the nasal cavity and only the ethmoturbinates on the right have been spared. The destroyed turbinates have been replaced by soft tissue opacity. The vomer bone has been destroyed rostral to the carnassial teeth, indicating that the septum has been breached. (B) Dorsoventral, intraoral view of the nasal cavity in a case of aspergillosis. The left turbinates have been destroyed rostrally and caudally, with only a small portion of the ethmoturbinates remaining. There is a relative increase in radiolucency due to the absence of turbinates.

sample is submitted. The agar gel double diffusion test is the most commonly used though it is not as rapid or as sensitive as the counter-immunoelectrophoresis test. A note of caution, however. The laboratory must test the sample against at least three, preferably six, different antigens and must maintain a quality control on the antigens used. In this way false negatives should be avoided.

HISTOPATHOLOGY AND CYTOLOGY

Examination of biopsy samples is sometimes the only way to confirm a diagnosis. The best samples are those obtained by rhinotomy, but this involves significant surgical intervention. A simple, yet effective, technique is to use a large male urinary catheter and obtain a suction biopsy of intranasal material.

Haematological and biochemical profiles are only of value in specific diseases where the common causes have been ruled out.

SPECIFIC CONDITIONS

NASAL NEOPLASIA

Tumours of the nasal cavity are, as a group, the most common affliction of the nasal cavity in the dog (Fig. 5.3). Although a large number of cell types have been identified, the clinical behaviour of all these tumours is similar. Tumours generally arise in the ethmoturbinate region and spread rostrally. They are locally invasive but rarely metastasize. The owners may note that the discharge was initially unilateral but that it has become bilateral. They may complain that the dog breathes excessively through its mouth, snorts when eating and has difficulty sleeping, because of occlusion of the caudal nares. Reduction in airflow is often, though not always, present. The tumour can erode through the bony case and appear as a soft painless swelling at the medial canthus of the eye, or produce convexity of the mucoperiosteum of the hard palate.

Radiologically, turbinate destruction is accompanied by an increase in soft tissue opacity which is generally homogeneous.

If the lesion is bilateral, absence of part or all of the vomer bone is apparent and the cartilaginous septum may be deviated. Destruction of the bony case may be visible as large superimposed areas of relative radiolucency, caused by defects in the hard palate or maxilla.

Endoscopy is frequently unrewarding, as the tumour generally originates in the ethmoturbinates. The otoscope may be too short if the tumour has not extended far enough rostrally. Further, the tissue which comprises the tumour is very friable and haemorrhage is easily induced. This, coupled with the discharge, blocks the field of view.

Confirmation of the diagnosis may be difficult in a very small number of cases as "early" tumours produce non-specific local radiological changes. These dogs should have further radiographs after an interval of 14 – 28 days. Samples for histological examination to support the diagnosis can be obtained by suction biopsy or, more accurately, at rhinotomy. Prognosis is poor, and recorded long-term survival rates do not generally justify treatment.

ASPERGILLOSIS

This mycotic infection, often considered to be a condition that affects farm dogs, is actually seen more frequently in dogs classified as suburban, with no specific access to heavy concentrations of fungal spores. It is still not clear why some dogs develop aspergillosis, since spores are present in the nasal cavity of most dogs, yet infection is uncommon. Certainly, both trauma and immune-incompetence have been implicated in some dogs, but the immune status of most cases has not been investigated. Dogs are usually presented with a history of unilateral nasal discharge or a sudden bout of epistaxis. The owner often reports an ocular discharge. Pain is often present when the affected side is touched or when the dog is chewing food. Rhinarial ulceration is a frequent feature. No reduction in airflow is present.

Radiologically, the main changes are of turbinate destruction accompanied by an increase in radiolucency in the rostral portion of the nasal cavity. This increased radiolucency may also involve the caudal compartment of the cavity, but in this area a mixed density pattern may be present. On rostrocaudal views of the skull, involvement of the frontal sinuses may be evident, producing opacification of the sinus cavity with thickening and mottling of the frontal bones.

Endoscopically the turbinate scrolls are absent, and dry fungal plaques (Fig. 5.7) are evident caudally in the ethmoturbinate region or laterally in the rostral compartment, the root of the ventral turbinates resembles a red walnut.

Serology by a reputable laboratory is the most accurate way of confirming infection and can be invaluable if radiology and endoscopy are equivocal. Prognosis is good following aggressive therapy with the current treatment of choice, enilconazole, instilled into the nasal cavity via drains implanted in the frontal sinuses (Imaverol; Janssen Pharmaceutical). This avoids turbinectomy and prolonged oral courses of antimycotic agents.

CHRONIC HYPERPLASTIC RHINITIS

Whippets and dachshunds appear to be particularly susceptible to this disease. These dogs are presented with a history of nasal discharge, which is more often bilateral than unilateral. The discharge never contains blood and is a nuisance to the owner rather than the dog. Radiologically, the changes are of turbinate masking, producing a mixed pattern of density.

The diagnosis in most cases is made by the elimination of other common causes. Treatment consists of a trimethoprim/ sulphonamide combination together with oral bromhexine hydrochloride (Bisolvon; Boehringer). Surgery should be

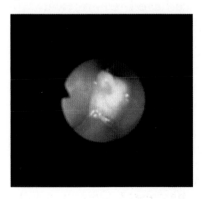

Fig. 5.7
Aspergillosis. A fungal plaque can be seen lying adjacent to the entrance of the frontal sinus. Turbinate destruction has permitted the passage of the rhinoscope this far caudally.

avoided, as there is a residual nasal discharge after turbinectomy. The prognosis is guarded.

In rare cases polyps, composed of chronic inflammatory
tissue, occur in the nasal cavity, producing radiological changes
indistinguishable from early nasal tumours.

RHINARIAL ULCERATION

A number of young dogs are presented with a chronic nasal
discharge which is often unilateral and in which there is
alar fold swelling, rhinarial ulceration and depigmentation.
Ancillary aids return normal results and biopsies are often
inconclusive.

FOREIGN BODY

The type of foreign body which may be present depends on
the area of the country. In the north and west of the UK the
obstruction is more likely to be caused by a twig or plant
stem (Fig. 5.8). In other areas grass awns are more commonly
encountered. Therefore, these animals are often working dogs
or dogs exercised in rough cover. They may have a history of
sneezing, of sudden onset nasal frenzy and unilateral epistaxis.
The discharge usually becomes mucopurulent if untreated.

Radiologically, the changes are not diagnostic, but an
increase in radiolucency in the region of the rostral common
meatus is suspicious.

Endoscopy is diagnostic in those cases where twigs are
present (Fig. 5.9). Grass seeds and pine needles may not be
visible because of the volume of discharge and a nasal flush
is therefore recommended.

The offending object should be removed, and the animal
discharged with a 14-day course of broad spectrum antibiotics.
The prognosis is good.

IDIOPATHIC DESTRUCTIVE RHINITIS

A number of cases are presented in which the signs are
clinically and radiologically indistinguishable from dogs with

Fig. 5.8 Nasal foreign body. Two parts of a 6 cm long twig removed from a young springer spaniel presented with unilateral nasal discharge, with a history of sudden onset of sneezing and nasal frenzy.

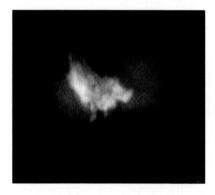

Fig. 5.9
Rhinoscopy. End-on view of a twig lying in the common meatus wedged by the surrounding turbinates.

aspergillosis. But sera from these dogs give negative results when tested for antibodies to *Aspergillus* and *Penicillium* species, and no fungus is detected endoscopically. These may be animals which have had a foreign body penetration of the nasal cavity, resulting in a severe turbinate necrosis, although the foreign body is no longer present.

ORONASAL FISTULAE

These animals should have the cleft palate or dental problem (usually periodontal disease) identified at clinical examination. The discharge is unilateral. The tooth most often responsible is the canine, though the incisors and, rarely, the carnassial tooth may be responsible. If the diagnosis needs confirmation then an oblique intraoral dorsoventral view of the incisor arcade or oblique lateral views of the maxillary arcade will demonstrate a radiolucent halo around the root, destruction of the lamina dura and rounding of the root apices.

Treatment is effected by repair of the cleft, by removal of the offending teeth, or in those cases where the canine tooth is absent and a large defect is present, mucosal flaps should be used to close the defect.

RARE CAUSES OF EPISTAXIS

A number of rare conditions can give rise to epistaxis as the main clinical finding. Coagulopathies such as autoimmune thrombocytopenia, von Willebrands disease, haemophilia and macroglobulinaemias with cryoglobulins are examples. These conditions require a thorough haematological and biochemical evaluation. Autoimmune thrombocytopenia - where evidence of regenerative anaemia, decreased platelet count, packed cell volume, and abnormal platelets on blood smears may be encountered. The majority of cases of macroglobulinaemia will have a plasmacytoma located somewhere in the body, though usually not in the nasal cavity. The excessive immuno-globulins and immunoglobulin complexes are precipitated in regions of the body where the temperature is below core temperature. However, the blood for investigation must be spun at as near to 38°C as possible so that the globulins which may precipitate, clot or flocculate are not lost. Despite full investigation there are still cases of epistaxis which currently defy accurate diagnosis.

FURTHER READING

Gibbs, C., Lane, J. G. & Denny, H. R. (1979) *Journal of Small Animal Practice* **20**, 515.

Lane, J. G. (1982) *ENT and Oral Surgery of the Dog and Cat*, p. 41. Bristol, P. S. G. Wright.

Lane J. G. & Warnock, D. W. (1977) *Journal of Small Animal Practice* **18**, 169.

Richardson, M., Warnock, D. W. & Lane, J. G. (1982) *Research in Veterinary Science* **33**, 167.

Sharp, N. J. H. & Sullivan, M. (1986) *Veterinary Record* **118**, 560.

Sullivan, M., Lee, R., Jakovlejic, S. & Sharp, N. J. H. (1986) *Journal of Small Animal Practice* **27**, 167.

CHAPTER 6

Cerebrospinal Fluid Sampling

JAYNE A. WRIGHT

INTRODUCTION

Indications for cerebrospinal fluid sampling include the following suspected conditions:

Encephalitis	Spinal cord neoplasia
Meningitis	Intracerebral haemorrhage
Myelitis	Subarachnoid haemorrhage
Toxoplasmosis	Spinal cord compression
Brain neoplasia	caused by epidural abscess

The site normally used for sampling is the cisterna magna.
The puncture is made using a spinal needle (Yale sterile
disposable; Becton Dickinson). These come in the following
sizes: 380 mm ($1\frac{1}{2}$ in) 20 and 22 gauge; 890 mm ($3\frac{1}{2}$ in) 19, 20
and 22 gauge.

The appropriate one is selected to suit the size of the dog,
e.g. for a dog or cat weighing 5 kg, use a 380 mm, 20 gauge
needle, or for a 60 kg dog, a 890 mm, 19 gauge needle.

TECHNIQUE FOR COLLECTING CEREBROSPINAL FLUID

(1)   Following premedication with acetylpromazine (0.1 mg/kg) and atropine (0.5–1 ml, 0.6 mg/ml), anaesthesia is induced with thiopentone sodium (1.0 mg/kg) and maintained with halothane and oxygen by means of an endotracheal tube.

(2)   The hair is clipped from the skin in the region of the occiput and the first cervical vertebra. Thè site is aseptically prepared for introduction of the needle.

(3)   The dog is placed in right lateral recumbency (assuming the operator is right-handed) at the end of the table. The head is held by an assistant, at a 90° angle to the neck, with the ear towards the table tucked underneath (Fig. 6.1).

(4)   With the usual aseptic precautions the following landmarks are identified with the left hand: external occipital protuberance, middle finger; the edge of the wing of the atlas, thumb; the region overlying the atlanto-occipital space, index finger.

The latter lies on the midline halfway between an imaginary line drawn through the external occipital protuberance and the wings of the atlas (point X). With experience it can be seen as a slight depression (Figs 6.2–6.4).

(5)   The needle, held in the right hand, is introduced at the

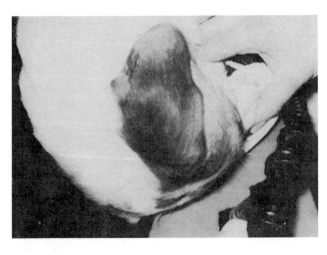

Fig. 6.1
Head held at 90°
angle.

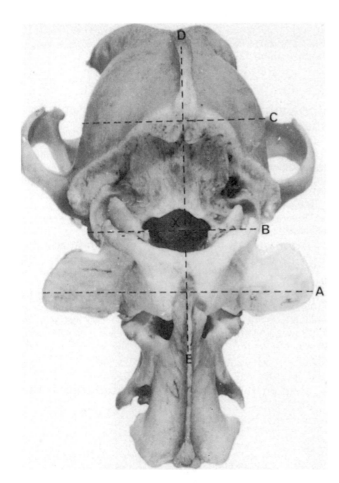

Fig. 6.2
Articulated atlas, axis and occiput. The skull has been flexed upon the atlas as in position for cisterna puncture. A, through the wings of the atlas; B, the atlanto-occipital space and C, external occipital protuberance respectively. D–E, midline; X, atlanto-occipital space.

point where the index finger has identified the underlying atlanto-occipital space (Fig. 6.5).

(6)   The needle is directed at 90° through the dorsal skin and musculature toward the atlanto-occipital interspace. The tough ligamentum flarum is then palpably pierced followed by the dura mater, which often results in a cutaneous "flinch".

(7)   The stylet of the needle is removed and cerebrospinal fluid should be seen to bubble up to the needle hub. It is essential that the needle is inserted into the midline to avoid penetrating one of the cervical venous sinuses which run

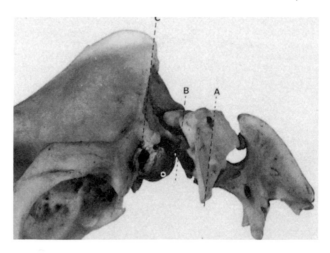

Fig. 6.3 Skull, atlas and axis viewed laterally. The bones are articulated in a position corresponding to that at cisternal puncture. The lines A, B and C are the surface markings as in Fig. 6.2.

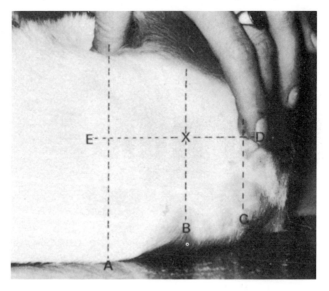

Fig. 6.4
Hair clipped and site aseptically prepared. Lines show positions as in Figs 6.2 and 6.3.

longitudinally on either side of the cord in this area. Should blood appear, the needle should be removed, and a fresh puncture made with a new needle.

(8)   Between 1 and 2 ml of cerebrospinal fluid is allowed to drip into a sterile Bijou bottle (Fig. 6.6).

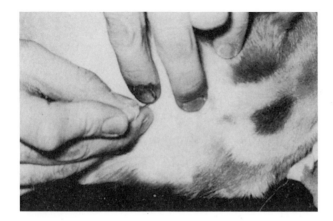

Fig. 6.5
Spinal needle being
introduced.

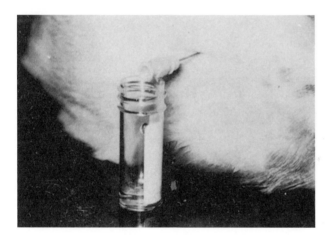

Fig. 6.6
Cerebrospinal fluid
being collected.

CONTRAINDICATIONS FOR CEREBROSPINAL ANALYSIS

(1)   Fractures, dislocations or subluxations involving the bony compartment housing the brain stem and cerebellum or the upper cervical vertebral column including the atlanto-occipital articulation.

(2)   Brain herniation when intracranial lesions have forced the cerebellum and brain stem into or below the foramen magnum.

(3) Lesions beneath the brain which distort its normal anatomy, e.g. posterior fossa neoplasm.
(4) Neurological and radiological examination will aid in determining the presence of these conditions.

It should be noted that neuropathological entities cannot be differentiated on the basis of cerebrospinal examination alone. Examination of cerebrospinal fluid is most valuable in confirming a clinical diagnosis of inflammatory or neoplastic disease.

CHAPTER 7

Myelography

JAYNE A. WRIGHT

INTRODUCTION

Indications for a myelographic study include:

Paresis	Forelimb knuckling
Ataxia	Quadriparesis
Lumbar pain	Cervical pain
Paraplegia	Quadriplegia

The conditions which may cause such signs and which may be diagnosed with the use of myelography include:

Intervertebral disc protrusion
Spinal tumours – spinal cord tumours
                    nerve root tumours
                    vertebral tumours
Lumbosacral spondylosis
Congenital/developmental vertebral anomalies
    wedge vertebra
    butterfly vertebra
    spina bifida
    cervical spinal stenosis ("wobbler" syndrome)
Traumatic injuries – fracture
                 dislocation
                 fracture/dislocation

A number of these conditions may be diagnosed on plain radiography, e.g. 50% of intervertebral disc protrusions; vertebral tumours, lumbosacral spondylosis, wedge vertebra, butterfly vertebra, spina bifida and traumatic injuries.

The myelogram aids in determining the extent of spinal cord impairment. It produces indirect evidence of pressure on the spinal cord by showing alterations to the normal flow of contrast medium in the subarachnoid space.

The contrast medium of choice is iohexol (Omnipaque; Nyegaard [UK]) at a dose rate of 0.15–0.3 ml/kg bodyweight of a solution containing 300 mg iodine/ml. The contrast medium may be administered following a cisternal or lumbar puncture. In practice the majority of myelograms (85%) are carried out via cisternal puncture; a lumbar puncture is only used when the contrast medium fails to outline the lesion, or its caudal flow is inadequate. A lumbar puncture may be carried out directly following a cisternal puncture.

TECHNIQUE FOR MYELOGRAPHY

(1)   The cisternal puncture is made in a similar way to that for cerebrospinal fluid sampling.

(2)   Following a successful cisternal tap, the radiology table is elevated to about 5°, head up.

(3)   When an equivalent volume of cerebrospinal fluid has drained, the injection of contrast medium is made (Fig. 7.1). A small quantity is injected initially followed, provided there is no adverse response, by the remainder.

(4)   The needle is withdrawn, the head and legs secured and an exposure made.

Calving ropes are used to secure the dog; they are applied to both forelegs and around the maxilla behind the canine teeth (Fig. 7.2). For a large dog a sling is used beneath the rump to support its weight.

(5)   The table is further tilted in gradations of 5° to 10° and exposures are made rapidly as required, with ventrodorsal projections as necessary.

(6)   Tilting the table to a final angle of 60° ensures that the

contrast medium flows beyond the caudal cervical regions, unless there is a lesion at this level.

LUMBAR PUNCTURE

A lumbar injection is usually made between L4–5, and occasionally L3–4.

(1) The dog is positioned in right lateral recumbency.
(2) The hindlegs are pulled cranially, so arching the lumbar region and increasing the space between the neural arches (Fig. 7.3).
(3) The spindle needle is inserted through the midline, cranial to the spinous processes of L5 and directed cranially at a 45° angle to pass through the spinal cord into the ventral subarachnoid space (Fig. 7.4).
(4) The stylet is withdrawn and cerebrospinal fluid should be seen to bubble up to the needle hub.
(5) Following withdrawal of a volume of cerebrospinal fluid, an equivalent volume of contrast medium is injected.
(6) It is sometimes not easy to be certain that the needle is correctly positioned. If this occurs, an exposure is made after

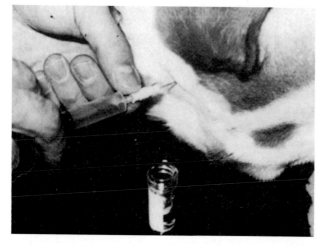

Fig. 7.1
Contrast medium
being injected into
the cisterna magna
after withdrawal of
cerebrospinal fluid.

J. A. Wright

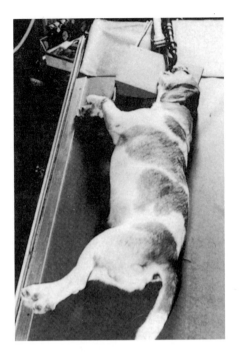

Fig. 7.2
Calving ropes tied around the forelegs and
maxilla with table elevated at 5°.

the injection of contrast medium with the needle still *in situ*.
Thus, if it is not quite within the subarachnoid space, it can
be repositioned (Fig. 7.5).
(7)   The table is tilted according to the direction of flow
required for the contrast medium, i.e. cranially or caudally.

TECHNICAL CONSIDERATIONS

(1)   During cisternal puncture if a spinal needle with too long
a bevel is used, or the needle is passed too deeply, penetration
of the central canal of the cord, with the subsequent injection
of contrast medium, may result.
(2)   In the course of lumbar puncture the needle may penetrate
the intervertebral disc, or the injection may enter both the

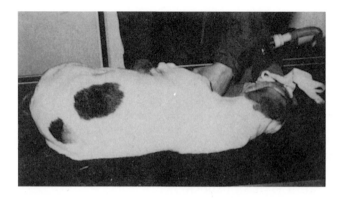

Fig. 7.3
Arching of the lumbar
region in preparation
for a lumbar
puncture.

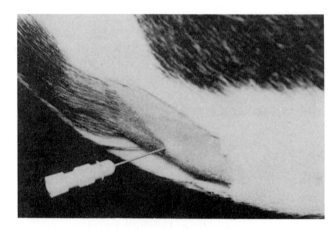

Fig. 7.4
Spinal needle
inserted for a lumbar
puncture, cranial to
the spinous process
of L5 and directed
cranially.

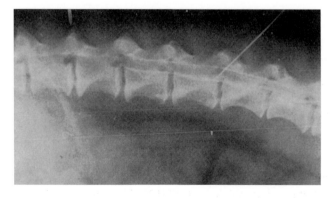

Fig. 7.5
Appearance when
contrast medium
injected inadvertently
into the central canal
of the spinal cord.

epidural and subarachnoid spaces simultaneously. It is also possible to enter the central canal at this site.

CONTRAINDICATIONS FOR MYELOGRAPHY

---

(1)   The conditions mentioned in cerebrospinal fluid analysis.
(2)   Immediately succeeding a traumatic incident, when the animal may be in a state of "shock".
(3)   Status epilepticus.

INTERPRETATION OF THE NORMAL MYELOGRAM (FIGS 7.6–7.9)

---

(1)   The width of the subarachnoid space is greatest at C2.
(2)   Slight indentations of the ventral contrast column, at C2–3 in particular, and also C3–4 and C4–5, are normal phenomena.
(3)   The ventral contrast column is quite a distance away from the floor of the neural canal from cranial C5 through to cranial C7.
(4)   In the lumbar area the ventral column is slightly elevated, or shows a slight break at the intervertebral discs.
(5)   Occasionally a small area of increased density occurs around the origin of the nerve roots in the lumbar area.
(6)   The spinal cord begins to narrow at caudal L5 and tapers rapidly to end in the first sacral segment.
(7)   Streaking of the column within L6 and L7 represents the cauda equina.

DIAGNOSTIC SIGNS ON THE MYELOGRAM

(1)   Obstruction – partial or total.
(2)   Dorsal uplifting of the ventral column only, or both dorsal and ventral columns together.

Fig. 7.6
Lumbar myelogram
indicating positioning
for lumbar puncture.

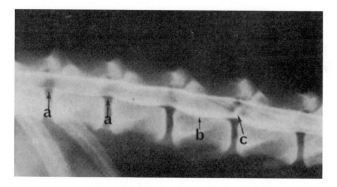

Fig. 7.7 Normal lumbar myelogram showing contrast medium in the subarachnoid and epidural spaces (b). The contrast medium is elevated and thinned over the intervertebral discs (a) and there is an increased density of contrast at the nerve root L4 (c).

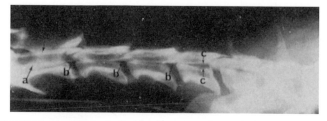

Fig. 7.8 Normal cisternal myelogram showing (a) a wide contrast column at C2; (b) indentations of ventral column at C2/3, 3/4, 4/5; (c) uplifting of the ventral column at the cranial edges of C5 to C7.

(3) Stricture of the column, dorsally and ventrally or laterally.
(4) Deviation to the right or left.
(5) A break in the column – dorsal, ventral or lateral.
(6) Narrowing of the column – dorsal, ventral or lateral.

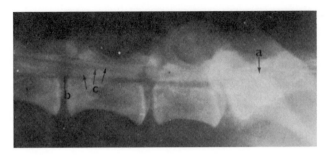

Fig. 7.9 Normal lumbar myelogram showing (a) contrast medium column ending at S1; (b) tapering of the column at the caudal edge of L5 through to S1; (c) streaking of the column representing the cauda equina.

(7)   A filling defect, i.e. failure of the contrast medium to fill part of or an entire vertebral area on serial films.

(8)   Expansion of the column – dorsally.

CHAPTER 8

Cervical Disc Surgery

SIMON WHEELER

INTRODUCTION

The clinical signs associated with cervical disc protrusions or extrusions are well recognized in dogs, neck pain being the most frequent. Affected dogs adopt a typical posture with the head carried low, with increased tone and fasciculations in the neck musculature (Fig. 8.1).

Signs of neurological dysfunction may be seen. Paresis or

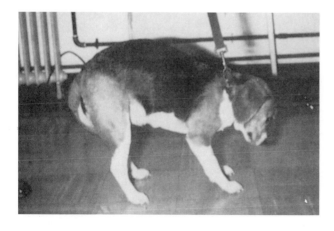

Fig. 8.1
Beagle suffering from a cervical disc extrusion.

lameness in one forelimb is the most common, although severely affected cases may display more serious signs, even quadriplegia.

The diagnosis is based on these clinical signs and is confirmed radiographically (Fig. 8.2). Differential diagnoses include atlanto-axial subluxation, traumatic lesions, discospondylitis, neoplasia and meningitis. Cervical disc disease is usually seen in adult dogs and rarely in dogs less than 2 years old. This should be borne in mind when a young dog is presented with neck pain. Smaller breeds are usually affected, typically beagles, dachshunds, corgis, etc. although any type of dog may be involved. It may be necessary to carry out myelography and cerebrospinal fluid analysis where the diagnosis is in doubt.

The first cervical disc (C2/C3) is the most frequently affected and the first four discs account for 90% of cases. Protrusions of the caudal discs are more likely to produce neurological signs.

Conservative treatment of cases involves strict cage confinement possibly accompanied by the use of anti-inflammatory drugs. In some dogs this may prove adequate for recovery to occur. However, some dogs will have a recurrence of neck pain once treatment is stopped and other cases suffer such severe pain that drug therapy fails to control the signs.

Thus many dogs with cervical disc disease are suitable candidates for surgical treatment. Two main procedures are used – disc fenestration and ventral decompression (ventral slot). Careful consideration of which to undertake is required (Figs 8.3 and 8.4).

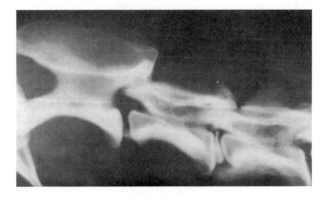

Fig. 8.2
Radiograph of C3/C4 disc extrusion. Note narrowing of the intervertebral space and dorsal displacement of mineralized nucleus pulposus.

SURGICAL TECHNIQUE (FIGS 8.5–8.17)

In both procedures a ventral approach to the neck is made. The patient is placed in dorsal recumbency with the neck well extended over a sandbag and the head taped to the table. It is important that the neck lies perfectly straight and upright, which is made easier by having the whole dog well aligned. The forelimbs may be tied back. It is useful to have an oesophageal stethoscope in position.

POST OPERATIVE CARE

Following surgery, cases are kept restricted for 2–3 weeks, with limited exercise allowed to let the dog urinate and defecate. Collars and chains should not be used; harnesses are suitable for controlling exercise. Dogs with severe neurological signs require a high standard of nursing care with particular attention to preventing the development of pressure sores and managing the bladder if incontinence is present.

Careful consideration of which to undertake is required.

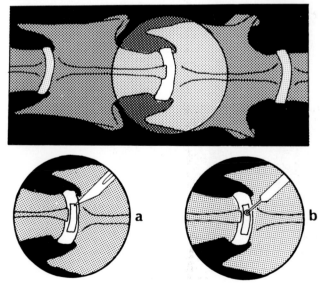

Fig. 8.3
Diagrammatic representation of ventral fenestration.
a, Annulus fibrosus incised with number 11 scalpel blade
b, Disc material removed with curette.

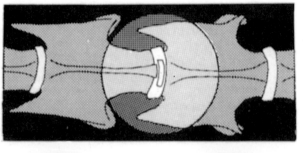

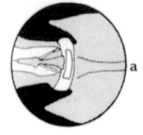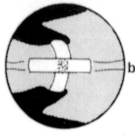

Fig. 8.4
Diagrammatic representation of ventral slot.
a, Removal of ventral spinous process.
b, Slot created to reveal disc material in vertebral canal.

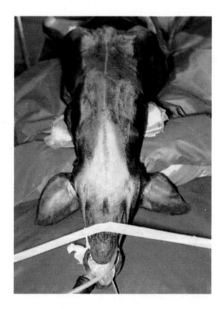

Fig. 8.5
Positioning of dog for ventral approach to neck.

Fig. 8.6 The skin is clipped and prepared from a couple of inches behind the manubrium to the middle of the mandible. A midline skin incision is made from the manubrium to the level of the larynx (this may be modified to suit the particular circumstances). The dog's head is to the left of the picture.

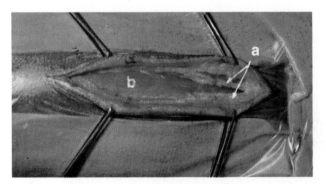

Fig. 8.7 The subcutaneous fascia is divided to expose the twin bellies of the sternocephalicus muscle (a) which are separated to reveal the paired sternohyoid muscles (b) which overlie the trachea and through which the cartilage rings can be palpated.

PROGNOSIS

Neck pain is usually resolved in most cases of cervical disc protrusion treated by fenestration. However, such dogs seem to fall into two well defined groups: those which have a very rapid recovery form the majority of cases. But some dogs take a month or more to recover following surgery and may require

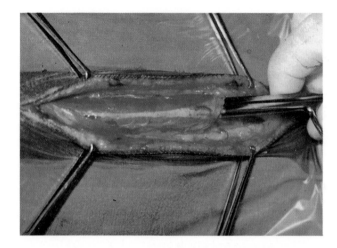

Fig. 8.8
The thin layer of fascia between the sternohyoid muscle bellies is divided – a small thyroid vein which lies there is conserved if possible.

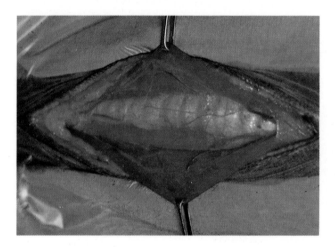

Fig. 8.9
This exposure reveals the trachea which, along with the oesophagus is displaced laterally, usually away from the surgeon.

medical treatment until that occurs, but they will usually recover given time. Ventral decompression leads to a rapid recovery from neck pain in the vast majority of dogs. It could be that those dogs experiencing a delayed recovery after fenestration were in fact good candidates for a slotting procedure. Cases that completely fail to respond after surgery may be suffering from a lateral extrusion, which is compressing the nerve roots.

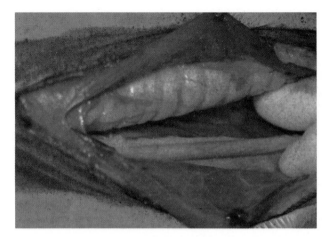

Fig. 8.10 The carotid sheath can be seen and this is mobilized towards the surgeon after careful dissection of the deep cervical fascia. Great care is required in handling the vital structures especially the carotid sheath and recurrent laryngeal nerve. Identification of the oesophagus is assisted if necessary by palpating the oesophageal stethoscope. The position of the vital structures is maintained laterally with a Gossett self-retaining retractor. The longus colli muscles are now visible and can be further exposed by blunt dissection of fascia.

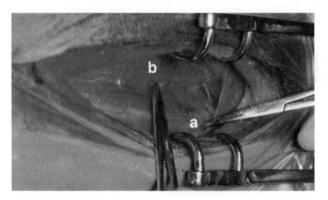

Fig. 8.11 The ventral spinous process of the vertebra, which is the caudoventral limit of the vertebral body, lies cranial to the intervertebral disc and can be palpated. The longus colli muscle bellies are paired and run from the transverse processes to the spinous process of the cranially adjacent vertebra, thus running over the intervertebral disc. Correct identification of the individual discs is important. The large ventrally projecting transverse processes of C6 (a) are easily identified – the C5 ventral process (b) lies between the cranial edges of these transverse processes. The other disc spaces can be identified by palpating the ventral processes cranially and caudally. Alternatively the very prominent ventral process of C1 may be noted (there is no disc at C1/C2) and the other ventral processes subsequently identified. It is wise to confirm the identity of the disc spaces by both methods if there is any doubt.

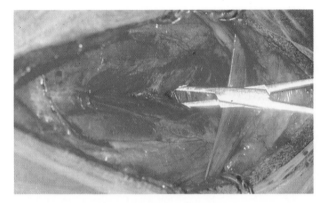

Fig. 8.12 For disc fenestration only limited exposure of the ventral annulus fibrosus is necessary. This may be achieved by placing a small curved haemostat between the bellies of the longus colli muscle just caudal to the insertion on the ventral process. Opening the haemostat separates the muscles giving adequate exposure for fenestration.

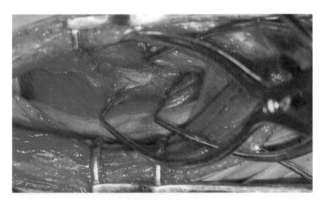

Fig. 8.13 In large dogs or if a ventral slot is being carried out, greater exposure is required. The insertions of the longus colli muscles are separated from the ventral process, a procedure which invariably leads to haemorrhage that must be controlled. The muscles are elevated from the vertebrae with a suitable instrument and retracted laterally using one or two Gelpi self-retaining retractors.

Mild neurological signs usually recover with time following either procedure. More severe neurological signs indicate a worse prognosis in all dogs. Ventral decompression will give these animals the best chance of recovery, which can occur even in some quadriplegic patients.

Fig. 8.14 Disc fenestration is accomplished by excising a rectangular piece of annulus fibrosus which should extend the full length of the intervertebral space, using a No. 11 scalpel blade. The full depth of the ventral annulus must be incised but care must be taken not to advance the blade too deeply. Nuclear material may then be removed using the scalpel blade or a suitable instrument. The depth to which the incision may be made should be evaluated from the radiographs. In disc fenestration it is usual practice to perform the procedure on the first four cervical discs – C2/C3 to C5/C6, as these account for the majority of cervical protrusions. The discs at C6/C7 and C7/T1 may be approached by extending the incision caudally if indicated.

Fig. 8.15 For ventral decompression correct identification of the disc involved is essential. Greater exposure is achieved by retracting the longus colli muscles laterally. A simple fenestration is initially carried out after which the ventral process is removed with rongeurs. The aim of the procedure is to create a bony defect for the full depth of the vertebral body to the spinal canal. The slot is usually approximately 30% of the width of the vertebra and 20–30% of the length and is best created using a high speed rotating burr, either electrically or air driven.

Fig. 8.16 The intervertebral space is angled craniodorsally and this must be considered when starting the slot, that is, more of the slot is started in the vertebra cranial to the disc than caudal and then advanced vertically down to the cord. The bone is removed using the burr or trephine until the dorsal cortex of the vertebral body (the floor of the vertebral canal) is reached. This can be identified by the character of the bone – the medullary bone is relatively soft and tends to bleed whereas the dorsal cortex is hard, dense bone. The burr is used in a gentle "painting" manner removing a thin layer of bone with each movement and maintaining a regular size and width to the slot. Haemorrhage from the bone is removed by suction and controlled with swab pressure or bone wax if necessary. Saline lavage of the site is continued throughout the procedure. On reaching the dorsal cortex it is thinned using the burr, but not penetrated. The final thin film of bone is removed with fine rongeurs or a small curette and is carried out with great care. Entry to the vertebral canal must be in the midline to avoid major haemorrhage from the vertebral sinuses. Should this occur swab pressure or the use of Gelfoam can arrest the haemorrhage although this can prove difficult. Once the canal is entered the dorsal longitudinal ligament may be identified, although it is often very tenuous or disrupted. Disc material may be visible in the canal and removed using a small curette, starting in the midline to avoid damage to the vertebral sinuses, until the dura mater is visible. The area is gently flushed with saline. After the removal of disc material has been completed the longus colli muscles are sutured. This is not necessary if the muscle bellies have only been separated as in a fenestration. The sternohyoid muscles and the caudal sternocephalicus muscles are apposed using a continuous suture of 2/0 Vicryl (Ethicon). The subcutaneous tissue is sutured similarly. The skin is closed with a subcuticular suture of Vicryl.

COMPLICATIONS

The ventral approach to the neck should present no major problems provided that great care is taken when handling the vital structures, particularly the carotid sheath.

The possibility of iatrogenic cord damage is a consideration in fenestration but is very unlikely. However, in carrying out a slot it is a far greater potential risk as the vertebral canal is actually entered. Great care must be taken during entry to and while exploring the canal.

Haemorrhage is usually minimal during the limited exposure required for fenestration and is readily controlled. In a slot there is greater potential for haemorrhage owing to the greater exposure required and the nature of the approach.

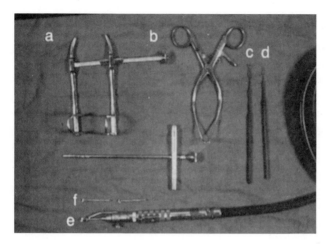

Fig. 8.17 Instrumentation for cervical spinal surgery. (a) Gosset self-retaining retractor, (b) Gelpi self-retaining retractor (Rocket, London)*, (c) Shea curette, (d) Rosen mobilizer (Seward Medical)*, (e) AO Pneumatic burr (Straumann, UK), (f) Michel trephine (Richard's Manufacturing)*

*Available through Veterinary Instrumentation, Sheffield

Cutting through the bone often leads to bleeding which can obscure the operation site for some time and may be a nuisance to control. Damage to the vertebral sinus easily occurs if the approach strays from the midline and the resultant haemorrhage may be difficult to control.

Strict aseptic precautions must be observed in either procedure – failure to do this may lead to the development of a secondary discospondylitis.

FENESTRATION OR SLOT?

There are several considerations to this question which may not easily be resolved – each individual case must be evaluated separately. Fenestration is technically an easy procedure to carry out – well within the range of most surgeons and little special equipment is required. Ventral slot contrasts directly with both these considerations – it is technically demanding and ideally requires the use of a powered burr. Some experience is desirable. Correct identification of the affected disc is essential in a slot, requiring myelography in many cases, but this requirement may be avoided by carrying out fenestration of a number of discs. The prospect for untoward complications is unlikely in fenestration but is appreciable in the slot.

The prolonged recovery following fenestration in some cases is clearly undesirable – a slot may well give these dogs a more rapid recovery – but it is impossible to predict which are the potentially quick recoverers and which are not. Thus a general recommendation would be that most cases of disc protrusion are probably most easily treated by fenestration. Some dogs in pain, those with severe neurological signs, or those which have radiographic/myelographic evidence of a large protrusion in the spinal canal are probably best treated by a slot if the facilities are available.

CONCLUSION

Dogs with cervical disc disease are good candidates for surgery. Fenestration is indicated in most cases although ventral decompression should be considered for some dogs if the facilities and expertise are available. Surgical treatment of cervical disc disease is frequently rewarding.

ACKNOWLEDGEMENTS

The author is grateful to Mr D. G. Clayton Jones for reading the manuscript, Mr D. Gunn for the illustrations and Miss O. Stagg for preparing the manuscript. Figs 8.6–8.8 appeared in *British Veterinary Journal* (1986) **142**, 95–115.

FURTHER READING

Denny, H. R. (1978) *Journal of Small Animal Practice* **19**, 25.
Robins, G. M. (1986) *The Veterinary Annual 26th Issue*. Bristol, J. Wright.
Walker, T. L. & Betts, C. W. (1985) *Intervertebral Disc Disease. Textbook of Small Animal Surgery*, Vol. 1, (ed D. H. Slatter). Philadelphia, W. B. Saunders.

CHAPTER 9

Thoracolumbar Disc Surgery

SIMON WHEELER

INTRODUCTION

Most small animal clinicians have been presented with dogs suffering from a thoracolumbar (TL) disc protrusion or extrusion. The method of treatment selected can have a profound influence on the dog's future mobility and in some circumstances the situation is as much an emergency as any other in veterinary practice.

Clinical signs vary with the severity of the lesion. Most affected animals display an acute or sub-acute onset of neurological deficits in the hind limbs, spinal hyperaesthesia and possibly bladder dysfunction. A method of categorizing the signs on the basis of the severity of the neurological deficit is given in Table 9.1.

Table 9.1 Severity of the neurological deficit.

I	Hyperaesthesia only
II	Ataxia, proprioceptive losses, paresis
III	Paraplegia
IV	Paraplegia, urinary retention with overflow (UR&O)
V	Paraplegia, UR&O, absent deep pain sensation.

Diagnosis of the condition is based on clinical signs and recognition that the problem predominantly occurs in the chondrodystrophic breeds. Differential diagnoses in adult dogs include traumatic lesions, discospondylitis, myelitis, neoplasia and ischaemic myelopathy. The occurrence of TL disc protrusions in dogs less than 1 year old is rare. In larger breeds of dog, disc protrusions can cause a chronic picture of clinical signs and the differential diagnosis includes degenerative myelopathy. Confirmation of the diagnosis is by radiography, the site of the lesion usually being apparent on plain films. In some instances myelography is indicated, either where the plain films are not diagnostic or where decompressive surgery is envisaged. The lumbar cistern is usually required for injection of the contrast medium as pressure must be applied to outline lesions where there is significant cord swelling.

An outline of treatments suitable for different categories of dogs is given in Table 9.2. Clearly, the course of action will depend on factors other than just the severity of the clinical signs. Financial constraints may make surgical treatment impractical. Also, in situations where decompression may be the ideal course of action, fenestration alone may be of some benefit.

The method of treatment has considerable influence on the prognosis for an individual case. Generally, the recovery rates for dogs in groups I–IV of the table are similar if conservative treatment or fenestration is employed. Decompression carries a significant benefit for dogs in groups III and IV where the time taken to recover is shorter. In group V, only 2–5% of dogs treated by conservative means or by fenestration will

Table 9.2 Summary of suggested treatment protocol based on severity and duration of clinical signs.

I	First episode	Conservative
	Subsequent episode	Fenestration
II	First episode	Conservative
	Subsequent episode	Fenestration or decompression
III	Surgical, preferably decompression	
IV	Surgical, preferably decompression	
V	Signs present < 48 h	Decompression
	Signs present > 48 h	Conservative

recover the ability to walk. However, if decompression is carried out within 48 h, approximately 50% of these dogs will walk again. Thus, the major potential benefits of decompressive surgery are a higher recovery rate in paraplegic dogs and a more rapid return to function, because of the removal of large amounts of disc material from the vertebral canal. Decompression is usually achieved by a dorsolateral approach with hemilaminectomy. However, this has disadvantages:

(1) While in most dogs the major component of the disc material lies in a lateral and ventral position in the vertebral canal, and is thus easily reached by a hemilaminectomy, retrieval of material from the opposite side of the canal can be difficult, although this can usually be achieved by careful exploration.
(2) It is possible to approach the wrong side of the spine which makes disc removal less easy. This situation can be avoided by making careful note of the clinical signs indicating the affected side and evaluation of a myelogram. Many dogs will have an asymmetric picture early in the episode.
(3) Fenestration of adjacent discs is less easy via a dorsal approach although it may be achieved with care.

SURGICAL TECHNIQUE: LATERAL FENESTRATION

The disc fenestration illustrated in Figs 9.1–9.6 is performed from the left side, the usual technique. The dog's head is to the left.

Once the disc is exposed the nuclear material is removed with a Rosen mobilizer, a tartar scraper or with the No. 11 scalpel blade. The T13/L1, L1/L2, L2/L3 and L3/L4 discs may be reached in a similar way; up to three discs may be approached from one muscle separation. Alternatively, individual approaches may be made to each disc.

Exposure of the T11/T12 and T12/T13 discs is a little more difficult. It is best achieved by following the convexity of the last two ribs with a finger and use this to dissect bluntly towards the vertebral column. The soft tissues are separated with haemostats. Care must be taken when inserting the Gelpi retractor not to tear the pleura. The levator costarum muscle crosses the lateral aspect of the disc and is retracted in a

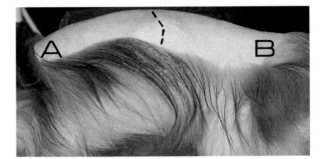

Fig. 9.1 The dog is placed in right lateral recumbency with a sandbag under the thoracolumbar region. The skin is clipped and prepared from the caudal border of the scapula (A) to the tuber coxae (B). The curvature of the thirteenth rib (T13) is shown by a dotted line.

Fig. 9.2 A skin incision is made at the level of the tips of the transverse processes, which can be palpated, from the mid thorax to the level of L5. This reveals an often thick layer of subcutaneous fat, which is divided to expose the lumbodorsal fascia. The forceps indicate the 13th rib.

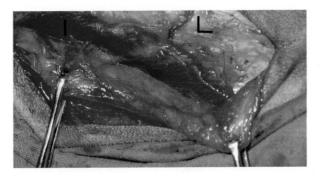

Fig. 9.3 The lumbodorsal fascia is divided longitudinally and retracted, shown here held by Aliss tissue forceps. Haemorrhage from segmental vessels must be controlled at this stage. This exposure reveals the longissimus dorsi muscles (L) and ventrally, the iliocostalis lumborum muscles (I). The transverse processes of the lumbar vertebrae can be palpated.

Fig. 9.4 The iliocostalis lumborum muscle fibres are divided along their length with haemostats. Initially, this is performed just cranial to the L2 transverse process, usually the first readily palpable bony structure caudal to the 13th rib. A Gelpi self retaining retractor is inserted in the muscle and the lateral surface of the vertebral body will become apparent. Exposure is improved by the use of a Langenbeck retractor held in the left hand.

Fig. 9.5 Once the vertebra is reached, the intervertebral disc may be identified just cranial to where the transverse process (T) inserts on the body of the vertebra (B). The position of these structures is outlined in the illustration. The annulus fibrosus appears yellow compared with the blue/grey tinted bone. Soft tissues are cleared off the annulus, this being accomplished best by a pushing motion in a cranio-dorsal direction with a swab held in forceps.

cranio-ventral direction. Again, the use of a Langenbeck retractor is useful. The disc is fenestrated as described in Figs. 9.1–9.6. The T11/T12 disc is approached in a similar way, although exposure may be limited and occasionally impossible in some barrel-chested dogs.

Wound closure is routine, with absorbable sutures in the lumbodorsal fascia, and in the subcutaneous tissues. The skin is closed with single interrupted sutures of nylon.

Fig. 9.6 A window is cut in the annulus using a No. 11 scalpel blade. Care must be taken not to advance too far dorsally, which would risk penetrating the vertebral canal. The incision should not extend dorsal to the top of the insertion of the tranverse process. A large enough window must be made in the annulus to allow the nucleus pulposus to be evacuated.

SURGICAL TECHNIQUE: DORSOLATERAL HEMILAMINECTOMY

Figures 9.7–9.14 illustrate a hemilaminectomy from the right side of the dog. The dog's head is on the right of all the photographs. The dog should be positioned in sternal recumbency, but slightly rotated with the side to be

Fig. 9.7 The skin incision is made just lateral to the dorsal mid-line and the subcutaneous tissues divided to expose the lumbodorsal fascia. The forceps are shown positioned at the 13th rib.

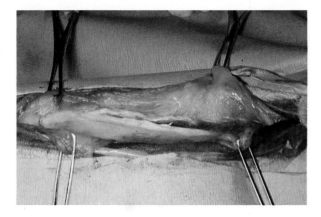

Fig. 9.8 The fascia is incised close to the dorsal spinous processes and the muscles elevated from the processes with a periosteal elevator.

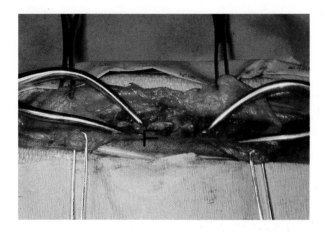

Fig. 9.9 The dorsal articular facets (F) are palpated and the muscular attachments incised close to the bone. Gelpi retractors are inserted to maintain the exposure. To expose the facet fully at the intervertebral space of interest, it is usually necessary to elevate the muscles from at least one vertebra cranial and caudal to the site of the entry into the vertebral canal. The facet is then removed with rongeurs.

approached uppermost. The skin is clipped and prepared from the caudal edge of the scapulae to the tuber coxae on each side of the midline.

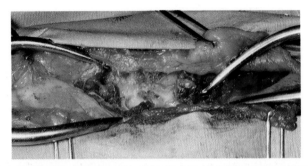

Fig. 9.10 The hemilaminectomy is commenced by drilling the bone with a pneumatic burr, starting at the site of removal of the facet and extending cranial and caudal to it. The hard, white external layer of cortical bone is penetrated to reveal the softer, red cancellous bone. This is removed to reveal the inner, white cortical bone. It is wise to remove all the cancellous bone and to thin the cortical bone prior to penetrating the vertebral canal. It is possible to thin the bone to a great degree with careful use of the drill. This inner sheet of bone is then gently removed with small instruments such as mosquito forceps, small rongeurs or a curette. (The process of performing the hemilaminectomy may be achieved using a trephine if great care is taken.)

Fig. 9.11 This exposure reveals the extruded disc material (arrowed) which is removed with a suitable instrument. Note the dorsal displacement of the spinal cord by the disc material.

Fig. 9.12 The vertebral canal is further explored with a dental tartar scraper to ensure that all disc material is removed. Gentle irrigation with saline through a narrow catheter is also useful.

Fig. 9.13 Fenestration of the affected space is performed by retracting the soft tissues ventro-laterally to expose the lateral annulus fibrosus (A).

Fig. 9.14 The annulus is incised with a No. 11 blade. Nuclear material can be seen escaping from the annular defect (arrow). Fenestration of adjacent discs may be achieved in a similar way. Alternatively, this may be performed by making a new approach via a lateral incision in the lumbodorsal fascia as described above. The hemilaminectomy site is covered with an autogenous fat graft and the wound closed in a routine fashion.

POST OPERATIVE CARE

Dogs which have only had fenestration should be cage confined for at least 2 weeks, or until limb function improves. Those that have had decompressive surgery may be encouraged to exercise a couple of days after the surgery. If urinary incontinence is present, it is vital that the bladder is kept empty of urine, either by manual expression or aseptic catheterization four times daily. If there is any suspicion of cystitis being present, urinalysis and bacteriological culture should be performed. Existing cystitis should be treated with appropriate antibiotics.

SUMMARY

Thoracolumbar disc disease is a common occurrence in dogs and surgical treatment is indicated in many cases. The procedures described are well within the capabilities of most surgeons engaged in small animal practice and the employment of the correct technique will ensure the optimum prognosis.

ACKNOWLEDGEMENTS

I am grateful to David Gunn (Royal Veterinary College), Wendy Savage and Chris Frazee (N.C. State) for taking the photographs.

FURTHER READING

Davies, J. V. & Sharp, N. J. H. (1983) *Journal of Small Animal Practice* **24**, 721.
Denny, H. R. (1978) *Journal of Small Animal Practice* **19**, 259–266.
Gage, E. D. (1975) *Journal of the American Animal Hospitals Association* **11**, 135.
Wheeler, S. J. (1985) *British Veterinary Journal* **141**, 222.
Wheeler, S. J. (1986) *British Veterinary Journal* **142**, 95.

CHAPTER 10

Urine Sampling in the Bitch

MIKE HERRTAGE AND LIZ WILLIAMS

INTRODUCTION

Collecting urine from the bitch is often restricted in practice to sampling during natural or induced micturition. While the urine collected in this manner is satisfactory for screening tests, the technique is not adequate for other purposes. Urinary catheterization and cystocentesis are very useful techniques which have both diagnostic and therapeutic applications. Neither technique is difficult or dangerous provided the patient is properly restrained and the operator is familiar with the technique and procedure.

The diagnostic indications, apart from collecting urine for urinalysis and bacterial culture, include radiographic contrast studies and evaluation of urethral patency. These last two procedures require urinary catheterization. Therapeutic indications include the relief of urethral obstruction, maintenance of bladder drainage and the instillation of medication into the bladder. Although cystocentesis can be used to decompress the bladder in urethral obstruction, urinary catheterization is necessary for the other therapeutic indications. Indwelling catheters are particularly useful in the nursing of paralysed or recumbent patients and for monitoring urine output in intensive care.

METHODS OF URINE COLLECTION

MICTURITION

Urine can be collected in a shallow sterile receptacle, such as a kidney dish or saucer, during urination. The obvious advantage is that the owner can collect the sample and there is no risk to the patient. The urine, however, can become contaminated with cells and bacteria located in the genital tract or on the skin and hair. Such samples, while adequate for screening tests, are less desirable for bacterial culture. Some patients, particularly aggressive or nervous ones, will not always oblige at the required times.

MANUAL EXPRESSION

Micturition can be induced by manually compressing the bladder through the abdominal wall. This is more likely to be effective in small dogs and cats but the bladder must contain a least 15–20 ml urine for the technique to be successful. Exert a steady continuous pressure over as large an area of the bladder as possible and try to direct the force towards the neck of the bladder. Moderate pressure should be sustained until the patient urinates. This may take several minutes. Excessive or vigorous intermittent pressure should be avoided as this can only increase the risk of iatrogenic damage and subsequent haematuria. If the bladder is overdistended as a result of urethral obstruction excessive pressure could lead to bladder or urethral rupture.

CATHETERIZATION

Inserting a urinary catheter is not a difficult procedure. It can be carried out safely in an atraumatic and aseptic manner provided the operator understands the technique. Urinary catheterization is useful for both diagnostic and therapeutic purposes.

CYSTOCENTESIS

This is a form of paracentesis using a needle to puncture the urinary bladder through the abdominal wall in order to aspirate a quantity of urine. The technique prevents samples from becoming contaminated with bacteria and cells from the lower genital tract. It can also be used to provide temporary decompression of the bladder in cases of urethral obstruction.

URINARY CATHETERIZATION

The equipment required for catheterization is listed in Table 10.1, however, the exact requirements will depend on the method of catheterization and the type of catheter being used.

TYPES OF CATHETER

Four types of catheter are commonly used (Fig. 10.1). They are available in a variety of different diameters and lengths. The diameter of the catheters is usually measured using the French gauge "FG", where each French unit is equivalent to 1/3 mm. Thus a 9FG catheter has an external diameter of 3 mm.

Table 10.1 Equipment required for urinary catheterization.

Catheter	3-way tap
Speculum	Syringe 20–60 ml
Sterile swabs	*Stylet
Kidney dish	*Sterile water
Gallipot	*Syringe 5–10 ml
Antiseptic solution	*Spigot
Lubricant jelly	

Items marked * are only required when using a Foley catheter.

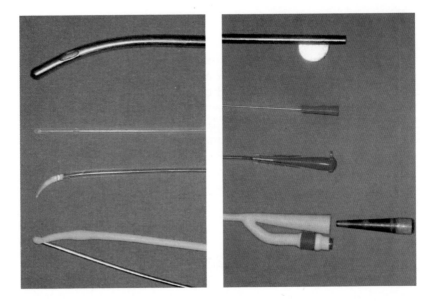

Fig. 10.1 Types of catheter showing both ends. From top to bottom: Rigid metal bitch catheter; dog catheter; Tiemann's bitch catheter; Foley balloon catheter with stylet in place. A spigot for use with a luer syringe is shown.

Rigid metal bitch catheter

These metal catheters are usually 20–25 cm long, 2–4 mm in diameter with a curved tip near the proximal end to facilitate introduction into the urethral orifice. Some have a luer connection to which a syringe or three-way tap can be attached, while others require the use of an irrigating syringe. They are reusable and can be autoclaved. These catheters should be used very carefully as their rigid structure can cause urethral and bladder damage.

Dog catheters

These straight plastic catheters are fairly rigid but do not have a curved end. They have two drainage holes at the proximal end near the rounded tip and a luer connection at the distal end. They are available in three sizes: 6FG (50 cm long), 8FG (60 cm long), and 10FG (60 cm long) and come double wrapped in a sterile packet. They can be resterilized with care, for further use. The increased rigidity makes them easier to use than the Tiemann's catheter.

Tiemann's bitch catheter

These catheters are made of soft plastic, 43 cm in length, with a curved and tapered tip to facilitate introduction into the urethral orifice. There are two holes, situated on either side of the curved tip and a luer connection at the distal end. They are available in three sizes 8, 10 and 12FG and come double wrapped in a sterile packet. Plastic catheters have the advantage that they are smooth, non-irritant and are transparent. The Tiemann's catheter, however, can sometimes prove difficult to use because of its flexibility.

Foley balloon catheter

These are soft latex rubber catheters with a polystyrene core. They have an inflatable balloon situated just behind the drainage holes at the tip of the catheter. A stylet is required to insert the catheter and for this reason it can only be used in female dogs. The balloon is inflated by introducing water through a valve fitted in the side-arm attached to the distal end. The syringe must be pressed firmly into the valve to inject or remove water. The inflated balloon keeps the catheter in the neck of the bladder and prevents it from falling out. Foley catheters do not have a luer connection and a spigot is required to attach them to a syringe. They are available in sizes 8 to 30FG, but are not reusable. The balloon must be deflated before removing the catheter from the bladder.

The main use for a Foley catheter is as an indwelling catheter to measure urine output and to maintain bladder drainage. The urine can be collected into a commercially available urine bag or an empty drip bag and giving set attached to the catheter. Both methods provide a closed system to reduce the possibility of ascending infection. If left in for a period of time, these catheters can become blocked with blood or debris in the drainage holes. Flushing the catheter with sterile water every 4 h will help prevent this.

SPECULA FOR BITCH CATHETERIZATION

Although the plastic and metal catheters can be inserted blind by digital manipulation in bitches which are large enough to permit vaginal examination, this technique is not easy and it is preferable to use a speculum in order to see the urethral orifice (Fig. 10.2).

Specula should be sterilized before use either by autoclave or by the Anprolene ethylene oxide gas system. After use they should be rinsed in cold water, washed in antiseptic solution, rinsed well, resterilized and stored carefully.

Technique

Place the patient in dorsal recumbency and, if conscious, restrain using two people, one supporting the head and forelimbs and the other holding the hindlimbs (Fig. 10.3). The hind legs should be held apart and pulled cranially to rotate the pelvis as this makes it easier to see the urethral orifice. The dog must be kept as asymmetrical as possible as this will facilitate the introduction of the catheter into the urethra. The person catheterizing the bitch should prepare their hands as

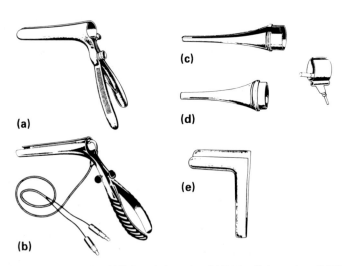

Fig. 10.2 Types of bitch speculum: (a) Sim's vaginal speculum; (b) McIntyre bitch speculum with light source to illuminate the interior of the vagina; (c) Speculum with cut away section which attaches to an auroscope; (d) Auroscope cone; (e) Human nasal speculum.

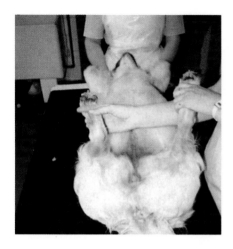

Fig. 10.3
The patient is held as straight as possible in dorsal recumbency by two assistants. The hindlimbs are pulled forwards so as to rotate the pelvis. This makes it easier to visualize the urethral opening.

for surgery. The vulva and surrounding area should be cleansed with a mild antiseptic solution (e.g. Savlon; ICI).

The lubricated speculum is introduced vertically into the vagina, a process which is helped by lifting the lips of the vulva (Fig. 10.4). With the handles of the speculum pointing cranially, the blades of the speculum are opened to expose the urethral orifice (Fig. 10.5). The urethral opening appears as a dark slit in a mucosal ridge on the ventral vagina floor close to the vaginovestibular junction. In some cases it is difficult to see the orifice even with a lighted speculum. It may be helpful in these cases to increase the rotation of the

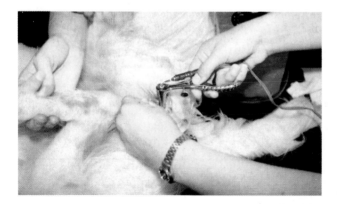

Fig. 10.4
The lubricated speculum is inserted vertically into the vagina, taking care to avoid the clitoral fossa.

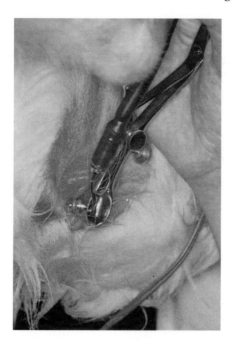

Fig. 10.5
With the handles of
the speculum
pointing cranially,
gently open the
blades. If the urethral
orifice is not visible,
try pulling the
hindlimbs further
forwards.

pelvis by pulling hindlimbs further cranially. If the presence
of the speculum is resented by the bitch, the vagina can be
filled with sterile Xylocaine Gel (Astra) to provide topical
anaesthesia.

Lubricate the catheter tip and insert it into the urethral
orifice. As soon as the catheter is in the urethra the hindlimbs
should be pulled caudally to allow the catheter to be advanced
into the bladder. Using a Foley catheter with the stylet in
place, the rounded end should slide along the ventral floor of
the vagina (Fig. 10.6). A common mistake is to try and
introduce the catheter vertically rather than horizontally. This
is particularly important if the urethral opening cannot be
seen. Provided the catheter is advanced along the floor of the
vagina in the midline, it should catch in the urethral orifice
(Fig. 10.7).

With any catheter other than a Foley, urine will pass back
along the catheter once it is in the bladder, provided the end
is not blocked. Urine will not pass back along a Foley catheter
until the stylet has been removed. To do this, the balloon is
inflated with sterile water injected through the valve using
the amount recommended and printed on the catheter. If there

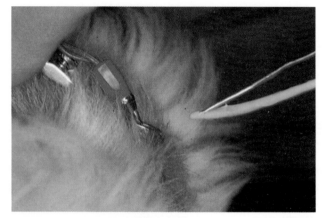

Fig. 10.6 The catheter is advanced along the vertical floor of the vagina using the hooked tip to catch in the urethral opening. To facilitate this the catheter should be virtually horizontal. Once in the urethra the hindlimbs must be pulled caudally to allow the catheter to pass along the urethra.

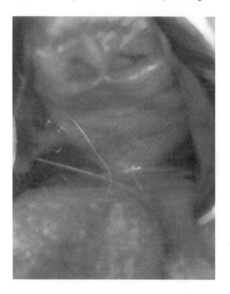

Fig. 10.7
The urethral orifice can be seen as a slit-like opening. Note the clitoral fossa at the top of the photograph.

is any resistance to injecting the water, the position of the catheter should be checked to make sure it is not in the vagina or urethra. Once the balloon has been inflated the stylet can be removed by twisting and withdrawal. To remove a Foley catheter, the balloon must be deflated first by removing the water via the valve.

The risks of urinary catheterization can be minimized by adequate restraint of the patient, an aseptic technique, plenty of lubrication on the speculum and catheter, topical anaesthesia if required, correct insertion of the catheter and the avoidance of repeated catheterization.

CYSTOCENTESIS

The only equipment required for this procedure is a 23 gauge hypodermic or spinal needle 2·5–7·5 cm in length depending on the size of the patient and a 5–10 ml syringe for sampling or a 20–60 ml one for decompression.

The patient can be placed in dorsal or lateral recumbency. If conscious, the patient must be restrained firmly in order to avoid any sudden movement which might lead to iatrogenic damage. Clip and clean the area over the bladder with an antiseptic solution. It is essential to localize and immobilize the bladder with one hand by gently grasping the bladder and holding it against the body wall. If the bladder cannot be palpated, it is unlikely that the technique will be successful. In any event, it is dangerous to stab blindly at the bladder. The needle is directed obliquely at an angle of about 45° to

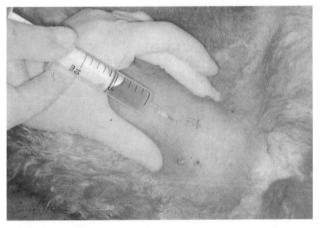

Fig. 10.8 With the patient firmly restrained, hold the bladder in position with one hand while directing the needle at an angle of 45° towards the bladder neck with the other, advance the needle gently into the bladder lumen and remove the urine by aspiration with a syringe. The bladder should remain fixed in position throughout the procedure.

the skin and advanced through the ventral bladder wall towards the bladder neck (Fig. 10.8). The oblique approach reduces the risk of urine leaking from the bladder after the needle has been removed. Slight discomfort may be noted as the needle passes through the abdominal wall.

In order to avoid possible leakage of urine into the peritoneal cavity, it is important not to apply excessive digital pressure to the bladder while the needle is in its lumen and to empty the bladder as completely as possible if the bladder wall is diseased or if there is urinary obstruction. If a large quantity of urine is to be removed, it is wise to use a three-way tap. Antibiotic cover is not usually required.

ACKNOWLEDGEMENTS

We are grateful to John Fuller for the artwork and Joss Herrtage for typing the manuscript.

CHAPTER 11

Urinary Incontinence

PETER HOLT

INTRODUCTION

Urinary incontinence is a common presenting sign in the dog and is associated with a variety of congenital, physical, infectious and neoplastic disorders. Apart from the clinical effects on the animal, incontinence presents serious management problems for the owner to the extent that euthanasia of the patient may be requested. In order to understand the causes and treatment of incontinence, a knowledge of the maintenance of continence in the normal animal is required.

MAINTENANCE OF CONTINENCE

The mechanisms involved in the control of urinary continence are complex and the present concepts may require revision in the future when vesico-urethral physiology is better understood. Contrary to popular belief, there is no true sphincter muscle encircling the bladder neck. Instead, during the period when the bladder is filling between micturitions (the storage phase), the whole urethra represents a tube of resistance to urine outflow.

Factors contributing to maintenance of urethral resistance are:

(1)   Tone in urethral smooth muscle (the "internal" sphincter);
(2)   Tone in urethral striated muscle (the "external" sphincter);
(3)   Elastic tissue in the urethral wall;
(4)   Mechanical properties of the urethral tube, e.g. length, diameter;
(5)   Engorgement of urethral venous plexuses.

As long as these factors result in intra-urethral pressure exceeding that within the bladder, continence is maintained.

There is neurological control of (1), (2) and probably (5), although the latter is thought to make only a minor contribution to urethral resistance in the dog. The neuromuscular control of continence is presented as a simplified diagram (Fig. 11.1).

During storage, tone in the urethral smooth muscle is maintained by sympathetic stimulation via the hypogastric nerve. The striated urethral muscle may also receive sympathetic innervation although its tone is under the voluntary control of the pudendal nerve. The effect of sympathetic innervation to the bladder is to reduce detrusor muscle tone, allowing the bladder to fill without a rise in intravesical pressure.

At the same time, there is reflex inhibition of parasympathetic activity which would normally result in bladder contrac-

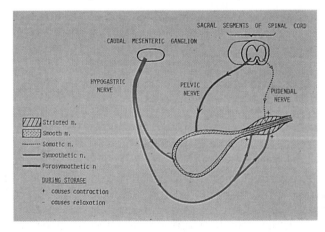

Fig. 11.1
Neuromuscular control of continence.

tion. A further, involuntary spinal reflex results in increased tone in the striated urethral muscle when intra-abdominal pressure suddenly rises (e.g. during barking, coughing), thus counteracting any resultant rise in intra-vesical pressure.

INVESTIGATION OF INCONTINENT ANIMALS

The clinical examination of incontinent animals is often unrewarding and little diagnostic information may be obtained. There are, however, a number of features which may suggest the type of incontinence involved.

HISTORY

The following information should be obtained from the owner of the animal:

(1) Sex — male, female, neutered?
(2) Duration of incontinence — since birth, since acquired as a puppy, recent onset, following neutering?
(3) Nature of incontinence — continuous, intermittent, copious leakage or only a few drops, positional, only when excited, worse when relaxed/asleep, loss of urine through the umbilicus?
(4) Micturition — normal urination observed, normal volume voided, increased frequency, nocturia, dysuria, haematuria?
(5) Other signs — e.g. paraplegia, polydypsia, tenesmus, dyschezia, vaginal discharge, perineal swelling, weight loss, hypersexuality (males)?

CLINICAL EXAMINATION

The external genitalia (and umbilicus in the juvenile animal) should be examined for evidence of incontinence such as wet hairs and skin excoriation. These signs are not pathognomonic and should be differentiated from urine scalding occurring during micturition associated with abnormalities of the external genitalia (Fig. 11.2).

If the history is insufficient for differentiation, it may be necessary to hospitalize the animal for observation. The bladder should be palpated for presence in or absence from its normal anatomical position, abnormal masses, increased wall thickness and size. The hypoplastic bladder cannot be distinguished on palpation from a partially filled, normal bladder but the distended bladder associated with urinary retention is more readily appreciated. Similarly, while the kidney(s) may be palpably enlarged if marked hydronephrosis is present, contrast urography is required to confirm the condition.

In male animals, the prostate should be palpated for evidence of disease and during rectal examination, the pelvic urethra investigated for the presence of calculi or tumours. At the same time, disruption of the pelvic diaphragm may be determined and anal sphincter tone assessed. The latter forms part of a neurological examination of the animal which should be performed when neurogenic incontinence is suspected.

In bitches, the vestibule and vagina should be examined for tumours, strictures and ectopic ureteral openings although the latter are rarely detectable (Fig. 11.3). The pelvic urethra may also be palpated through the vaginal wall.

Finally, it must be emphasized that the remainder of the animal should not be neglected. Evidence of renal failure or widespread malignancy may appreciably alter the prognosis

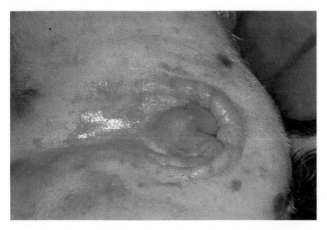

Fig. 11.2
Perineum of an incontinent Shetland sheepdog bitch with bilateral ureteral ectopia.

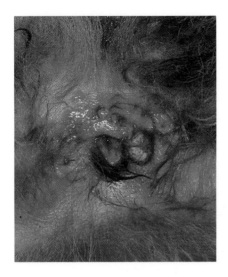

Fig. 11.3
Urine scalding associated with infantile vulva in
a continent spaniel puppy.

and enable a decision on management to be made before
extensive investigative procedures are undertaken.

LABORATORY EXAMINATIONS

Urine analysis is the cheapest and often the most useful test.
Usually, urine samples are best obtained by catheterization
which may also reveal complete or partial urethral obstruction.
In such animals, abdominal cysto-centesis may be required
to obtain a urine sample and empty the bladder. It may be
useful to compare catheterized with mid-stream samples in
dogs with suspected prostatic or urethral disease.

Stored or posted urine samples may be preserved with boric
acid (Boricon; Sterilin Universal). Samples should be subjected
to biochemical, cytological and bacteriological examinations
and the antibiotic sensitivities of cultured organisms determined. Any calculi obtained should be analysed as an aid to
subsequent prophylactic therapy.

Blood biochemistry may reveal evidence of renal failure
(elevated urea, inorganic phosphorus, creatinine) and serum
potassium may be raised in cases with acute urethral obstruction.

Haematology is not of specific value but is a useful parameter
in suspected inflammatory diseases.

RADIOLOGY

Preparation of the patient

Almost invariably, contrast radiographic investigations (intravenous urography, retrograde urethrocystography and vagino-urethrography) are required to differentiate conditions resulting in incontinence.

To facilitate radiographic interpretation, the gastrointestinal tract should be empty. This is accomplished by starving the animal for at least 12 h and the use of an enema. Soapy water enemas should be avoided — they are time-consuming and may leave residual bubbles in the large bowel which make radiographic interpretation difficult. More convenient is the Fletchers' phosphate enema (Pharmax Ltd). A full enema (128 ml) is administered to animals over 15 kg bodyweight, half an enema is sufficient for dogs of 5–15 kg and in patients below 5 kg, a 5 ml Micralax enema (Smith Kline) may be used. The enema can be administered at the same time as the anaesthetic premedication and is effective within 5–20 min. The animal is allowed to defecate in a kennel run or taken for a short walk by the owner during which the time the necessary anaesthetic and radiographic equipment can be prepared. This type of enema should not be used in dogs with dyschezia which require excavation of the large bowel under general anaesthesia.

Intravenous urography (IVU)

Under general anaesthesia, plain ventrodorsal and lateral radiographs are taken, the latter with the animal on its right side (this reduces the degree of superimposition of the kidneys).

Following a test dose of 0·5 ml, 70% sodium iothalamate (Conray "420"; May & Baker) is administered by rapid intravenous injection at a dose rate of 1 ml/kg bodyweight; Conray "280" may be used in small dogs at a dose of 2 ml/kg. A ventro-dorsal radiograph is taken immediately after injection (the nephrogram).

Lateral and ventro-dorsal radiographs are usually taken 5 and 15 min after contrast medium administration although further exposures may be required in individual animals for complete examination of the ureters.

An optional procedure is partially to fill the bladder with air before IVU, to improve the contrast between the distal ureters and the bladder neck.

Urethrocystography and vagino-urethrography

In males, a low iodine content water-soluble contrast medium (e.g. Urografin "150"; Schering Chemicals) is introduced via a catheter inserted into the bladder (for cystography alone) or distal urethra (for urethrocystography). In the latter case, the distal urethra must be occluded around the catheter to prevent leakage of contrast medium during injection.

Alternatively (and in bitches) a paediatric Foley catheter may be used. All catheters should be pre-filled with contrast medium to prevent injection of air bubbles which may be mistaken radiographically for calculi or tumours.

The bladder should be filled with contrast medium but over-distension is avoided to prevent vesico-ureteral reflux or bladder rupture. (Fig. 11.4). In bitches, contrast medium can be injected through a Foley catheter into the vagina to obtain a vagino-urethrogram (Fig. 11.5). Great care should be taken during retrograde techniques if ureteral ectopia (Fig. 11.6) or fistulation is suspected to avoid introducing excessive contrast medium into the ureter and the consequent risk of renal damage or infection. Incremental doses, each followed by a

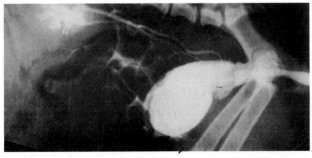

Fig. 11.4 Iatrogenic bladder rupture and vesico-ureteral reflux in a male West Highland white terrier puppy following urethro-cystography.

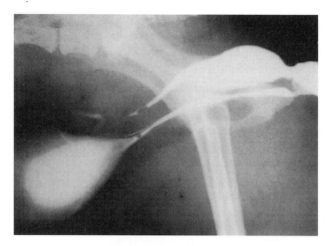

Fig. 11.5
Ureteral ectopia
demonstrated by
vagino-
urethrography in an
incontinent labrador.
A mild vestibulo-
vaginal stricture is
also present.

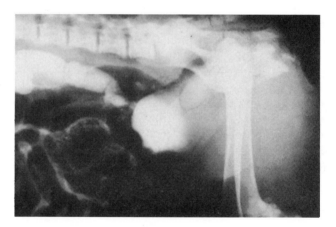

Fig. 11.6 Renal pelvic and ureteral dilatation demonstrated by IVU in a labrador bitch. The dilated portion of the ectopic ureter within the bladder wall (a ureterocoele) can be seen but not its termination.

radiographic exposure, should be used or, better still, screening facilities employed if available.

If retrograde techniques are performed soon after IVU, the possibility of confusing contrast medium flowing down the ureter with retrograde filling should be borne in mind.

Following positive contrast cystography, the bladder may be emptied and air introduced to obtain a double-contrast cystogram.

BIOPSY

In cases of suspected neoplasia, a biopsy is required for diagnosis and prognosis. In many cases, material will be obtained at the time of surgery but useful, non-invasive techniques are prostatic punch biopsies (Weaver, 1977) and biopsy via a urethral catheter (Melhoff & Osborne, 1977).

DIFFERENTIAL DIAGNOSIS OF INCONTINENCE

Current concepts of micturition physiology suggest that incontinence may occur under the following circumstances:

(1) Normal urethral resistance but abnormally high intra-vesical pressure.
(2) Normal intra-vesical pressure but abnormally low urethral resistance.
(3) Abnormally high urethral resistance overcome by even higher intra-vesical pressure.
(4) Normal intra-vesical pressure and urethral resistance but urine outflow partially or completely by-passes the urethral sphincter mechanism.
(5) Leakage of residual, voided urine from internal genitalia between normal micturitions.

In the juvenile animal, conditions which may result in incontinence (with the relevant, above circumstances in brackets) are:

Ectopic ureter (4)
Congenital sphincter mechanism incompetence (2)
Bladder hypoplasia (1)
Previous urachus (4)
Intersexuality (5)
Congenital neurological problems, e.g. spina bifida (3)

In the adult, the differential diagnosis is:

Prostatic disease (3 or 2)
Bladder neoplasia (1 or 3)
Acquired sphincter mechanism incompetence (2)
Uretero-vaginal fistula (4)

Acquired neurological conditions producing urinary retention with overflow incontinence (3)
Overflow incontinence associated with chronic retention, e.g. lithiasis (3)
Detrusor hyperactivity (e.g. cystitis) or instability (1)

JUVENILE INCONTINENCE

ECTOPIC URETER

The cause is unknown but hereditary factors and vitamin imbalances in the dam may play a role. Incontinence may be continuous or intermittent and even in bilateral cases, normal micturition usually occurs. Diagnosis is by contrast radiography when a ureterocoele may be detected.

Treatment involves transplanting the ureter into the bladder or excision of the ureter and associated kidney if severe secondary disease is present. Approximately 50% of animals are completely cured and in most of the remainder, the incontinence is markedly reduced. A few animals show no improvement after surgery, possibly due to undiagnosed bilateral ectopia (Fig. 11.7), concomitant sphincter mechanism incompetence, bladder hypoplasia or anomalous ureteric branches.

Fig. 11.7
Gross left hydronephrosis and hydro-ureter in a golden retriever male with bilateral ureteral ectopia.

CONGENITAL SPHINCTER MECHANISM INCOMPETENCE

The sphincter mechanism may be inadequate when the urethra is too short and/or wide, when urethral diverticula are present or when the urethra opens ectopically or is absent (Figs 11.8–11.10). In many instances (particularly in bitches), no abnormalities are found on clinical and radiographic investigations and diagnosis relies on the history and elimination of other possible causes of incontinence.

Treatment is unsatisfactory but some bitches become continent following their first oestrus, presumably as a result of oestrogen influence on the urethra (see acquired sphincter mechanism incompetence later).

BLADDER HYPOPLASIA

This is not uncommonly associated with other congenital causes of incontinence but may, rarely, occur alone. The diagnosis is confirmed by contrast radiography and only a small amount of contrast medium is required to fill the bladder during retrograde techniques (Fig. 11.11).

It is important to eliminate other causes of incontinence which may also be present.

Treatment of this condition is also unsatisfactory.

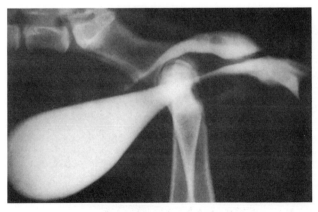

Fig. 11.8 A short, wide urethra demonstrated by vagino-urethrography in a golden retriever with congenital sphincter mechanism incompetence. Marked vestibulo-vaginal stenosis is also present.

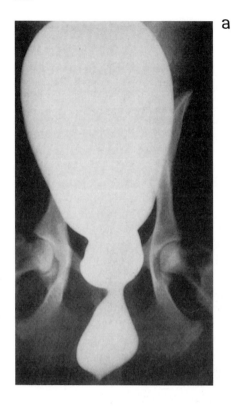

a

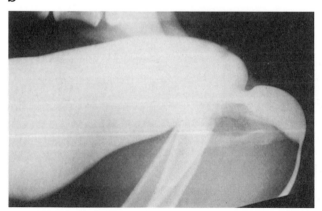

b

Fig. 11.9
A male alsatian with
congenital sphincter
mechanism
incompetence.
Ventro-dorsal (a) and
lateral (b)
radiography during
urethrocystography
demonstrates marked
urethral dilatations.

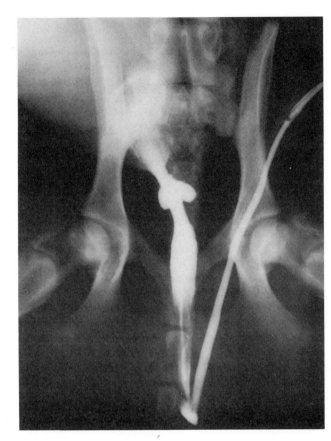

Fig. 11.10
Diverticula of the
prostatic urethra
demonstrated by
urethrocystography in
a golden retriever.

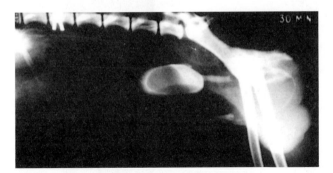

Fig. 11.11 Bladder hypoplasia and leakage of contrast medium through a wide urethra in an Italian greyhound puppy with congenital sphincter mechanism incompetence (IVU — 30 min).

PREVIOUS URACHUS

This condition is easily diagnosed since incontinence occurs through the umbilicus which may be scalded with urine. Contrast cystography confirms the diagnosis. Treatment involves excision of the urachus and repair of the resulting cranial bladder wall defect.

INTERSEXUALITY

Rarely, intersex animals may be incontinent. This is usually associated with the anatomical abnormalities illustrated (Holt *et al.*, 1983) (Figs 11.12, 11.13). It is likely that urine accumulates

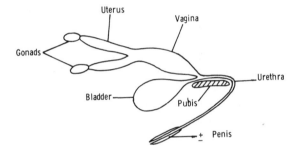

Fig. 11.12 Diagrammatic representation of the commonest anatomical abnormalities resulting in incontinence in intersex dogs.

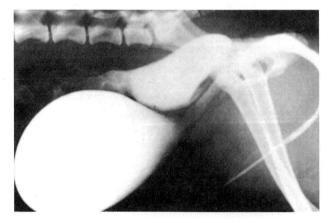

Fig. 11.13
Anatomical abnormalities shown in Fig. 11.12 demonstrated by urethrocystography in an incontinent Yorkshire terrier cross intersex.

in the vagina during micturition and subsequently leaks out via the urethra between micturitions. Diagnosis relies on contrast radiography.

Treatment involves excision of the vagina, uterus and gonads via a laparotomy (Fig. 11.14), taking care to preserve the blood supply to the bladder.

CONGENITAL NEUROLOGICAL CONDITIONS

Affected animals usually present as obvious neurological cases (e.g. paraparetic) but faecal and urinary incontinence may be present. Upper motor neurone lesions result in spasticity of the external urethral sphincter muscle. Increased urethral resistance leads to urinary retention with overflow incontinence (Fig. 11.15).

Lower motor neurone lesions result in interruption of the sacral reflex arc. Thus, reflex bladder contraction and urethral relaxation do not occur and urine is retained in the bladder with overflow incontinence. Spinal radiography may confirm the diagnosis and euthanasia of the animal is required if the symptoms persist.

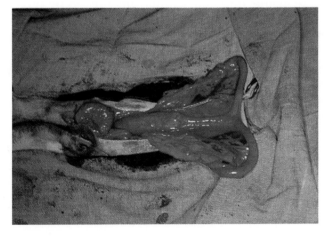

Fig. 11.14
Internal and external genitalia of incontinent intersex dog at laparotomy.

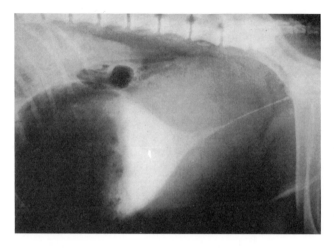

Fig. 11.15
Paraprostatic cyst
and emphysematous
cystitis demonstrated
by
urethrocystography in
a border collie with
urinary retention with
overflow
incontinence.

VESTIBULO-VAGINAL STENOSIS

Vestibulo-vaginal stenosis may be detected in continent and incontinent bitches and the author now believes this to be a complicating factor rather than a cause of incontinence.

In recumbent, incontinent animals, urine leaking via the urethra is often observed passing into the cranial vagina during IVU, even if a stenosis is present. The stenosis prevents drainage of this urine from the vagina when the animal stands and vaginitis may result.

Cranial flow of urine into the vagina did not occur when micturating cystography was performed in affected bitches supported in a normal squatting position (rather than recumbency).

Dilation of the stenosis or vaginectomy may prevent pooling of urine in the vagina but it is difficult to explain how these procedures could have cured the incontinence present in previously reported cases (Holt & Sayle, 1981).

ADULT INCONTINENCE

PROSTATIC DISEASE

Although haematuria and dysuria are the most common presenting signs, nearly a quarter of dogs referred to the department of veterinary surgery at Langford with prostatic disease are said by their owners to be incontinent. In more than half of these cases, prostatic haemorrhage had been mistaken for incontinence of bloody urine but true incontinence, with or without urinary retention, also occurred. This was associated with paraprostatic cysts, prostatitis or malignancy (Fig. 11.16) but prostatic hyperplasia may also result in incontinence (Table 11.1).

The diagnosis and treatment of prostatic disorders are well-documented and examination of the prostate should always be performed in adult, male, incontinent dogs.

BLADDER NEOPLASIA

One third of animals referred to the Langford clinic with bladder neoplasia were incontinent and all had carcinomas at various sites in the bladder (Table 11.2).

Interestingly, even with bladder neck tumours, urinary retention with overflow incontinence was rare. It is likely that incontinent dogs with bladder neck/urethral neoplasia have impairment of the sphincter mechanism whereas bladder wall tumours probably result in detrusor hyperactivity (see later).

Diagnosis is confirmed by contrast urethrocystography, Fig. 11.17, but the possibility of malignancy should be eliminated before surgical excision is attempted. Even in the absence of evidence of malignancy, histopathological examination of the excised tumour is essential to obtain a prognosis.

ACQUIRED SPHINCTER MECHANISM INCOMPETENCE

This usually follows spaying in the bitch although, rarely, cases of castrated males becoming incontinent are recorded.

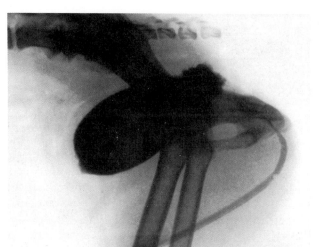

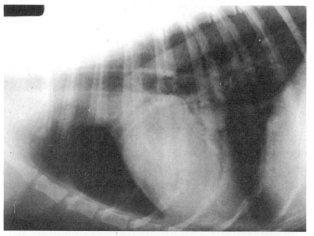

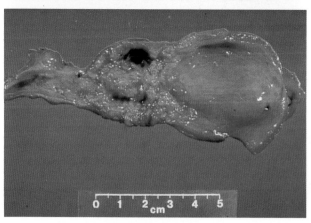

Fig. 11.16
Urethral transitional cell carcinoma invading the prostate of a crossbred demonstrated by urethrocystography (a). Thoracic radiography (b) revealed pulmonary metastases and the post-mortem specimen (c) illustrates the disruption of the urethral sphincter mechanism which resulted in incontinence.

Table 11.1 Nature of incontinence in eight dogs with prostatic disease.

Nature of incontinence		Diagnoses
Urinary retention with overflow incontinence	5	3 Paraprostatic cysts 1 Prostatitis 1 Prostatic carcinoma
Incontinence without urinary retention	3	1 Paraprostatic cyst 1 Prostatitis 1 Urethral carcinoma invading prostate

Table 11.2 Location of tumours in eight incontinent dogs with bladder carcinoma.

Bladder neck	4
Bladder neck + whole urethra	1
Anterior bladder wall	1
Dorsal bladder wall and proximal urethra	1
Whole bladder wall	1

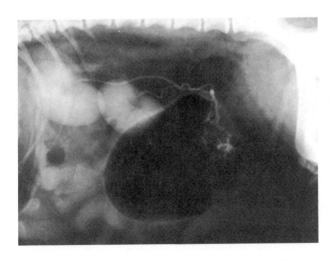

Fig. 11.17
Bladder neoplasia in
a corgi demonstrated
by double-contrast
cystography and IVU.
Prostatic enlargement
is also present.

Confirmation of diagnosis is difficult and relies upon elimination of all other causes of incontinence.

Although in theory sympathomimetic (or parasympatholytic) agents should improve continence control, there are no published clinical trials of their use in animals. The results in treated humans are poor and often temporary. Many of the sympathomimetics are present in proprietary combinations of drugs used to treat respiratory conditions and it may be difficult to obtain the pure agent. In the present state of knowledge, such chemotherapy cannot be recommended.

Many incontinent spayed bitches respond favourably to oestrogen treatment. The exact mechanism of action is unclear but oestrogens may stimulate maturation of the urethral squamous epithelium, improve mucosal elasticity, act directly on urethral muscle or sensitize it to sympathetic stimulation. Similarly, there are instances of castrated dogs responding to androgen therapy although the author's experiences in a limited number of cases are disappointing.

Surgical urethral sling procedures have been described in the dog but in human surgery where they have been employed more extensively, they are losing favour; it is thought that fibrosis occurs in the region of the sling and that any apparent return to continence is due to the dysuria which results.

URETERO-VAGINAL FISTULA

This condition also follows spaying and probably results from inclusion of a ureter during ligation of the cranial vaginal stump (Pearson & Gibbs, 1980). An acquired ectopic ureter draining into the vagina results and can be diagnosed by contrast radiography.

Treatment is identical to that for congenital ureteral ectopia.

ACQUIRED NEUROLOGICAL CONDITIONS

As with congenital neurological conditions, acquired urinary retention with overflow incontinence may result from upper or lower motor neurone dysfunction, usually as a sequel to spinal lesions (e.g. intervertebral disc prolapse, tumours).

Other neurological abnormalities are usually apparent and the diagnosis may be confirmed by radiography (Fig. 11.18). Treatment is conservative or surgical (orthopaedic) depending on the cause, severity and duration of signs. In the case of tumours, euthanasia is usually performed.

Rarely, displacement of the bladder into a perineal defect

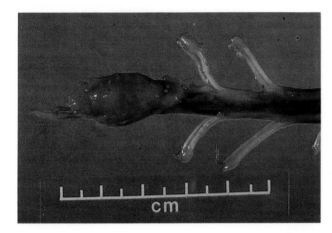

Fig. 11.18
Extradural
osteosarcoma of the
cauda equina of a
10-year-old Welsh
terrier with
neurogenic
incontinence.

may result in a lower motor neurone lesion leading to urinary retention with overflow incontinence although urethral kinking may also contribute to these signs. Fortunately, resolution usually occurs following replacement of the bladder, repair of the perineal rupture and regular bladder expression but it may take several weeks.

OVERFLOW INCONTINENCE WITH CHRONIC RETENTION

Animals with urethral obstructions (calculi, tumours) may, paradoxically, become incontinent when the intra-vesical pressure becomes high enough to overcome the urethral resistance. Such cases are primarily presented with dysuria and should be investigated and treated as such (Figs 11.19 and 11.20).

DETRUSOR HYPERACTIVITY/INSTABILITY

In these cases, uncontrollable bladder contractions occur, resulting in voiding of urine. In dogs, the condition is often secondary to lesions leading to excessive bladder wall stimulation (e.g. cystitis, bladder tumours, adhesions between vaginal stump and bladder after spaying). Such stimulation may also occur in animals with bladder hypoplasia, especially

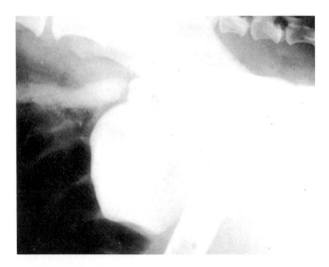

Fig. 11.19
Uretero-vaginal fistula
in an Irish setter
demonstrated by
vaginography.

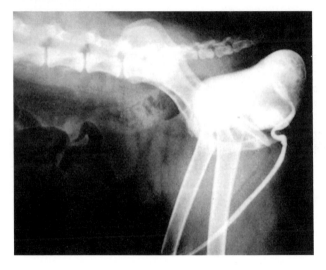

Fig. 11.20
Neurogenic urinary
retention with
overflow incontinence
in an alsatian cross
with bladder
displacement into a
perineal rupture
(demonstrated by
urethrocystography).

if they are housed for long periods (e.g. overnight) and unable to inhibit the detrusor reflex. The owners of such animals may report nocturia or marked bed-wetting overnight.

Occasionally, as in man, detrusor instability occurs with no obvious underlying cause. It may be present alone or in conjunction with sphincter mechanism incompetence. Diagnosis depends upon the taking of a detailed history and elimination of other causes of incontinence.

In cases secondary to other disorders, such as cystitis, treatment of the primary condition alone usually results in a return to continence. Animals with bladder hypoplasia and primary detrusor instability are much more difficult to treat. In theory, anti-cholinergic (parasympatholytic) or smooth muscle anti-spasmodic drugs should be useful but, in the absence of results of clinical trials, cannot yet be recommended for use in the dog.

ACKNOWLEDGEMENTS

I am grateful to Mr J. Conibear for the photography and Mrs C. Francis, Mrs V. Beswetherick and Mrs M. Hughes for typing this paper. Dr C. Gibbs and Professor H. Pearson kindly commented on the manuscript and I am also grateful to Professor Pearson for allowing me to use material from two of his cases.

REFERENCES AND FURTHER READING

Holt, P. E. & Sayle, B. (1981) *Journal of Small Animal Practice* **22**, 67.
Holt, P. E., Gibbs, C. & Pearson, H. (1982) *Journal of Small Animal Practice* **23**, 195.
Holt, P. E., Long, S. E. & Gibbs, C. (1983) *Journal of Small Animal Practice* **24**, 475.
Melhoff, T. & Osborne, C. A. (1977) *Current Veterinary Therapy VI. Small Animal Practice*, (ed. R. W. Kirk), p. 1173. Philadelphia, W. B. Saunders.
Pearson, H. & Gibbs, C. (1980) *Journal of Small Animal Practice* **21**, 287.
Weaver, A. D. (1977) *Journal of Small Animal Practice* **18**, 573.
Weaver, A. D. (1980) *The Veterinary Annual, 20th Issue*, (eds C. S. Grunsell & F. W. G. Hill), p. 82. Bristol, Scientechnica.
Webbon, P. M. (1982) *The Veterinary Annual, 22nd Issue*, (eds C. S. Grunsell & F. W. G. Hill), p. 199. Bristol, Scientechnica.

CHAPTER 12

Infertility in the Bitch

W. EDWARD ALLEN

INTRODUCTION

The term infertility is difficult to define in the bitch, mainly because of our lack of knowledge concerning the maximum number of offspring each breed can produce. Bitches are often mated at selected heats in order to try to provide puppies at a time which is convenient for management and when a demand for the puppies is anticipated.

For the clinician the definition of infertility is less crucial, as a problem can be considered to exist once advice is sought. This is usually after an individual bitch has been mated apparently normally at two or three heats and has not conceived or when, in a breeding kennels, the rate of puppy production is less than in previous years.

Investigation to try to elucidate the cause of breeding failure is somewhat urgent because in any event a bitch has relatively few chances of becoming pregnant. This is because the interoestrous period is long and variable and because there is usually a reluctance to use a bitch for breeding after it has reached middle age.

Most cases of infertility fall into one of three main groups: delay of oestrus, mistiming of mating and possible interference from non-specific bacteria.

DELAY OF OESTRUS

The time of onset of first oestrus varies from between 6 months to 2 years of age, although most bitches have exhibited their first oestrus by 15 months. Most owners do not like to breed from their bitch at the first heat, even when this occurs relatively late. The average period between successive heats is 7–8 months although periods of 4 months to well over a year are not uncommon. Although there may be a trend towards a seasonal influence bitches will come into heat spontaneously at all times of the year.

It is interesting to speculate on what stimulates the occurrence of oestrus after the long and variable anoestrus exhibited by the bitch. The possible effect of season of the year and the probable influence of pheromones in groups of bitches are two factors. However, they do not explain, for example, why an individually housed bitch comes into heat in the winter after a 9-month interoestrous interval. It is probable that, before domestication, bitches were seasonally anoestrus but selection over many years for appearance, with little or no reference to breeding patterns, has resulted in the present situation.

INDUCTION OF OESTRUS

Equine chorionic gonadotrophin (eCG) can be used at doses of 20 IU/kg administered subcutaneously daily for 5 days, with 500 IU (total dose) of human chorionic gonadotrophin being given intramuscularly on the fifth day. The length of pro-oestrus is unpredictable so that it is difficult to plan a mating time in advance. It is therefore necessary to monitor vaginal cytology and plasma progesterone concentrations, although even then, the chances of obtaining live pups are not great.

To induce oestrus using oestrogens, low doses, which in themselves do not stimulate signs of heat, are administered repeatedly. Using this system, endogenous hormone production is similar to that during normal oestrus.

MISTIMING OF MATING

Traditionally, bitches are mated between 10 and 14 days after the onset of pro-oestrus, i.e. during the first few days of oestrus. One mating, or two matings 48 h apart, is usually permitted. In general this system works well and most bitches conceive when mated to fertile dogs (Fig. 12.1). In fact, the exact day of mating is probably not critical because spermatozoa appear to live for a relatively long time in the bitch's genital tract. This complements the fact that bitch ova are shed when only halfway through the meiotic division and a number of days must elapse (during which the second polar body is shed) before fertilization can occur.

Laparoscopic studies on bitch ovaries have accurately defined the time of ovulation in the bitch. There is a relatively stable temporal relationship between the peak of oestrogen production, the peak of luteinizing hormone release and the period of time during which most ovulations occur. However, the exhibition of behavioural change, especially that of accepting coitus, does not seem to be so firmly coupled to the

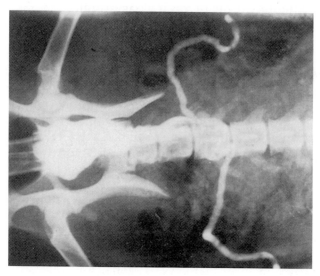

Fig. 12.1 Radiograph (ventrodorsal) of the posterior abdomen of a bitch in heat. Contrast material (12·5% sodium diatrizoate solution) has been introduced into the vagina under general anaesthesia and has entered the uterine horns. The bitch was mated on the same day and became pregnant. (From the *Journal of Small Animal Practice*, with the permission of the editor).

endocrine changes so that some bitches may ovulate before accepting the dog, and others ovulate as long as 9 days after this event. Thus, in individual bitches which do not conceive, the possibility that mating has occurred at a time which is not related to ovulation must be considered. It is also important to appreciate that the timing of events in pro-oestrus and oestrus are not repeatable from one cycle to the next even in the same bitch.

It has been customary to examine smears of vaginal discharge in order to monitor the process of keratinization of the superficial epithelial cells. As pro-oestrus progresses the vaginal wall becomes thickened and the cells impregnated with keratohyalin (or cornified) owing to the stimulus of oestrogens. Because the peak of oestrogen production by the ovary occurs during the middle of pro-oestrus, the change seen in vaginal epithelial cells is a delayed one, although it has recently been confirmed that the maximum number of keratinized cells is present at the time when ovulation is expected. A characteristic crystallization pattern of the cervicovaginal mucus is also observed (similar to that seen in the cow) during the fertile period; this can be seen on an air dried unstained smear of vaginal discharge.

In problem bitches, examining smears from the vagina every 2 or 3 days can be useful for ensuring that mating occurs around the optimal time. In the bitch, unlike most species, follicles undergo luteinization prior to ovulation. During this period progesterone is produced. The measurement of peripheral plasma progesterone concentrations will therefore allow the detection of impending ovulation. It is now possible, using enzyme-linked immunosorbant assay test kits, to determine rapidly the plasma progesterone concentration in the majority of practice laboratories. It has been claimed that ultrasound examination may also allow the accurate determination of the time of ovulation. Recent studies have however shown that this method is at present of little value, since in the bitch follicles do not collapse at ovulation.

POSSIBLE EFFECT OF NON-SPECIFIC BACTERIA

Certain bacteria, particularly β-haemolytic streptococci and *Escherichia coli*, have been incriminated as causing infertility by producing conception failure, vaginal discharge and early puppy deaths. These organisms are also often isolated from uterine contents in cases of pyometra. It has become customary for some dog owners to ask for bitches to have vaginal swabs taken for culture before they go to stud, and the isolation of β-haemolytic streptococci in particular is viewed with suspicion.

These swabs are usually taken from the vestibule, i.e. caudal to the urethral opening. However, streptococci and coliforms are part of the normal vaginal and vestibular flora and it has been found that the uteri of apparently normal bitches can harbour bacteria. There is however no evidence to suggest that if bacteria are isolated from the vagina there are necessarily bacteria within the uterus. Because the cervix of the bitch only opens during oestrus, parturition and the post partum period, it is probable that these are the times when bacteria are most likely to enter from the vagina; this is particularly so during coitus, although the antibacterial action of prostatic fluid may reduce contamination to some extent.

Although there is no direct evidence that the persistence of bacteria in the uterus is a hindrance to early pregnancy development in the bitch, it is a possibility which cannot be excluded. In trying to prevent this situation from arising it appears unrealistic to attempt to make the vagina bacteriologically sterile before coitus, especially since the dog's penis is likely to have a similar bacterial flora to that of the bitch's vagina, and since its penis will inevitably touch other parts of the bitch before it enters the vagina.

The author's policy is to swab the bitch in early pro-oestrus for bacteriological culture and sensitivity. The isolation of *Pseudomonas aeruginosa* is viewed with suspicion and the bitch is not bred from. Otherwise an appropriate antimicrobial drug is selected. Trimethoprim is the drug of choice as this is concentrated in vaginal fluids. Treatment begins orally 1–2 days before the expected (first) mating date and is continued for at least 4 days after the last mating. The rationale for this treatment is that it may help the uterus to become clear of the microorganisms which are introduced during coitus.

It is probable that isolating an organism in pure culture from the vagina is more significant than finding a mixed flora. In groups of infertile bitches the common history is that bitches come into heat less frequently and that pro-oestrus is short and terminates in vaginitis (as judged by vaginal smears).

The administration of an autogenous vaccine has, on occasions, been of benefit although in some cases it has been necessary for the whole kennels to move to a new premises (which have never housed dogs) before improvements in conception rates occur.

MISCELLANEOUS CONDITIONS WHICH CAUSE INFERTILITY

PSYCHOLOGICAL INABILITY TO MATE

Some bitches which are in heat (as confirmed by vaginal smears) will not entertain sexual interest by male dogs. In some cases a dominant dog may achieve copulation if the bitch is merely timid, but on occasions bitches will not stand for any dog. Tranquillization of the bitch is usually ineffectual and the only way of achieving pregnancy is by artificial insemination. Before this is resorted to Kennel Club permission must be obtained and the bitch should be examined per vaginum for any constriction at the vestibulovaginal junction.

In this context, it is considered that a tie should occur if copulation is to be successful. However, although this is probably desirable, there are many recorded instances of "non-tie" matings resulting in conception.

PHYSICAL INABILITY TO MATE

This can be caused by vestibulovaginal barriers (constrictions and remnants of the hymen), tumours and prolapse of the hyperplastic vagina; all require surgical correction.

ABORTION AND FETAL DEATH

The term reabsorption (resorption) refers to a process whereby embryos (fetuses) which die *in utero* are subsequently dehydrated. At some stage the tissue remnants are expelled per vaginum although these are probably eaten by the bitch or otherwise lost. The causes of early embryonic death are unknown but some may be linked to genetic abnormalities.

Later fetal death is followed by a similar biological process, but if skeletons have been formed, the dehydrated puppies retain a recognizable shape; they are usually expelled at a later date. Although herpesvirus has been incriminated as a cause, many abortions in bitches are of unknown aetiology. There is no direct evidence of *Brucella canis* infection in this country, but many bacteria have been isolated from cases of spontaneous abortion. Figure 12.2 shows six conceptuses removed from a rough collie bitch at term. She was presented with a black tarry discharge from the vulva but no signs of labour. The conceptuses were removed at hysterotomy and it was evident that they died at different fetal ages. The bitch was mated at the next heat and produced eight normal puppies. Frequently the investigation of such cases is unrewarding. Subsequent pregnancies may however be monitored during real-time ultrasound.

VAGINAL SMEARS

There are several methods of obtaining samples of vaginal fluid for cytological examination. The author favours using a plastic or glass pipette (at least 15 cm long) attached to a 2 ml syringe. The pipette is introduced into the posterior vagina by first inserting it through the vulval lips in a vertical direction. At the vestibulovaginal junction the pipette is redirected cranially. Cells are obtained by gentle traction on the plunger of the syringe as the pipette is withdrawn. A drop of the suspension is placed on a microscope slide and spread with another slide, as when making a blood film. A drop is placed onto a second slide which is tilted to allow the material to spread. Both slides are air dried. The second is not stained

Fig. 12.2 Mummified (dehydrated) fetuses removed from the uterus of a rough collie bitch at term. The three fetuses at the bottom are still encased in their membranes.

and is examined for mucous ferning.

There are several ways of staining vaginal smears but the authors finds Leishman's method both simple and effective. The dried smear is flooded with Leishman's stain (about 2 ml) and left for 3 min. An equal volume of phosphate buffer (pH 6·8) is then added. This produces a metallic-looking film on the surface of the stain (Fig. 12.3). After 10 min the slide is washed in water and allowed to dry. The smear may be examined under high and low power.

During pro-oestrus there is an increase in the number of round (small intermediate) vaginal epithelial cells present (Fig. 12.4). These cells have an obvious nucleus. Also present are erythrocytes and some polymorphonuclear leucocytes

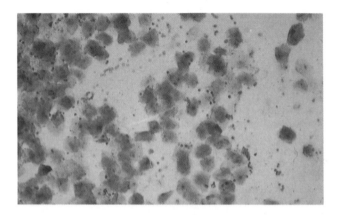

Fig. 12.3
Vaginal smear from a bitch in early oestrus, stained by Leishman's method. Cornified epithelial cells and erythrocytes are present.

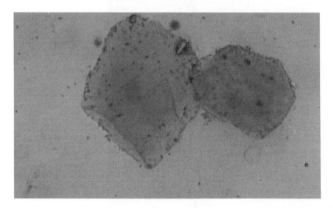

Fig. 12.4
Two cornified epithelial cells (Leishman's stain) with bacteria on their surfaces.

(neutrophils) (Fig. 12.5). As pro-oestrus proceeds the neutrophils disappear from the smear and the epithelial cells become larger, polygonal in outline and their nuclei become smaller. At the beginning of oestrus, 60–80% of the epithelial cells are polygonal and have no visible nucleus (squames). They have undergone cornification or keratinization. Neutrophils are absent and there are variable numbers of erythrocytes. Bacteria are also visible on high power examination, usually associated with epithelial cells.

At the beginning of metoestrus the smear changes dramatically; the epithelial cells become round and nucleated and masses of neutrophils appear. There is also a rapid reduction in the number of bacteria. It has been confirmed recently that the period of maximal cornification coincides with the time of ovulation.

ENDOCRINE CHANGES THROUGHOUT THE OESTROUS CYCLE

These changes are shown diagrammatically in Fig. 12.6. During pro-oestrus there is a peak of oestradiol production which precedes a similar peak of luteinizing hormone. Most ovulations occur 24–72 h after the luteinizing hormone peak. However, follicles luteinize extensively during pro-oestrus and begin to secrete progesterone at this time. Blood concentrations of progesterone rise throughout oestrus and peak

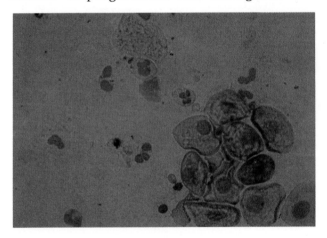

Fig. 12.5
Vaginal smear from a bitch in early metoestrus (Leishman's stain). Epithelial cells are round and nucleated (intermediate cells) and polymorphonuclear leucocytes are present.

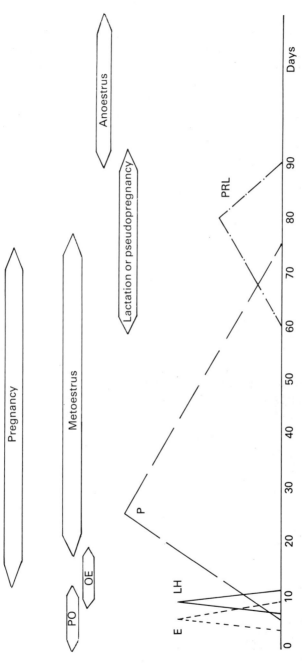

Fig. 12.6 Changes in hormone levels throughout the oestrous cycle of the bitch. PO Pro-oestrus; LH Luteinizing hormone; E Oestradiol; OE Oestrus; P Progesterone; PRL Prolactin.

during early metoestrus. Thereafter values fall slowly. Progesterone production by both pregnant and non-pregnant bitches is similar. At the end of metoestrus there is a rise in circulating prolactin. This is most marked in bitches which whelp and feed their puppies, but also occurs in non-pregnant bitches and is associated with pseudopregnancy. Anoestrus lasts for a variable period until the next pro-oestrus occurs.

The time when the bitch will first accept the dog (the beginning of oestrus) is very variable in relation to the hormone changes and it is clear that sexual behaviour is controlled by factors other than the endocrine system.

FURTHER READING

Allen, W. E., Noakes, D. E. & Renton, J. P. (1984) *Canine Medicine and Therapeutics*, 2nd edn, (eds E. A. Chandler, J. B. Sutton & D. J. Thompson) p. 442. Oxford, Blackwell Scientific Publications.

CHAPTER 13

Infertility in the Dog

W. EDWARD ALLEN

INTRODUCTION

Infertility in the male dog is more easily investigated and quantified than that in the female. This is because male dogs used at stud usually have more opportunities to mate than females, and because an assessment can be made of the quality of gamete (sperm) production.

Most male dogs start to produce ejaculates considered capable of fertilization at 8–12 months of age, although sexual activity, such as mounting and copulatory movements, begins to be practised much earlier.

The testes of male dogs are usually descended soon after birth and should be in the scrotum when the puppy is first presented for routine vaccination at 8–12 weeks of age. Non-descended testes may become scrotal after this time, although the likelihood diminishes with increasing age.

Owners of potential stud dogs should be warned of this, as dogs without two scrotal testes and their parents (carriers) should not be used for breeding because of the inheritability of the condition. Dogs with only one scrotal testis can still be fertile.

Infertility in male dogs may be caused by either inability to copulate and, or, failure in sperm production.

INABILITY TO COPULATE

PHYSICAL

Acquired injuries such as loss of a limb, fractures, lumbosacral spondylosis, etc. may render a dog unable to copulate and the only way of effecting fertilization is by artificial insemination. It is important to ensure that dogs which are unable to copulate are not suffering from inherited conditions such as hip dysplasia.

PSYCHOLOGICAL

Some otherwise fertile dogs are reluctant to copulate because of either having experienced a negative stimulus to mating in the past, or having become too "humanized" during puppyhood. In either case patience is required and it is an advantage if the bitch to be mated is presented to the dog in advance of its calculated oestrus.

The interaction between the dog and the bitch is also crucial, and in general experienced bitches are more tolerant of reluctant males. In the author's experience, collection of semen in the presence of a bitch in oestrus can eventually evoke a normal copulatory response from the dog, although on occasions this may also depend on the location of these activities and the humans involved.

FAILURE IN SPERM PRODUCTION

SPERMATOGENIC ARREST

This condition has only been described in the UK and typically is characterized by a dog which has been mated with several bitches at about 1 year of age with some success. It is then used infrequently whilst being shown and on completing a satisfactory show career is returned to stud; the first two to four bitches do not then conceive.

When presented for examination the dog typically exhibits

good libido and is fit and healthy, with no history or signs
of disease. However, examination of the ejaculate reveals that
it is composed of clear prostatic secretion and is azoospermic.
Physical examination shows that the testes are small and soft,
and the tails of the epididymides (usually palpated on the
dorsocaudal aspect of the testis) are shrunken or absent.

The aetiology of this condition is not understood; it may
be multifactorial. However, there is evidence that the problem
can be inherited, and that it involves an autoimmune response
to testicular tissue.

There is no known method of treatment or prevention and
experience shows that such dogs remain sterile.

POOR SEMEN QUALITY

The fertility of dogs which produce semen of poor quality is
difficult to assess because the standards applied to dog semen
are arbitrary, and because knowledge of what constitutes an
infertile dog is inadequate.

A dog which produces only a few normal shaped and live
sperm cannot be said to be sterile because it is always possible
that some ova will become fertilized. Conversely a dog with
an ejaculate full of progressively motile and morphologically
normal sperms would be expected to have good fertility. It
has been shown that males with as few as 16% morphologically
normal live staining sperm can produce pups in some circumstances.

The dividing line between these two extremes cannot be
defined and probably depends on the timing of mating relative
to ovulation, the frequency of matings, the expected fertility
of the bitch and other unknown factors.

Experimental evidence suggests that stud dogs can be mated
at least once a day without detriment to fertility, although
there is one report of overuse causing temporary cessation of
sperm production. No information exists on the effect of daily
ejaculation on dogs with poor semen quality, although in our
laboratory we have seen improvements in both motility and
the percentage of live staining sperm following daily collection
from an infertile stud dog, but the author has on several
occasions suggested that dogs with this problem should be

allowed to mate with bitches at least once daily throughout oestrus, which has been successful.

There is no proven way of improving seminal quality in dogs although a second sperm evaluation, 3 months or more later, may reveal improvement if a specific cause has been involved. The synthetic androgen mesterolone has been shown by some workers to stimulate testicular function in men, but unlike most exogenous androgens it does not significantly reduce gonadotrophin release. In our laboratory mesterolone increased the daily sperm output of normal laboratory beagles.

MISCELLANEOUS CAUSES OF INFERTILITY IN DOGS

ORCHITIS

Orchitis is usually traumatic and may be caused by bites during fights, or abrasions to the genital area in hunting dogs and hounds. The degree of damage varies with the degree of trauma, and the adjacent testis, if not affected, can also be expected to become aspermic for a while because of local elevation of temperature.

Three months should be allowed to elapse (the approximate time between the beginning of spermatogenesis and the appearance of sperms in the ejaculate) before the function of affected and adjacent testes can be assessed. Specific orchitis caused by *Brucella canis* has not been detected in the UK.

NEOPLASIA

Interstitial tumours are the most common to affect the testes of dogs. They do not cause an increase in size of the testis and are asymptomatic except that they interfere with spermatogenesis during later life. They are usually only diagnosed at post mortem examinations.

Sertoli cell tumours and seminomata usually cause testicular enlargement and, in the case of the former, signs of feminization. Both interfere with spermatogenesis.

TORSION

Testicular torsion or torsion of the spermatic cord can occur in both abdominal and scrotal testes. Initially there is massive swelling of the testis because of congestion and subsequently the testis atrophies and becomes non-functional.

PROSTATIC DISEASE

Evidence of prostatic disease is seen in the ejaculate as either erythrocytes or neutrophils. There are no data on the effect of this disease on fertility, although it is not uncommon for the third fraction of the ejaculate (of prostatic origin) to contain erythrocytes in dogs over 7 years of age; this may signify that there is subclinical prostatic change.

The presence of neutrophils in the ejaculate does not necessarily indicate prostatic infection as most sexually mature dogs have a degree of discharge from the prepuce, which is produced inside the sheath and contains neutrophils. This discharge is normal and can contaminate the ejaculate. Large macrophages are also seen in the ejaculates of dogs with both normal and suboptimal seminal quality.

ECZEMA

Scrotal eczema causes very intense pruritus resulting in self trauma. Although there is no evidence that this condition affects spermatogenesis, it is possible that it has some effect in the short term due to a local rise in temperature.

DRUG ADMINISTRATION

The effects of drugs on spermatogenesis in dogs have been poorly studied. However there is evidence that adrenocorticosteroids affect semen quality and it is probable that oestrogens, androgens and anabolic steroids are also detrimental to fertility.

Progestogens used to control libido and behavioural problems may also adversely affect spermatogenesis by inhibiting the production and, or, release of pituitary gonadotrophins.

SEMEN COLLECTION

A quiet room with a non-slip floor should be chosen. Extraneous noise and movement often distract dogs, especially those which are shy or nervous.

Ideally a bitch in heat should be available as this not only increases the libido of most dogs, but also improves the quality of the ejaculate. Failing this any quiet bitch may stimulate an otherwise reluctant dog. The bitch is best restrained by an assistant who can direct the bitch's vulva towards the dog, control its tail and prevent it from sitting.

The ease with which a dog can be induced to ejaculate under artificial circumstances depends on its experience, temperament and libido. Most older stud dogs are readily induced to ejaculate by digital pressure in the absence of a bitch, although at the other extreme young or nervous dogs often appear completely uninterested and may on occasions be impossible to collect from.

Right handed collectors should kneel on the dog's left side and encircle the penis (in its sheath) firmly between forefinger and thumb behind the bulbus glandis. In many dogs this will stimulate partial erection of the bulbus but if no response is evident to and fro massage is necessary. In keen dogs, initial swelling of the bulbus glandis is accompanied by vigorous thrusting but in quieter dogs there may be little physical movement and the dog appears to be unaware that it is ejaculating.

When the bulbus glandis has begun to swell the whole penis should be protruded from the sheath and gripped again behind the bulbus. It is often difficult to decide on the best time to protrude the penis. If the dog is reluctant, premature extrusion of the penis results in loss of the erection.

Conversely, if the bulbus is allowed to swell too much (and this can occur very rapidly in experienced dogs), then extrusion will not be possible because of restriction by the preputial orifice. In this event semen collection should be discontinued as the sheath will not expand sufficiently to accommodate the fully erect bulbus glandis, and this is therefore painful to the dog. When the erection has subsided a further attempt may be made to collect, but if the dog has been hurt it may be some time before this is possible.

The semen is collected into two test tubes via glass funnels. During the period of thrusting (i.e. after extrusion of the penis), the first (clear) fraction is ejaculated. If the dog is thrusting vigorously collection is difficult and is best not attempted as it may cause trauma to the penis against the collecting funnels.

Before ejaculation of the second (white) fraction the dog stops thrusting. Either just before, during or just after ejaculation of this second fraction the dog indicates its desire to turn round by lifting the left hindleg. An assistant should then lift the hindleg and place it in front of the collector's right arm. At the same time the collector bends the penis downwards and backwards so that it protrudes between the dog's hindlegs and allows the penis to rotate, so that the dorsal surface of the penis remains dorsal.

Ejaculation then usually proceeds uninterrupted, and the third fraction appears as a clear fluid. In long haired dogs it is difficult to hold the penis without including hair in the grasp, and this may cause pain when the penis is deflected backwards.

In reluctant dogs it is often beneficial to deviate the penis as soon as a partial erection has been achieved as this will help to prevent loss of the erection if the dog is distracted. However, even then, the erection may subside before full ejaculation has occurred.

An attempt is made to collect the second (sperm-rich) fraction into one test tube and the first, and part of the third, fraction into the other. It is only necessary to collect the first portion of the third fraction.

In all cases it is advisable to allow the dog to lick its penis so that return of the penis into the sheath does not cause inversion of the integument. If this occurs the dog is very uncomfortable and may resist manual correction.

The change from the first to second and second to third fractions may not be obvious; in some dogs at either the beginning or the end of the second fraction successive urethral contractions may expel alternatively sperm-rich and non sperm-rich emission. If a dog is interrupted during ejaculation of the second fraction it may produce clear fluid for a period and then conclude ejaculation of the second fraction. It appears that the prostate gland is the main source of the whole ejaculate, and that the sperm-rich fraction from the epididymides interrupts this evacuation, usually towards the beginning of coitus.

Collection from miniature breeds is hampered by the lack of room under the dog and difficulty in maintaining pressure on the base of the penis. In these breeds (e.g. chihuahua, Yorkshire terrier and Pomeranian) the author uses a small test tube (7.5 × 0.8 cm internal diameter) attached to a 5 ml rubber pipette bulb, the blind end of which has been cut off (Fig. 13.1). Once the dog's penis has been exposed from the sheath the pars longa glandis is introduced into the pipette bulb, which it completely fills when fully erect. After the second fraction has been collected, the test tube is removed but difficulty may be experienced in replacing it with a clean one for collection of the third fraction. With small dogs it is most convenient to have both dog and bitch on a table with a non-slip surface, and the collector and an assistant sitting either side.

SEMEN EVALUATION

The volumes of the three fractions are as follows: first fraction = 0.25–2.0 ml; second fraction = 0.5–3.5 ml; and third fraction = 3–20 ml. A rough indication of the quality of an ejaculate can be gained by looking at the second fraction, which should be milky white. An assessment of motility is made immediately or after the semen has been placed in a water bath at 37°C by putting a drop of semen on a clean warmed slide, adding a coverslip and looking at it under the microscope. Sperms which are oscillating or moving sluggishly are not considered motile.

Sperm concentration is usually measured using a haemocytometer although a colorimeter or spectrophotometer may also

Fig. 13.1 A 5 ml pipette bulb, with the end cut off, attached to a small test tube for collecting semen from small dogs.

be used. The average concentration in the whole ejaculate from various breeds is 125×16^6 sperms/ml with a range of 4–540×10^6 sperms/ml. However, the total number of sperms (100–$3\,000 \times 10^6$) in the ejaculate is the most reliable criterion as variation exists in the accuracy with which each fraction is collected, and the volume of third fraction which is included in the ejaculate.

The ratio of live to dead sperm is most easily estimated using nigrosin/eosin stain. Seven drops of stain (pH 6.8–7.4) are added to one drop of semen (both at 37°C) and a smear is prepared. Dead sperms are stained by the eosin. A smear prepared in this way may be conveniently used to study the morphology of the sperms under the oil-immersion microscope lens (Fig. 13.2).

The present state of knowledge regarding the significance of morphological defects in dog sperms is poor. Settergren (1971) considered that a fertile semen sample should contain at least 60% motile sperms. Examples of normal and abnormal spermatozoa are shown (Figs. 13.3–13.5).

SEMEN PRESERVATION

The use of fresh undiluted semen is the only form of artificial insemination via which puppies can be registered with the Kennel Club. Usually only the second fraction is inseminated,

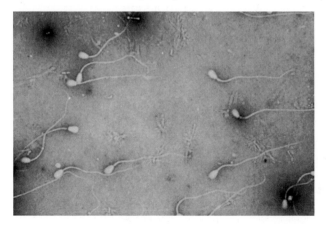

Fig. 13.2
Normal sperms from a fertile dog (nigrosin/eosin).

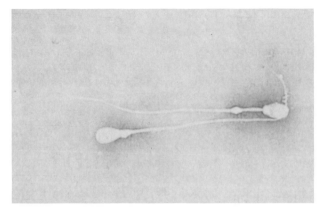

Fig. 13.3
Two dog sperms with cytoplasmic droplets. The upper sperm has a distal droplet (at the end of the mid-piece) and is considered normal. The lower sperm has a proximal droplet (at the neck) and is immature (nigrosin/eosin).

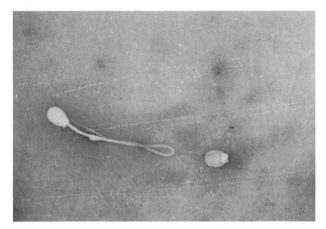

Fig. 13.4
Two abnormal dog sperms. One has a dead detached head and has taken up the eosin stain. The other has a bent tail (nigrosin/eosin).

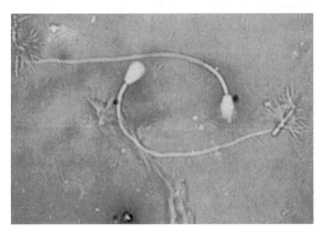

Fig. 13.5
Two dog sperms. The head on the left is normal. The head on the right has an oedematous acrosome and it is abnormal (nigrosin/eosin).

although some part of the third fraction may then be introduced to help in the transport of sperm to the Fallopian tubes.

When the insemination is not to be made immediately, however, methods of short-term (cooled and extended) and long-term (frozen) storage have been devised. Semen can only be imported into the UK from countries which are free from rabies and must be frozen because the donor dog has to be re-examined 14 days after collection and certified free from disease.

REFERENCES AND FURTHER READING

Allen W. E., Noakes, D. E. & Renton, J. P. (1984) *Canine Medicine and Therapeutics*, 2nd edn (eds Chandler, E. A., Sutton, J. B. & Thompson, D. J.) pp. 442–462. Oxford, Blackwell Scientific Publications.
Settergren, I. (1971) *Veterinary Clinics of North America* 1, 103.

CHAPTER 14

Therapy using Reproductive Hormones in the Dog and Bitch

G. C. W. ENGLAND AND W. EDWARD ALLEN

INTRODUCTION

Reproductive hormones, particularly steroids, are commonly used in dogs and bitches in the control of reproduction and some pathological disorders. In many cases gonadectomy is an alternative method of treatment. Factors such as the age of patient, possibility of side effects and attitude of the owner will influence the decision.

Although some conditions may be amenable to treatment by all members of a group of drugs, only a few may be licensed for such use. In this article the drugs specifically recommended for particular purposes in the Compendium of Data Sheets for Veterinary Products are listed.

TERMINOLOGY

There is disagreement over the correct terminology for describing the oestrous cycle of the bitch. In this article the following system is used:

Pro-oestrus commences with the first signs of vulval oedema and blood tinged vaginal discharge; it terminates with the first acceptance of the male. This lasts 9 days on average, with a range of 3–16 days.

Oestrus is limited to the period of male acceptance. It lasts for a similar period to pro-oestrus. Ovulation most commonly begins 1–3 days after first acceptance of the male. *Metoestrus* commences with the last acceptance of the male and ends with the regression of the corpora lutea. This period averages 75 days, with a range of 60–90 days.

Metoestrus gradually merges into *anoestrus* which is characterized by ovarian inactivity. The average period of anoestrus is 125 days with a range of between 15 and 265 days.

REPRODUCTIVE STEROIDS

The reproductive steroids which include oestrogens, androgens and progestogens are produced by the testes, adrenal glands, ovaries and placenta.

PROGESTOGENS

Progestogens (Table 14.1) (compounds with progesterone-like activity) are widely used to control reproductive activity. They exert a powerful negative feedback effect upon the hypothalamus/anterior pituitary gland, inhibiting gonadotrophin release and suppressing cyclical activity. They can be given parenterally or orally.

USES OF PROGESTOGENS (BITCH)

Terminology

The term *prevention* is used here when progestogens are administered to an anoestrous bitch to prevent the occurrence of oestrus. The term *suppression* is used when progestogens are used during pro-oestrus or oestrus to abolish the signs of that particular oestrus.

Table 14.1 Progestogens.

Agent	Preparation	Formulation	Manufacturer
Delmadinone acetate	Tardak	I 10 mg/ml	Syntex
Medroxyprogesterone	Anoestrolin	I 50 mg/ml	Berk
acetate	Perlutex	T 5 mg	Leo
		I 25 mg/ml	Leo
	Promone E	I 50 mg/ml	Upjohn
Megestrol acetate	Ovarid	T 5 mg	
		20 mg	Glaxovet
	Syntex	T 5 mg	Syntex
	Supress	20 mg	
Progesterone	Progesterone	I 25 mg/ml	Intervet
	Progesterone	Implant	
		50 mg	Intervet
		100 mg	
Proligestone	Covinan	I 100 ml/mg	Intervet
	Delvosteron	1 100 mg/ml	Gist-brocades

I Injection
T Tablets

♀ Control of the oestrous cycle of the bitch

Subcutaneous injections of long-acting preparations (medroxyprogesterone acetate, progesterone and proligestone) allow
slow release of progestogen and are used during anoestrus to
prevent the subsequent oestrus. Delmadinone acetate has
been used in a similar manner. Regular dosing will give long-
term prevention; however, in the authors' opinion anoestrus
should not be extended for more than 2 years. These preparations may also be given in early pro-oestrus to suppress
the signs of that oestrus. Depot injections have variable
duration of action, making the prediction of the next oestrus
or the timing of subsequent injection difficult. Following
this regime bitches will eventually return to fertile oestrus,
although some manufacturers do not recommend use in
breeding animals. Contact with other animals in oestrus may
cause failure of contraception.

Oral administration of a low dose of orally active progestogen
(medroxyprogesterone acetate, megestrol acetate) during
anoestrus will postpone the subsequent oestrus. The requirement for constant oral medication is the main disadvantage
of this regime. However, anoestrus is ensured during treatment

and there is the option to stop medication should side effects occur. The progestogen should be given in late anoestrus if treatment is to coincide with the next expected oestrus. However, if the animal enters oestrus during the first few days of medication, the dose can be increased to that required for oestrus suppression. Oestrus usually returns 3–9 months after the end of medication, depending on the stage of anoestrus when the tablets were administered. Administration of a higher dose of orally active progestogen (medroxyprogesterone acetate, megestrol acetate) for 8 days starting early in pro-oestrus will suppress the signs of that oestrus within 5 days. Correct timing of treatment is essential. Late dosing is often inadequate to cause follicular atresia. Subsequent return to oestrus usually occurs 4–6 months after treatment (range 1–7 months).

♀Treatment of pseudopregnancy

Progestogens (megestrol acetate, proligestone) inhibit the release of prolactin from the pituitary gland and are thus effective in treating false pregnancy in the bitch. Delmadinone acetate, medroxyprogesterone acetate and progesterone are also effective. Normal behaviour usually returns within 3 days, although relapse can occur in some bitches.

♀Treatment of oestrogen-dependent mammary neoplasia

Oestrogen and progesterone receptors are present in both malignant and benign mammary tumours. Progestogens (megestrol acetate) administered for 10–15 days may control the growth of some of these tumours but should be used with care (see below).

♀Prevention of habitual abortion

Daily to weekly injections of progesterone, daily oral medroxyprogesterone acetate and subcutaneous progesterone implantation have all been recommended for the prevention of spontaneous abortion. However there is little evidence to support the theory that progestogen deficiency is an important factor in pregnancy loss.

♀Treatment of irregularities of the oestrous cycle

Prolonged pro-oestrus and oestrus, and ovarian cysts have all been treated with a variety of progestogens. The results have been variable but signs may disappear with a return to normal cyclical activity.

USES OF PROGESTOGENS (DOG)

In the dog, testicular function is influenced by two gonadotrophins which are released from the anterior pituitary gland. Follicle stimulating hormone acts on the seminiferous tubules to promote spermatogenesis and luteinizing hormone (interstitial cell stimulating hormone) stimulates the interstitial cells of Leydig to produce testosterone and dihydrotestosterone. Progestogens inhibit gonadotrophin release and are therefore antiandrogenic in effect.

♂Control of antisocial and other behavioural problems

Problems such as aggression, roaming, territory marking, copulatory activity, destruction and excitability exhibited by both entire and castrated dogs may be controlled by the administration of progestogens (delmadinone acetate, medroxyprogesterone acetate and megestrol acetate). They have both anti-androgenic properties and a central effect on the cerebral cortex. Depot therapy may need to be repeated at least every 1–6 months, while oral preparations have the advantage that the dose may be adjusted to effect. Progestogens suppress spermatogenesis, an effect which should be reversed when therapy is stopped.

Various regimes are suggested for the use of oral preparations; usually the drugs are given for 2 weeks with a gradual reduction in dose over subsequent months although results can be very variable. Behaviour modification training is an essential adjunct to progestogen therapy.

♂Treatment of epilepsy

Castration and progestogen therapy (delmadinone acetate, medroxyprogesterone acetate) have been used for the control of some epileptiform seizures; their mode of action is probably via a central effect on the cerebral cortex. Dosage regimens vary but repeated injections are usually necessary.

♂Control of prostatic hyperplasia

Benign prostatic hyperplasia develops in dogs from middle age. The enlarged gland may encroach on the structures within the pelvic canal producing constipation or dysuria.

Depot progestogens (delmadinone acetate, medroxyprogesterone acetate) usually produce clinical improvement within 4 days, although a second treatment 1 week later may be necessary. Effects last up to 3 months. Oral therapy with other progestogens should be similarly effective.

♂Reduction of circumanal adenomata

These benign tumours of the perineal region of male dogs respond to repeated progestogen therapy (delmadinone acetate) provided that areas of necrosis are not present.

♀ADVERSE EFFECTS♂

In both the dog and bitch transient side effects have been noted which cease once therapy is withdrawn. These include increased appetite and weight gain, lethargy, mammary enlargement and occasionally lactation, hair and coat changes and temperament changes. They occur in less than 10% of animals treated with megestrol acetate.

Progestogen-induced lesions which give the greatest concern are cystic endometrial hyperplasia, mucometra and pyometra. The risk can be related to both the amount and the duration of administration, the latter being the most important single factor. For this reason the depot preparations of medroxyprogesterone acetate and progesterone are recommended only for use during deep anoestrus. Delmadinone acetate and proligestone have been shown to be safe when given at almost any stage of the cycle, although delmadinone acetate is only licensed for use in the male dog.

Oral therapy with both medroxyprogesterone acetate and megestrol acetate produces a low incidence of side effects on the uterus. No preparation is recommended for use in the first oestrous period or in prepubertal dogs.

Progestogens have been implicated in causing benign mammary nodules and mammary neoplasia, although this does not appear to be the case with proligestone. This is somewhat paradoxical because progestogens are recommended for the control of some cases of mammary neoplasia.

Progestogens are also diabetogenic. Progesterone acts as a potent insulin antagonist and can induce acromegaly in entire bitches. Progestogen therapy for the prevention of habitual abortion can produce masculinized female and cryptorchid male puppies.

The subcutaneous administration of progestogens may produce hair discoloration and local alopecia. It is recommended that injections should be in an inconspicuous site, although this is not always practical. Because of their adverse effect on spermatogenesis, careful consideration should be given to the use of progestogens in stud dogs.

OESTROGENS (TABLE 14.2)

Naturally occurring oestrogen oestradiol is only effective parenterally as it is partially inactivated in the gut. The

Table 14.2 Oestrogens.

Agent	Preparation	Formulation	Manufacturer
Oestradiol benzoate	Oestradiol benzoate	I 5 mg/ml	Intervet
Ethinyloestradiol (and Methyltestosterone)	Sesoral	T 0.005 mg (4.0 mg)	Intervet

I Injection
T Tablets

synthetic oestrogens ethinyl oestradiol and diethylstilboestrol may be given orally or parenterally. The purchase of injectable stilbenes is illegal in the EEC because of concern about residues in human food products. However, veterinary surgeons may still obtain and prescribe oral preparations for small animals. The efficacy of ethinyloestradiol when given orally to dogs is equivocal.

Oestrogens are responsible for the female sexual characteristics, including uterine growth and mammary development. They also influence mineral and protein metabolism. In high doses they inhibit the output of gonadotrophins, while in low doses there is an enhancement of follicle stimulating hormone (FSH) output.

Both the indications and dose rates of oestrogen therapy in small animals are mainly empirical.

USE OF OESTROGENS (BITCH)

♀Prevention of pregnancy following misalliance

Following an unwanted mating, nidation may be prevented by the oral or parenteral administration of high doses of oestrogens (oestradiol benzoate). Oestrogens interfere with progesterone dominance during the tubular phase of development of the fertilized ova, altering transport time in the oviduct and creating a uterus hostile to continued pregnancy. Generally, oestrogens are effective when administered up to 5 days after mating.

Until recently the parenteral administration of diethylstilboestrol after mating was used to prevent implantation. Oestradiol benzoate is now used in a similar manner up to 96 h after mating, although treatment too early may fail to prevent pregnancy. The oestrogen may cause animals to continue to show signs of oestrus or appear to return to oestrus and thus be remated. Such a mating may be fertile. However this is unlikely unless treatment was given in prooestrous (i.e. there will not be a second crop of ovulations). Oestrogens used for such a purpose should only be administered once, to avoid toxicity. Daily oral diethylstilboestrol has been suggested for 7 days after mating. Differences in absorption and, or, metabolism of diethylstilboestrol and oestradiol benzoate may influence their relative efficacy in the treatment of misalliance.

♀Treatment of pseudopregnancy and suppression of post partum lactation

The negative feedback effect of oestrogens on the hypothalamic/pituitary axis means that they are effective in reducing prolactin levels. Both oral diethylstilboestrol and parenteral oestradiol benzoate are used, although neither is specifically licensed for this use. Ethinyl oestradiol (with methyltestosterone) is marketed for this purpose but the suggested dose seems to be arbitrary and the large number of tablets required makes it unsuitable for anorexic bitches.

♀Urinary incontinence

Urinary incontinence is frequently described as a complication of ovariectomy in the bitch. The aetiology is unknown, but onset occurs months to many years later. Some cases respond well to oestrogen therapy while in others success is short lived or absent. The precise role that oestrogens play is unclear, although the major action is probably on the urethra.

Oestrogen therapy (oestradiol benzoate) is recommended at daily intervals for 3 days with subsequent injections every third day. Oral preparations (diethylstilboestrol and ethinyl oestradiol) are usually administered daily for 3 week periods, with a response being observed after the first few days.

♀Induction of oestrus

Oestradiol given two to four times at intervals of 2–3 days in very low doses (0.05–1.0 mg) followed by equine chorionic gonadotrophin therapy has been used for the treatment of delayed puberty or prolonged anoestrus in the bitch with variable success.

♀Alopecia in ovariectomized bitches

The epitheliotrophic action of oestrogens may be useful in cases of alopecia following ovariectomy. The primary effects on skin are to promote keratinization and to suppress sebum production. The effective therapeutic agent is usually found by trial and error, but the dose used must be low enough to avoid stimulating sexual attractiveness.

♀Other uses of oestrogens

(1)   Treatment of vaginitis in prepubertal and mature bitches (sometimes combined with antibiotics).
(2)   For vulval hypoplasia, particularly in spayed bitches.
(3)   Obesity following ovariohysterectomy.
(4)   Acute postpartum metritis (with antibiotic and fluid replacement therapy).

USES OF OESTROGENS (DOG)

In the dog, the negative feedback mechanism which inhibits gonadotrophin release means that oestrogens are anti-androgenic.

♂Control of antisocial and other behavioural problems

Oestrogens (oestradiol benzoate) may be used to control libido and other testosterone stimulated conditions in the dog. However, because of the possible side effects of long-term oestrogen therapy and because the superior action of progestogens, the latter are more commonly used in practice.

♂Reduction of circumanal adenomata

Daily or weekly therapy with oestrogens (oestradiol benzoate) is suggested for the control of anal adenomata. Diethylstilboestrol and ethinyloestradiol can also be given orally to effect.

♂Treatment of prostatic hyperplasia

Repeated parenteral oestrogen therapy (oestradiol benzoate) will cause a reduction in the size of the prostate gland. Oral therapy with diethylstilboestrol or ethinyloestradiol may prove more convenient. Oestrogen therapy may also provide temporary improvement in some cases of prostatic neoplasia.

♀ADVERSE EFFECTS♂

When presented with a bitch that may have been mated, examination of a vaginal smear should confirm that the animal is in oestrus. However, sperm may not always be seen in the smear, even after a recent mating. Oestrogens may increase the risk of pyometritis by potentiating the stimulatory effect of progesterone and causing cervical relaxation, allowing vaginal bacteria to enter the uterus.

Oestrogens suppress bone marrow function, resulting in severe anaemia and thrombocytopenia which may be fatal. There is considerable individual variation in the toxic dose, which may lie within the manufacturer's recommended dose range. Toxicity is generally dose related, being less likely with lower doses given over a period of time, rather than one large single dose.

Oestrogens administered during pregnancy may cause urogenital abnormalities in the developing fetuses, or cervical relaxation and abortion. Prolonged oestrogen therapy may produce signs of bilaterally symmetrical alopecia, epidermal hyperpigmentation, vulval enlargement, gynaecomastia and squamous metaplasia of the prostate gland. The latter may lead to prostatic enlargement.

ANDROGENS (TABLE 14.3)

The naturally occurring androgens testosterone and dihydrotestosterone are produced by the interstitial cells of the testis. The duration of activity of synthetic androgens is related to the nature of the ester (propionate, phenylpropionate, etc.). Androgens are divided into those with virilizing actions and

Table 14.3 Androgens.

Agent	Preparation	Formulation	Manufacturer
Drostanolone propionate	Masteril	I 100 mg/ml	Syntex
Methyltestosterone	Orandrone	T 5 mg	Intervet
Methyltestosterone (and Ethinyl oestradiol)	Sesoral	T 4 mg (0·005 mg)	Intervet
Testosterone	Testosterone	Implant 25 mg	Intervet
Testosterone phenylpropionate	Androject	I 10 mg/ml	Intervet
Testosterone propionate phenylpropionate isocaproate deconoate	Durateston	I total 50 mg/ml	Intervet

I Injection
T Tablets

those with anabolic actions. Drostanolone and methyltesto-sterone are virilizing while the naturally occurring androgens have both properties.

Virilizing effects include the development of the secondary sexual characteristics and the promotion of libido and sperma-togenesis. Anabolic effects stimulate protein synthesis, muscle deposition and mineral metabolism as well as appetite. High doses will inhibit gonadotrophin release in a similar manner to oestrogens and progestogens.

USES OF ANDROGENS (DOG)

♂Anabolic therapy

Various androgens (methyltestosterone, testosterone, testoster-one esters) are used for their anabolic effect in debilitated and aged dogs. They can also be used as supportive therapy in traumatic injury, delayed fracture healing, etc.

♂Treatment of hypogonadism and cryptorchidism

Hypogonadism may be secondary, for example to Cushings syndrome, or can be a primary non-development following puberty. The efficacy of androgens (testosterone, testosterone esters) has not been proved in these cases. A response is also unlikely in cryptorchid animals. If successful, dogs should not be used for breeding owing to the hereditary nature of the condition and the high frequency of neoplasia in undescended testes.

♂Deficient libido and poor semen quality

Although direct androgenic stimulation might be expected to cure impotence, the negative feedback effect upon gonadotrophin release contraindicates such treatment. None the less, androgens (testosterone, testosterone esters) are recommended by some manufacturers. No androgens are recommended for animals with poor semen quality, contrary to the situation in man.

♂Feminization

The feminizing effect of Sertoli cell tumours may be suppressed by the antioestrogenic properties of various androgens (methyltestosterone, testosterone, testosterone esters) although the treatment of choice is castration. Therapy may be useful to reverse the oestrogen effects after castration, although these should subside naturally; either depot preparations or daily oral therapy can be used.

USES OF ANDROGENS (BITCH)

♀Oestrogen-dependent mammary neoplasia

The antioestrogenic effects of androgens (drostanolone proprionate, testosterone, testosterone esters) may be used in the control of certain mammary tumours. Weekly to monthly parenteral administration is recommended, whilst oral therapy is given daily.

♀Control of the oestrous cycle

Testosterone implants and both oral and parenteral androgens have been used to prevent oestrus, especially in the greyhound. Although successful, these regimes may produce side effects that are not acceptable to some owners. A synthetic androgen, mibolerone, is available in the USA and elsewhere for the long term prevention of oestrus.

♀Treatment of pseudopregnancy

Androgens as well as oestrogens and progestogens inhibit prolactin release and are thus effective in the treatment of pseudopregnancy. Androgen therapy (methyltestosterone +/− ethinyloestradiol, testosterone phenylpropionate, testosterone implants, mibolerone) may be used either parenterally or orally for the suppression of pseudopregnancy. Androgens may be more useful than progestogens or oestrogens, since they lack adverse effects on the uterus.

♀ADVERSE EFFECTS♂

In the female, overdosing or prolonged therapy may produce virilizing effects such as clitoral hypertrophy and vaginitis. These may be more severe in prepubertal animals, and premature epiphyseal growth plate closure may occur.

Anabolic effects cause both sodium and water retention, thus contraindicating androgens in nephrotic conditions and hepatic dysfunction. Severe urogenital abnormalities may develop in female puppies if androgens are administered to pregnant bitches.

GONADOTROPHINS (TABLE 14.4)

Equine chorionic gonadotrophin (eCG) is produced by the mare during pregnancy. It is mainly FSH-like in action but does have some LH-like activity; it thus promotes growth and maturation of ovarian follicles in the female and stimulates

Table 14.4 Gonadotrophins.

Agent	Preparation	Formulation	Manufacturer
Equine chorionic gonadotrophin	Folligon	Injection	Intervet
Human chorionic gonadotrophin	Chorulon	Injection	Intervet

spermatogenesis in the male. Human chorionic gonadotrophin (hCG) is extracted from the urine of pregnant women and is primarily LH-like in effect. It causes final maturation and ovulation of follicles and the formation of corpora lutea in the female and stimulates Leydig cells to secrete androgens in the male. There are several gonadotrophin-releasing hormone preparations and their analogues available, but they are not licensed for use in small animals.

USES OF GONADOTROPHINS

♀Induction of oestrus and ovulation

The use of eCG in cases of delayed puberty or prolonged anoestrus in the bitch gives variable results. If ovulatory oestrus is achieved it may be followed by a short luteal phase; hCG has been similarly used. Induction of oestrus with eCG may also cause ovulation because the production of oestrogens resulting from follicular growth will initiate a natural LH surge. However, the most consistent results have been achieved when repeated dosing with eCG is used to induce oestrus and then hCG is given to control the timing of ovulation.

♂Treatment of genital hypoplasia and cryptorchidism

Sometimes hCG administration appears successful in promoting testicular descent, and may be of some use in stimulating hypoplastic testes. However, the probability that cryptorchidism is inherited should be considered.

♀Failure to hold to service and fetal resorption

Bitches which repeatedly fail to conceive are often given hCG on the assumption that ovulation has not occurred or that early development of the corpea lutea is inadequate – there is no evidence of the efficacy of these regimes.

♀♂Other conditions in which gonadotrophins have been used

Prolonged prooestrus and oestrus   Theoretically the LH-like activity of hCG will cause final maturation of slow growing follicles; however it is not always effective.

Suboestrus   eCG is said to improve the manifestation of weak oestrus in bitches.

Stimulating libido and sperm production   eCG should stimulate spermatogenesis, and both eCG and hCG should increase the production of testosterone, but their value in impotent and infertile male dogs has not been proven.

♀ADVERSE EFFECTS♂

The LH-like activity of CG may cause luteinization of follicles before the onset of behavioural oestrus or ovulation. Hyperstimulation of the ovary may also occur, resulting in cystic follicles or prolonged oestrous behaviour. There is a risk of inducing both anaphylactoid reactions and antibody formation following the injection of these protein preparations.

PROSTAGLANDINS

There are no naturally occurring or synthetic prostaglandin analogues specifically licensed for use in the dog. Preparations available for other species include the naturally occurring prostaglandin dinaprost (Lutalyse; Upjohn) and the analogues cloprostenol (Estrumate; Coopers and Planate; Coopers), fenprostalene (Synchrocept B; Syntex), luprostiol (Prosolvin; Intervet) and tiaprost (Iliren; Hoechst).

The reproductive prostaglandins are synthesized in the endometrium. They are generally considered to be luteolytic in nature although in man, dog and cat the normal lifespan of the corpus luteum is unaltered by the absence of the uterus. Since the corpora lutea of bitches are not readily lysed by prostaglandin action the uses of such compounds are related to their presumed ability to produce myometrial contractions and relaxation of the cervix.

USES OF PROSTAGLANDINS

♀Treatment of pyometra

Cases of open pyometra may respond to prostaglandins given for 5 days parenterally and combined with antibiotic therapy, although there may be severe adverse effects (see below) and the success rate varies.

♀Termination of pregnancy

Canine corpora lutea are unresponsive to prostaglandin therapy for the first 3 weeks of pregnancy. However, after this time repeated doses or slow-release devices may be effective, although adverse effects are still common.

♀Treatment of postpartum endometritis

Acute metritis following parturition has been treated successfully by inducing uterine evacuation with prostaglandins.

♀ADVERSE EFFECTS

The administration of prostaglandins may be followed by restlessness, hypersalivation, vomiting, abdominal pain, pyrexia, tachycardia and diarrhoea. These effects occur rapidly after injection and last for up to 3 h.

OXYTOCIN (TABLE 14.5)

Oxytocin stimulates ductal myoepithelial cells within the mammary gland and thus induces milk letdown. It also causes contraction of uterine smooth muscle. Posterior pituitary extract contains both oxytocin and antidiuretic hormone.

♀OXYTOCIN IS USED TO TREAT THE FOLLOWING CONDITIONS

(1) Uterine inertia (primary or secondary): the compound has a short half-life and repeated administration may be needed, provided that re-examination reveals no physical obstruction.
(2) Failure of milk letdown: hormonal agalactia requires prolactin treatment; however oxytocin is helpful in promoting milk letdown.
(3) Placental retention.
(4) Postpartum haemorrhage.
(5) Postpartum endometritis.
(6) Antidiuretic activity of the posterior pituitary extracts is recommended for a variety of purposes including the management of diabetes insipidus and shock.

Table 14.5 Oxytocin.

Agent	Preparation	Formulation	Manufacturer
Oxytocin	Oxytocin S	I 10 iu/ml	Intervet
Pituitary extract	Hyposton	I 10 iu/ml	Paines & Byrne
	Pituitary (posterior lobe)	I 10 iu/ml	Arnolds
	Pituitary (posterior lobe)	I 10 iu/ml	Univet
	Pituitary extract	I 10 iu/ml	Vet Drug

I Injection

♀ADVERSE EFFECTS

Oxytocin is contraindicated in obstructive dystocia, since uterine rupture may result; it may also promote placental separation which jeopardizes the survival of unborn fetuses. Subcutaneous administration of oxytocin may cause skin sloughing or abscess formation.

ERGOT PREPARATIONS

ERGOMETRINE

This is not licensed for use in the dog, although both parenteral and oral preparations of ergometrine maleate are available (Ergometrine maleate; Evans Medical and Syntometrine; Sandoz). Ergometrine produces a prolonged myometrial spasm with relaxation after 1–2 h when the uterus starts rhythmical contractions similar to those induced by oxytocin. It has been used to treat:

(1) Postpartum haemorrhage.
(2) Postpartum endometritis.
(3) Uterine inertia.

BROMOCRIPTINE

Bromocriptine (Parlodel; Sandoz) is a synthetic ergot alkaloid which inhibits prolactin secretion; it is not specifically licensed for use in dogs. Daily oral administration of small doses is often successful in the treatment of pseudopregnancy, but it may cause vomiting. This can be prevented by minimizing the dose, mixing the drug with food or using antiemetics.

TOCHOLYTIC AGENTS

Drugs including hyoscine and dipyrone (Buscopan Compositum; Boehringer), monzaldon (Monzaldon; Boehringer) and proquamezine fumarate (Myspamol; RMB Animal Health) may be used to cause myometrial and urethral relaxation.

NON-HORMONAL ABORTIFACIENTS

Non-hormonal substances which cause pregnancy failure in bitches have been shown to be effective but are not available in the UK.

CONCLUSION (TABLES 14.6 AND 14.7)

Table 14.6 Common conditions treated with hormones in the bitch.

Condition	Common treatment	Other possible treatments
Oestrus prevention or suppression	Progestogens	Androgens, Oestrogens
Pseudopregnancy	Conservative	Progestogens, Oestrogens, Androgens, Bromocriptine
Misalliance	Oestrogens	Prostaglandins
Induction of oestrus	Gonadotrophins	Oestrogens
Urinary incontinence	Oestrogens	Emepromium bromide
Pyometra	Surgery	Prostaglandins, Millophyline
Vaginitis	Oestrogens	
Uterine inertia	Oxytocin	Ergometrine
Milk letdown	Oxytocin	
Retained placenta	Oxytocin	Ergometrine
Postpartum haemorrhage	Oxytocin	Ergometrine

Table 14.7 Common conditions treated with hormones in the dog.

Condition	Common treatment	Other possible treatments
Prostatic hyperplasia and secondary prostatitis	Castration	Progestogens Oestrogens
Hormone related behavioural problems	Castration Behaviour modification	Progestogens
Circumanal adenomata	Castration	Oestrogens

CHAPTER 15

Diagnosis and Treatment of Common Disorders of Newborn Puppies

TONY BLUNDEN

INTRODUCTION

It is estimated that one in three puppies dies within the first 3 weeks of life. The diagnosis and treatment of illness in newborn puppies presents a difficult challenge to the clinician. Sick puppies are often referred to as "faders" with little discrimination over the possible cause of illness. In a BSAVA East Anglian Regional Survey (1980) on neonatal mortality in the dog, veterinary surgeons did not expect to reach a diagnosis in over 80% of cases. The aim of this paper is to review some of the most common disorders of newborn puppies in the UK in order to assist more accurate diagnosis, treatment and prophylaxis.

The neonatal period is normally taken as the first 7–10 days of life but it must be remembered that growth and development is a continuous process following birth. This period represents the time of greatest vulnerability, although the perinatal period as a whole, when the puppy is entirely dependent on its dam for its survival, should extend to the first 3 weeks of life.

The newborn puppy, unlike other more precocious neonates such as the foal or calf, is very vulnerable to a whole range of adverse conditions and demonstrates its immaturity in a number of ways. For instance its thermoregularity mechanisms are poorly developed and shivering mechanisms do not begin until after the first week. The eyelids begin to open from the tenth day onwards but vision is poor until 4–5 weeks old. The immunological system, though capable of stimulation, does not become fully competent until 3–4 months old. Therefore, because of immaturity, small size and often non-specific signs of malaise it is difficult to make a clinical assessment. Other aids to diagnosis usually employed in the adult are difficult to undertake and frequently a puppy is presented in a state of extremis, making any interference, for example blood sampling, a hazardous procedure.

GENERAL APPROACH TO DIAGNOSIS OF NEONATAL DISORDERS

The approach to the case will vary depending on whether the problem involves an individual puppy or a whole litter, or is a recurring problem involving many litters. A full investigation of illness and deaths in the perinatal period should take into account the following:

(1)   The breeding history of the kennels, especially in the previous 2 years, e.g. any associated seasonal/breed/incidence, association with particular dams/stud dogs, infertility, abortion, stillbirths, illness and deaths in the perinatal period and in older puppies and the general health status in the kennels.
(2)   Assessment of the management, including:
      Kennel construction and whelping facilities.
      Type of heating (it is good to encourage temperature recording in the whelping environment), risk of draughts and heat loss.
      Whelping routine and supervision, especially over the first 2–3 days.
      Hygiene policy.
      Staff capability.
      Presence of disease vectors, i.e. mice, birds, ectoparasites.
      Risk of infection by introduction of outside animals, e.g. stud dogs.
      Worming programme.
      Vaccination policy.
(3)   The health of bitches through pregnancy, parturition and

lactation, e.g. to detect metritis, mastitis.

(4)   Clinical pattern of illness and deaths in litters.

(5)   Individual examination of sick puppies (Table 15.1 shows normal physiological data). Routine clinical examination has to be modified because of small size and relative immaturity but careful observation of the behaviour of the sick puppy or litter (*in situ* at the kennels if possible) and a thorough physical examination can provide some valuable clues to aid diagnosis.

(6)   Post mortem examinations and appropriate histopathology and microbiology.

Table 15.1 Physiological data for young puppies.

Average body temperature	At 24 h = 35.5°C (96°F) By the 7th day, this rises to 38°C (100°F) and by the 4th week it reaches 38.5°C (101°F)
Respiration rate	Variable 15–38/min
Heart rate	Variable approx. 200/min
Kidney function	Glomerular filtration increases from 21% at birth to 53% at 8 weeks old. Tubular secretion matures at 8 weeks
Urine specific gravity	1.006–1.017
Water requirement	60–90 g/450 g bodyweight/day. The turnover is about twice that of adult
Caloric requirement	60–100 kcal/450 g bodyweight/day
Weight gain	Bodyweight is usually double that of birthweight by 10 days old
Shivering reflex	Develops 6–8 days after birth
Muscle tone	Firm. Flexor dominance involving body and neck muscles at birth is replaced by extensor dominance by the third day of life. Pups can stand at 3 weeks with normal tone and postural reflexes. Walking and running by 4 weeks
Hyperkinesia (body twitching)	Normal 1–3 weeks Disappears after 4 weeks
Eyes open	10–15 days
External auditory canals open	12–14 days

CLINICAL EXAMINATION

EXTERNAL APPEARANCE AND BEHAVIOUR

The healthy newborn puppy will appear round and full in the abdomen, with a sleek coat and the skin will feel warm and elastic if pulled away from the body. Normally the puppy will spend about 90% of its time asleep, showing an activated sleep pattern indicated by body twitching (only present in the first 3 weeks of life). The pup will only cry when disturbed or before a feed and then only for a period of a few minutes. There is a strong suck reflex. The newborn pup will gain weight regularly usually doubling its birthweight by the 10th day. The eyelids remain closed until 10–14 days.

Obvious departures from normal are a bony, ribby appearance, slackness of the abdominal wall, an empty stomach and inelastic skin (indicating dehydration). Alternatively, a swollen, tight abdomen suggests ascites or intestinal tympany. A dirty, unkempt coat indicates ill mothering or poor management. Other indicators of poor health are persistent crying, loss of body twitching, flexor dominance involving body and neck muscles (after day 3), a fall in body temperature, and changes in the appearance of the visible mucosae (e.g. cyanosis) (Table 15.2).

It is useful to have some idea of normal birthweight ranges. In general terms, small breeds range between 100 and 150 g, medium-sized breeds between 200 and 300 g, and large breeds between 400 and 600 g. It is helpful to obtain the normal range of birthweights for the specific breed concerned in order to judge which puppies are at risk from low birthweight. If the puppy is small compared to the breed average, then it is likely to be physiologically immature relative to puppies of more normal birthweight and therefore disadvantaged compared to stronger litter mates. The failure to gain weight at a regular rate for more than 24 h indicates some health problem or difficulty over feeding. Wilsman & Van Sickle (1973) found a low survival rate in pointer puppies (born in a series of normal whelpings) when individuals lost more than 10% of their birthweight.

Table 15.2 External examination of the newborn – some common features of diagnostic significance.

External features	Comment
Bodyweight and development	Compare with birthweight and assess low birthweight/progressive weight loss. Dehydration, starvation
Lack of body hair	Prematurity
Dirty unkempt coat; ectoparasites; skin pustules	Poor management/poor mothering. Pyoderma – check for possible associated skin/oral lesions in dam
Inelastic skin	Dehydration; also indicated by weight loss
Signs of injury (e.g. bruising, oedema, bleeding, fractures)	Poor management/poor mothering/dystocia
Mucous membranes	Cyanosis with cardiopulmonary failure. Pale with haemorrhage; jaundice is rare – can occur in haemolytic disease of newborn
Appearance of umbilicus, tail docking, dew claw sites	Check for signs of infection/damage and haemorrhage; this can be due to excessive maternal interference
Congenital abnormalities, e.g. cleft palate, limb deformity, microphthalmia; generalized subcutaneous oedema in anasarcous puppies, imperforate anus, encephalocoele	There can be a variety of possible causes, i.e. genetic/nutritional infectious agents/drugs and environmental chemicals. A specific cause is usually not found
Discharges from external orifices, e.g. haemorrhage, exudate, diarrhoea, milk from nose in cleft palate	Assess type of injury, infection or other abnormality
Swelling around eyelids	"Ophthalmia neonatorum". Pus formation beneath eyelids, often a *Staphylococcus* species infection

FADING PUPPY COMPLEX

About 50% of neonatal deaths have no obvious cause and most of these are classified as death due to fading puppy complex or syndrome. These are puppies of normal birth-weight which at birth are expected to survive but subsequently fail to thrive and usually die within the first 5 days without obvious cause. The dams are usually in good health and have unremarkable pregnancies of normal gestational length. The bitches do not have whelping difficulties, are good mothers and are considered to be in an adequate state of lactation.

Although apparently normal at birth, the puppies lose weight, show poor suckling responses and display either lassitude or unusual restlessness, with plaintive and persistent crying; this progresses to generalized weakness and death (usually between day 3 and day 5). Common post mortem features include bodyweight well below birthweight, the stomach and intestines largely devoid of contents and a general absence of gross lesions or defects. The liver to bodyweight ratio changes from 1 : 10 to 1 : 20. Histopathological examin-ation of all main organ systems does not reveal any specific lesions.

There are no common management-linked factors that are associated with the deaths, although there is a strong tendency for certain dams in certain kennels to have successive fading litters, while others experience no problems.

Although the clinical signs and post mortem findings are not diagnostic, there is a common pattern of signs and the deaths do constitute a large group within a narrow time period. It is not known if the aetiology is related to one predominating factor or if it is multifactorial.

DIAGNOSIS OF SPECIFIC DISORDERS

Although clinical signs observed in neonatal puppies will often distinguish between ill and healthy puppies, specific disease is much harder to diagnose. In one study (Blunden, 1986), the author found that one third of cases described by the owner as fading puppies had a specific, predominant cause. The most common causes of neonatal death were ascribed to:

(1) Infections.
(2) Maternal/management related factors.

(3)   Low birthweight.
(4)   Gross congenital abnormalities.

INFECTIONS

The main routes and sources of infection are prenatal (via the placenta or cervix), intrapartum (from the birth canal), immediate post partum from the general environment.

Bacterial

Many fatal infections result from peritonitis and septicaemia (often through infection of the umbilicus) and from pneumonia and pleurisy. Potential pathogens commonly isolated are β-haemolytic streptococci, *Staphylococcus* and *Pasteurella* species and *Escherichia coli*. The puppies are not necessarily debilitated from some other cause.

Enteritis does not occur as commonly in the neonatal period as in the post weaning period, probably because of passive antibody protection. Infection is more likely to occur if the pups are colostrum deprived (they receive 95% of passive antibody protection via the colostrum), for example if the whelping is prolonged and the firstborn pups are removed and do not suck in the first 12–24 h. Salmonella, campylobacter and *E. coli* infections may be considered although the enteropathogenic strains of *E. coli* have not been well investigated in the dog. Probably the *E. coli* isolated in most cases forms part of the normal intestinal flora. Predisposing causes of diarrhoea include unsuitable dietary supplements and the use of antibiotics, which can upset the balance of the bowel flora, especially at a stage when it is first becoming established.

It may be difficult to detect diarrhoea in the newborn pup without close observation, because of the regular cleaning activities of the bitch. Sometimes diarrhoea is indicated by inflammation around the perineum and a wet tail. Meconium is passed soon after birth and is normally a green-brown colour; this is followed by semi-solid yellow faeces once the pup starts sucking. Very watery, green or bloody faeces are abnormal.

Viruses

There is little evidence that viral infections are responsible for many neonatal/perinatal mortalities. Acquired colostral antibodies from vaccinated dams should provide immunity against canine distemper virus, canine hepatitis virus and canine parvovirus infections. Myocarditis associated with parvovirus infection in 3–6 week-old pups is now rarely seen, presumably because of the general level of immunity in the canine population. Occasional cases of enteritis seen in neonates are probably associated with colostrum deprivation and endemic virus in kennels. Canine herpesvirus (CHV) infection is a sporadic disease causing high mortality in 7- to 14-day-old pups. The virus replicates well in the neonatal pup because of the relatively low body temperature compared to the adult, and systemic disease is not seen after 3 weeks. Probably, in most cases, infected dams develop immunity which is conferred upon subsequent litters.

The role of respiratory viruses in neonatal infections is unknown. Distemper virus infection may cause fetal death in pregnant bitches and a runting syndrome has been associated with neonatal infection, but not specific respiratory disease.

Protozoa

There is little evidence that toxoplasmosis is important in the canine neonate in the UK, although intra-uterine infections have been produced experimentally.

Parasites

Toxocara canis is a common prenatal infection, but migration of larvae does not give rise to significant lesions in the fetus or newborn pup. However, larvae in the small intestine grow quickly (from 2 to 3 mm long in the first week to 4–5 cm or more by the third to fourth weeks) and can cause severe bowel obstruction or irritation by 3–4 weeks of age. Prenatal infection by hookworms is not thought to be common in the UK.

MATERNAL AND MANAGEMENT RELATED FACTORS

The dam should always be considered in addition to examination of sick puppies. There may be:

(1) *Temperament factors* related to the inexperience of a bitch at its first whelping or excessive disturbance of the bitch by interested family members, neighbours, etc., and occasional aggression or excessive clumsiness (large breeds).
(2) *Concurrent illness* in the dam resulting in poor lactation and mothering, e.g. mastitis, metritis.
(3) *Some abnormality of lactation.* Primary agalactia is uncommon, but there may be teat abnormalities or insufficient milk production to meet the requirements of the pups, especially for a large litter.
(4) *Injuries and reduced viability due to dystocia/caesarean section.*

LOW BIRTHWEIGHT

Pups of low birthweight are likely to be physiologically immature (even if they are born at full term) and at a physical disadvantage. Reduced viability is especially attributable to poor function of lung, kidney and liver. Inadequate nutrition of the dam can lead to low birthweight pups.

Placental disorders are poorly documented in the bitch, but it is possible that small placenta size, overcrowding of the uterus, placental disease and vascular anomaly could retard fetal growth.

CONGENITAL ABNORMALITIES

Congenital abnormalities resulting in death or euthanasia occur at a rate of 1–2% of pups born (Figs 15.1 and 15.2). Congenital defects may be genetic in origin, although other causes, such as nutritional factors, infectious agents, drugs and environmental chemicals should always be considered. The fetus is at particular risk in the first half of pregnancy

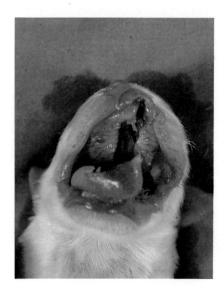

Fig. 15.1
Cleft palate in a labrador puppy.

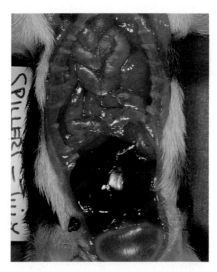

Fig. 15.2
Congenital diaphragmatic hernia in a beagle puppy.

before organogenesis is complete. A sudden increase in congenital anomalies in a breeding kennels should give cause for concern and further investigation.

PATHOLOGY

POST-MORTEM EXAMINATION

Many puppies are presented either in extremis or dead, and therefore necropsy is very important in diagnosis. Ideally, when dealing with large-scale illness and mortalities, as many puppies as possible should be examined to obtain a comprehensive view, as a variety of causes of death can sometimes be found even in one litter.

For post-mortem examination it is essential to be systematic and record details of external appearance, bodyweight, abdomen, thorax, structures of head, neck and spine. Examination should be carried out as soon as possible after death or, if that is not possible, the cadaver should be chilled (*not frozen*) to prevent post-mortem changes from obscuring further investigation. Post-mortem examination will be helpful to confirm livebirth/stillbirth, and reveal evidence of injury, poor mothering, congenital abnormalities, infections, low birthweight and prematurity or it may suggest fading puppy complex. A list of more common post-mortem findings and their significance is given in Table 15.3. (See also Figs 15.3–15.5.)

BACTERIOLOGY

Bacteriology is best performed on heart blood swabs or from sites where there are lesions suggesting infection or from unusual discharges, e.g. diarrhoea. The significance of potential pathogens that are isolated must be judged in the context of macroscopic and microscopic lesions and the degree of autolysis in the carcase. The association between certain

Table 15.3 Common post-mortem features of diagnostic significance in canine neonates.

	Post-mortem feature	Comment and interpretation
Abdomen		
Peritoneal cavity	Excess sero-sanguineous fluid Fibrinous adhesions	Usually occurs following a bacterial peritonitis (often via an umbilical infection) or as a result of an adenovirus type 1 infection (infectious canine hepatitis [ICH]) or canine herpesvirus infection (CHV)
	Haemorrhage	Result of dystocia or maternally induced injury. Also consider an inherited clotting defect, e.g. Von Willebrand's disease in German shepherds and cocker spaniels
Liver	Enlargement, mottling, petechiae White-yellow foci	ICH and CHV infections. Histopathology useful. Microabscesses; coagulate necrosis due to bacterial infection often associated with umbilical infection, e.g. β-haemolytic streptococci (BHS)
	Rupture of capsule and frank haemorrhage	The sequel sometimes to dystocia or maternally induced injury
Kidneys	Multiple petechiae/ecchymoses	Characteristic of CHV: histopathology of kidney, liver, lung, thymus and adrenal can be helpful. Sometimes smaller, less numerous petechiae are present in septicaemia
	Congenital anomalies	Occasionally one or both kidneys missing
Spleen	Enlargement/haemorrhages	CHV infection
Bladder	Haemorrhage	Occasional, following dystocia
Stomach	Empty stomach. Usually few lesions seen	Starvation (check state of lactation/concurrent illness in dam/poor mothering) Fading puppies invariably have empty stomachs (although stomach tubing may be practised by some breeders)
Intestines	Congestion/haemorrhages	Not to be confused with autolytic discoloration. Bacterial (*Campylobacter* species, *Salmonella* species, *E. Coli*, ?*Clostridia* species) and viral enteritis (parvovirus, ? coronavirus, ? rotavirus)
	Round worms in small intestine	Large numbers may be found, first in the duodenum and then gradually lower down the alimentary tract and stomach as a result of prenatal infection. They may cause bowel obstruction and ascites

	Intussusception	Of the small intestine at the ileo-caecal junction: sequel to enteritis. Sometimes hairs swallowed from the region of the mammae have been found in the intussuscepted portion
	Congenital absence of a gut segment	Intestinal obstruction; (gut anterior to the obstruction is usually full of gas and fluid). Also imperforate anus
	Retained meconium	Usually only present in stillbirths, or pups dying immediately after birth. May be a sign of poor mothering, due to lack of urinogenital stimulation
	Constipation	Usually only found in hand reared pups on artificial diet, given insufficient urinogenital stimulation
Thorax	Thoracic effusions	Present in pleuritis
Lungs	Oedema, congestion, consolidation, fibrinous adhesions between lung and chest wall; occasional lung abscesses	Pneumonia/pleuritis not uncommon in neonates; may be result of inhaled vaginal fluids, septicaemia, aspiration of milk, etc. BHS and *Pasteurella* species are common isolates. Float lung in water to test aeration; if pieces sink, this indicates consolidated pneumonic lung or primary atelectasis in stillbirths; not all pneumonic lung sinks, may need histopathology
Trachea-Bronchi	Milk clots, haemorrhage, excess fluid	Inhaled fetal/vaginal fluids/milk/blood from injury/fluid from lung
Thymus gland	Small, shrunken gland	Atrophy due to starvation/infection, possibly immunodeficiency
Heart	Specific lesions uncommon. Pericardial effusions and petechial haemorrhages	May occur in septicaemia/viraemia
	Congenital defects	Unless the defects are severe, these are not fatal in early life but become gradually apparent from the post-weaning period onwards, e.g. patent ductus arteriosus, pulmonic stenosis, aortic stenosis
Diaphragm	Congenital absence or represented as a thin membrane	Cause of severe respiratory distress
Head and spine	Congenital defects	e.g. Cleft palate, hare lip, spina bifida
	Injuries – oedema, bruising, haemorrhage	Dystocia/maternally induced injury

A. Blunden

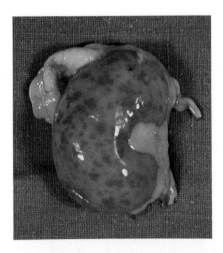

Fig. 15.3
Kidney. Typical petechial haemorrhages of canine herpesvirus infection in a 2-week-old West Highland white puppy.

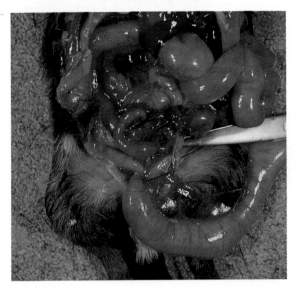

Fig. 15.4
Segmental agenesis of small intestine in a German shepherd dog.

organisms and disease is strengthened if they are linked with specific lesions (and if possible with ante-mortem blood cultures from sick puppies). An association may also be made with bacteria isolated from the dam, e.g. vaginal or tonsilar swabs, although a distinction has to be made between normal flora/opportunist pathogens and bacteria definitely implicated in disease.

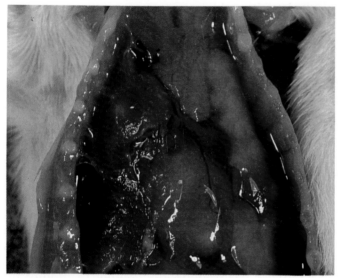

Fig. 15.5 Pleuritis and pneumonia in a 3-day-old West Highland white puppy.

HISTOLOGY

Histology is best performed on small pieces of tissue and preserved in 10% buffered formol saline. Thymus, heart, lung, liver, kidney, spleen and intestine are likely to be of most value, unless specific lesions are seen in other organs. As the neonatal brain is very soft it is best to fix the brain *in situ* after removing the top of the skull, if CNS lesions are suspected.

Although the placenta may not always be readily available or identified for each puppy, examination can be of value, especially in cases of abortion or stillbirth where there might be some associated placental lesions.

Histopathology can confirm or clarify the nature of macroscopic lesions or discover lesions that are only obvious at a microscopic level, e.g. it may be difficult to distinguish between pneumonia and generalized congestion by naked eye observation.

VIROLOGY

Virology is not commonly carried out on a routine basis in most diagnostic laboratories, and the evidence of virus infection in the canine neonate is usually suggested from a combination of clinical history, serology, post-mortem appearance and histopathology.

PREVENTATIVE MEASURES AND GENERAL THERAPY OF THE SICK NEONATE

Whether or not it is possible to identify specific causes of disease, it is important to reduce the number of possible adverse factors that could contribute to overall morbidity and mortality (Fig. 15.6).

A decision also has to be made whether to attempt therapy on individual puppies or to carry out euthanasia. In making a judgement account should be taken of the physical state of the neonate, the wishes of the owner and the economics of any treatment. Some large scale breeders may not desire any therapy, but require advice regarding treatment of other puppies in the litter or other litters in the kennel, in which case post-mortem examination may be more appropriate in the first instance. Alternatively, the treatment of an individual pup might be in the interest of good client relationship.

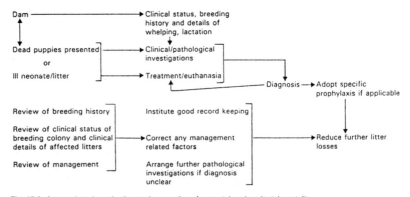

Fig. 15.6 Approach to investigation and prevention of neonatal and perinatal mortality.

The health status of the dam should always be considered when contemplating treatment of puppies to determine if any maternal factors are involved. Good management is also essential, especially careful supervision of the puppies over the whelping and immediate post natal periods; early sucking of colostrum (first 12–24 h) is important for antibody transfer and energy requirements. It is also important to recognize early signs of ill health, e.g. abnormal behaviour and weight loss, so that therapy can be instituted before the pup is moribund.

GENERAL CARE OF THE SICK NEONATE

Whatever the primary cause of illness, the neonate is soon at risk from hypothermia, dehydration and hypoglycaemia. Primary hypothermia is not usual provided the dam is allowed to carry out normal mothering and nesting activities. In normal circumstances the microenvironment of the nest area should provide sufficient heat for the pups to maintain their body temperature. Excessive heat, poor ventilation and malpositioned heat lamps are self-defeating because of discomfort caused to the bitch. Hand reared pups require an environmental temperature of 30–32°C (85–90°F) during the first 4 days, reducing to 28°C (80°F) by 7–10 days. Chilled puppies should always be warmed slowly to prevent tissue hypoxia. Starvation and hypoglycaemia may add to the risk of hypothermia as brown fat reserves (required for normal thermoregulation) become utilized. Glycogen reserves in the liver are used up very rapidly and the neonate is at risk from hypoglycaemia by the second day of anorexia. As water constitutes 80% of the bodyweight, with a turnover rate twice that of the adult, this, as well as immature kidney function, makes the neonate particularly at risk from dehydration. Texts recommend the use of 50 : 50 5% glucose/normal lactated Ringer's solution by subcutaneous injection at a rate of 1 ml/30 g bodyweight followed by oral 5–10% glucose at the rate of 0·25 ml/30 g until urine flow is normal.

The composition of milk substitutes should approximate to bitches' milk as far as possible. There is no commercial milk replacer that exactly corresponds, but Whelpi (Hoechst) and Canovel Milk mix (Beecham Animal Health) are probably the nearest. A detailed study on milk substitutes and the hand rearing of orphan puppies and kittens was carried out by Baines (1981). Most puppies are only able to ingest around 10–20 ml of milk depending on body size. Normally large volumes are not consumed in one feed but smaller amounts are ingested at regular intervals. However, they can adapt to larger less frequent meals (i.e. five times a day) if the composition of nutrients is adequate. Massage of the urinogenital region (to mimic the bitch's licking) is necessary to stimulate defecation and urination. Any puppies that fail to gain weight over a 24 h period, or lose weight, should be given supplementary feeding. Low birthweight puppies are at particular risk and should be considered for special nursing care and extra feeding.

INFECTIONS

Vaccination of the dam and acquisition of maternal antibody via the colostrum, together with good management, ought to provide adequate protection against the major infectious diseases. There is no commercial vaccine available to protect against canine herpesvirus infection, although evidence suggests that previously infected dams can confer immunity to subsequent litters. Application of antiseptic to the umbilicus after birth should help prevent abscesses and peritonitis. Antibiotics should not be used unless there is a good indication from pathological investigations and should be selected carefully because of the increased hazard of adverse effects in the neonate. The penicillins (or their derivatives), erythromycin, tylosin and lincomycin are among the safer antibiotics in the neonate. Antibiotics administered to the dam are not likely to reach therapeutic levels in the bitch's milk. Prenatal infections by *Toxocara canis* are common and treatment from 2 weeks old is recommended (e.g. with piperazine). Fenbendazole is recommended for treatment of bitches to reduce numbers of somatic larvae and the incidence of prenatal infection.

FADING PUPPY COMPLEX

The largest group of neonatal deaths (over 50%) is attributable to the fading puppy complex (FPC) where no specific aetiology has yet been found. As the first signs of fading can often be detected during the first 24 h of life, it is possible that this group of puppies is not completely viable from birth, i.e. there may be prenatal factors involved in the aetiology. There are no consistent reports of successful treatment for these puppies. Antibiotics appear to have little value. As these pups probably enter a fatal cycle of dehydration and hypoglycaemia, and fail to thrive soon after birth, *early* supplementary feeding of suspected FPC litters might improve survival. Otherwise treatment has to be symptomatic. In practice any supportive therapy is often given too late to alter the situation.

In a study of lung surfactant composition (Blunden, 1986) there was found to be a significant reduction in the phosphatidylcholine (lecithin) component in the fading puppy group. Abnormality of lung surfactant could predispose to hypoxia and breathing/suckling difficulties. It was not determined if abnormal surfactant was fundamental to the death of the puppies or a by product of some other pathological process. However, it does raise the possibility of the use of respiratory stimulants known to enhance surfactant production (e.g. Millophyline; Dales) as an adjunct to therapy.

The use of a paraimmunity inducer – a modified avian pox virus which stimulates non-specific immune mechanisms (Pind-Avi; Duphar, Netherlands) has led to apparent success in reducing deaths in German breeding kennels (Bibrack, 1975) but the product is not available in the UK.

CONCLUSION

Neonatal disorders in the dog present a difficult challenge in terms of diagnosis, therapy and prophylaxis. They are best investigated in the context of kennel environment and management and the health of the dam. Cooperation of the breeder is very important to obtain sufficient history and to implement any changes, which have to be both practical and economic.

Although many deaths in the fading puppy complex group cannot yet be ascribed to a particular aetiology, there are probably many cases of neonatal illness and death remaining undiagnosed because of insufficient investigation.

REFERENCES AND FURTHER READING

Baines, F. M. (1981) *Journal of Small Animal Practice* **22**, 555–578.
Bibrack, B. (1975) *Kleinterpraxis* **20** (80), 258–263, German (English summary).
Blunden, A. S. (1986) *Veterinary Annual* **26**, 264–269.
Lawler, D. F. & Colby, E. D. (eds) (1987) *Paediatrics. The Veterinary Clinics of North America* **17**, 3. W. B. Saunders.
Mosier, J. E. (ed.) (1978) *Canine Paediatrics. The Veterinary Clinics of North America* **8**, 1. W. B. Saunders.
Wilsman, N. J. & Van-Sickle, D. C. (1973) *Journal of the American Veterinary Medical Association* **163** (8), 971–975.

CHAPTER 16

The Pruritic Dog

DAVID GRANT

INTRODUCTION

Pruritus is a common problem in the dog. Important factors in its management are an accurate diagnosis, from which follows specific, logical treatment. A policy for the use of glucocorticoids is most important.

WHAT IS PRURITUS?

Pruritus may be defined as an unpleasant sensation which provokes a desire to scratch. It is considered, along with heat, cold, pain and touch, as a primary cutaneous sensation. A distinction should be made between physiological pruritus, which is normal, and pathological pruritus – a more severe, persistent and poorly understood phenomenon. Occasionally, careful questioning of the owner will reveal that the pruritus is not pathological and extensive investigations and therapy may thus be avoided.

Receptors for the stimulus of pruritus are found especially in the dermo-epidermal junction. Impulses are carried along slow conducting unmyelinated C fibres and ascend in the spine via the ventrolateral spinothalamic tract to the sensory cortex. Proteolytic enzymes are now thought to be the major mediators of pruritus. These enzymes arise from bacteria, fungi, mast cells, damaged epidermal cells and leucocytes, and may also be released by capillary dilation.

It is important to realize that more than one condition can occur on the same dog. A careful history and physical examination of the dog and treatment of at least one of these conditions will frequently reduce the pruritic threshold to a more acceptable level from the owner's point of view. This will make subsequent investigations easier.

CAUSES OF PRURITUS

Some important causes of canine pruritus are:

Ancylostoma, Uncinaria species
Trombicula species
Lice
Allergy (atopy, food, contact, bacterial)
Seborrhoea complex
Autoimmune disease
Neoplastic conditions
Fleas (allergy, irritant)
Bacterial infection
Fungal infection
Cheyletiella species
Otodectes species
Sarcoptes species
Demodex species (with secondary infection)

INVESTIGATION

In all but the simplest case, it is advisable to adopt a careful logical approach to the investigation of the pruritic dog. Absolute recognition of clinical signs is frequently unreliable since many skin conditions look identical, especially if there has been delay in requesting veterinary advice. A logical approach to the investigation of skin conditions has been described by many authorities, that of Lloyd (1985) is shown in Table 16.1.

History is the single most useful procedure in making a diagnosis. It is commonly stated that it supplies 70% of the diagnostic information. Frequently a specific diagnosis is not made initially, but arrived at by a process of elimination. It is important to explain this to the owner from the outset, since many arrive at the clinic with an unjustified expectation of instant diagnosis and cure.

Some key facts in taking the history are:

Age, sex and breed
Age of onset of pruritus, whether intermittent
Site and nature of lesions – if any
Severity of pruritus, response to glucocorticoids
Evidence of transmission
Diet
Have fleas been seen?

Table 16.1 Pruritus – investigative steps.

1 Take history
2 Make physical examination
3 Evaluate differential diagnosis
4 Do initial diagnostic tests
5 Narrow differential diagnosis
6 Do definitive tests
7 Arrive at a diagnosis

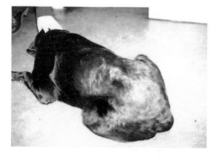

Fig. 16.1
Chronic flea allergic dermatitis in an 8-year-old labrador.

Fig. 16.2
Generalized sarcoptic mange in a cocker spaniel.

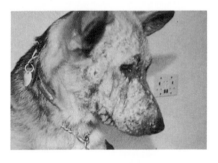

Fig. 16.3
Skin lesions on the owner of a dog with cheyletiella
infection.

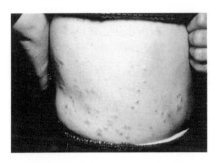

Fig. 16.4
Generalized pustular demodectic mange in a 14-
month GSD (photo: Keith Thoday).

Fig. 16.5
Pedal dermatitis caused by hookworm larvae.

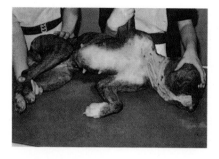

Fig. 16.6
Two-year-old boxer with facial, pedal and ventral erythema.

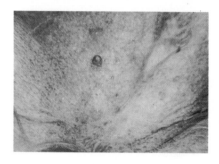

Fig. 16.7
Secondary pyoderma of the ventral abdomen in a 2-year-old crossbred with atopy.

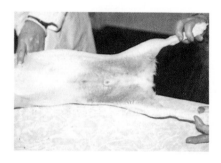

Fig. 16.8
Allergic contact dermatitis in a 4-year-old labrador. The allergen was grass pollen.

Fig. 16.9
Acute moist dermatitis ("hot spot") in a 9-year-old crossbred dog.

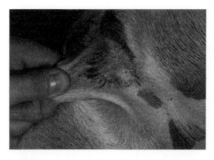

Fig. 16.10
Vulval fold pyoderma in a 1-year-old bulldog.

Fig. 16.11
Pustular and papular lesions in 4-month-old dog with impetigo.

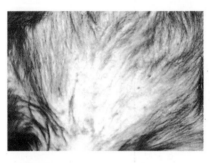

Fig. 16.12
Severe papular pyoderma lesions in an 18-month-old GSD.

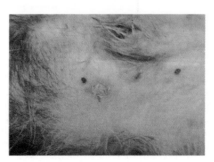

Fig. 16.13
Inflammatory pyoderma in a 2-year-old dog.

Fig. 16.14
Nasal pyoderma in a 3-year-old crossbred.

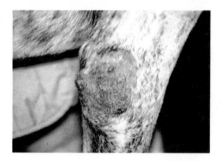

Fig. 16.15
Callus pyoderma in a 9-year-old great dane.

PRINCIPAL FEATURES OF IMPORTANT PRURITIC CONDITIONS IN THE DOG (FIGS 16.1–16.15)

ECTOPARASITES

Fleas

Flea infestation is the single major cause of pruritus in the dog in the UK. The pruritus may be induced by simple mechanical irritation from bites, (flea dermatitis) or by hypersensitivity to flea saliva (flea allergic dermatitis). Flea dermatitis is not difficult to diagnose, on finding lesions in typical sites – the gluteal region, ventral abdomen and the backs of the hind legs, and the presence of fleas or their faeces.

Flea allergic dermatitis, which is thought to be more common, is frequently difficult to diagnose. Explain this to the owner. Classical cases of flea allergic dermatitis are relatively straightforward from the diagnostic point of view. If treatment is inadequate, hyperpigmentation and acanthosis of the lesions may result.

Many dogs, however, present with non-specific generalized pruritus, and the diagnosis can only be made when there is a good response to proper flea eradication. In the eradication of fleas it is important to treat all animals in the house, especially cats (the cat flea is the most common flea on dogs in the UK). The environment should also be thoroughly treated with appropriate insecticides. Failure to adhere to these simple basic principles will result in therapeutic failure, and introduce doubt into the owner's and veterinary surgeon's minds.

Sarcoptes scabiei

Sarcoptes scabiei var. *canis* causes sarcoptic mange in the dog. It is an intensely pruritic condition, which is poorly responsive to glucocorticoids. Sometimes the source of infestation is suggested in the history – a recent visit to kennels or a grooming parlour for example. Usually the pruritus starts around the head, especially the pinnae. Failure to treat infection adequately allows the condition to become generalized, first to the elbows, hocks and ventral parts, and eventually the entire body.

Sarcoptic mange is contagious to other dogs and to humans. About 50% of the author's cases' owners also showed lesions, the development of which is favoured by close bodily contact, for example, allowing the dog in the bed or on the lap. Diagnosis is by skin scrapings and demonstration of the mite and, or, eggs. This is a difficult task, and numerous scrapings from lesion sites are necessary. Even with more than 10 scrapings per dog positive identification of the mite is only made in approximately 50% of cases. It follows that if sarcoptic mange is suspected it should be treated even if a thorough search for the mite is unsuccessful. A retrospective diagnosis is permissible if specific treatment is followed by cure.

In the treatment of sarcoptic mange it is advisable to clip long haired dogs to allow proper penetration of medicaments. Suitable washes are benzene hexachloride (Quellada; Stafford Miller) or bromocylcen (Alugan; Hoechst).

Glucocorticoids are not normally necessary except in the advanced case. Proper therapy with appropriate acaricidal drugs rapidly results in a dramatic lessening of the pruritus.

Cheyletiella species

Cheyletiella species are most commonly seen in puppies. The predominant clinical sign is dandruff. Frequently there is minimal pruritus in the early stages, but older animals may exhibit intense pruritus caused by the development of hypersensitivity. Owners commonly develop a characteristic pruritic rash in areas of contact.

Diagnosis is made by microscopic examination of coat brushings or of superficial skin scrapings.

Most acaricidal shampoos are effective in the treatment of the mite, e.g. benzene hexachloride (Quellada; Stafford Miller), selenium sulphide (Seleen; Ceva). The author routinely treats the environment with iodofenphos/dichlorvos (Nuvan Staykil; Ciba-Geigy).

Otodectes cynotis

Otodectes cynotis is principally a parasite of the ear canal. Aberrant infestations, however, may occur on the head, back and tail tip. Treatment of the ears with an acaricidal preparation and spraying the entire coat with insecticide is usually effective.

Trombicula autumnalis

This mite induces a seasonal (late summer and autumn) pedal and ventral dermatitis. Only the third stage larvae are parasitic and these can easily be identified as orange dots in the affected areas. Short-term glucocorticoids and acaricidal washes such as bromocyclen (Alugan; Hoechst) are effective.

Demodex canis

Localized demodicosis is rarely pruritic, but the generalized form of the condition is severely pruritic when associated with secondary pyoderma. It is essential, therefore, to perform skin scrapings on all cases of superficial or deep pyoderma. It should also be noted that dogs with the generalized form of demodicosis and secondary pyoderma have T-cell lymphocyte suppression. The use of glucocorticoids in these cases in an attempt to alleviate pruritus is *absolutely contraindicated*, since the immunosuppression will be worsened, favouring further multiplication of mites and bacteria.

In the treatment of generalized demodicosis there is needless controversy. The method described by Thoday (1981) using rotenone in spirit and systemic antibiotics is effective in over 90% of cases.

Amitraz (Derasect Demodectic Mange Wash; Beecham Animal Health), recently introduced to the UK market, considerably improves the clinical appearance of cases, but its long term effectiveness has to be established.

Lice

The sucking louse (*Linognathus setosus*) and the biting louse (*Trichodectes canis*) cause pruritus. Most cases occur in puppies from pet shops, and the diagnosis is easily missed if examination is not made with a hand lens under adequate illumination.

Lice are relatively easy to treat – virtually any insecticide is effective in shampoo form.

Hookworm dermatitis

Hookworms (*Ancylostoma caninum, Uncinaria stenocephala*) may cause pedal and ventral pruritus, particularly in kennelled dogs on grass or earth runs. Diagnosis is made on physical examination and microscopical examination of faeces. In some cases biopsy is helpful. Treatment is by means of anthelminthics such as nitroscanate (Lopatol; Ciba-Geigy), together with disinfection of the run with salt or borax solution.

ALLERGY

Allergies are important causes of canine pruritus. The three most common forms are atopy (inhalant) dermatitis, contact allergy, and food allergy.

Atopy (Table 16.2)

Also known as inhalant allergic dermatitis or atopic dermatitis. Allergy develops predominantly to inhaled allergens such as house dust mite, pollens, human and animal danders. Affected animals are genetically predisposed to form certain antibodies (IgE and IgGd) to these environmental allergens. The antibodies localize on the mast cells, and antigen/antibody interaction causes degranulation of the mast cell, with release of vaso-active amines. The resulting inflammation initiates pruritus and is an example of type 1 (Gell and Coombes) hypersensitivity. The incidence in practice is reported to be between 3 and 8% of dermatological cases.

Pruritus in atopic dogs tends to be in specific facial, pedal and ventral sites. Secondary otitis and pyoderma are common complicating factors.

The role of secondary pyoderma should be assessed by rigorous antibiotic therapy (see below). Resolution of the pyoderma lesions, but continuing pruritus, suggests an underlying allergy. Before considering allergy skin testing other causes of pruritus, such as parasites, food and contact allergy

Table 16.2 Typical clinical features of an atopic dog.

Age of onset	1–3 years (range 6 months to 7 years)
Predisposed breeds	Include boxers, terriers, English setters, dalmatians, pugs, Lhasa apso and miniature schnauzer
Cause	Allergy to inhaled allergens
Signs	Pruritus +/− secondary pyoderma, excoriation
Diagnosis	Clinical signs + allergy skin testing
Treatment	Avoidance of the allergen (rarely practicable) Hyposensitization Glucocorticoids

should be ruled out. Allergy skin testing is a specialized task, and is not considered further in this article. It is best performed in a centre where atopic dogs are investigated frequently.

Contact allergic dermatitis (Table 16.3)

Primary irritant dermatitis is more common than allergic contact dermatitis, which is thought to account for approximately 1% of dermatological cases. Many substances have been incriminated as allergens. These include pollens, soaps, shampoos, insecticides, drugs, mordants and finishes used in the manufacture of carpets and blankets, rubber and plastics. The allergens are generally of low molecular weight (haptens) and combine with skin proteins to form high molecular weight antigenic molecules. These are transported to regional lymph nodes where specific T-cell lymphocytes are stimulated. Sensitized lymphocytes migrate to the area of contact and an inflammatory response is initiated. This is an example of a Type 4 (Gell and Coombes) hypersensitivity.

Diagnosis is by means of physical examination allied to the history. This is accomplished predominantly by elimination of the suspected allergen from the environment, followed by provocative exposure. Patch testing, which is routine in man, is technically difficult in the dog and is rarely attempted in veterinary practice.

Allergic contact dermatitis is best treated by removal of the offending allergen if it can be identified. Glucocorticoids are only moderately effective and have side effects. Note that hyposensitization is not effective in dogs.

Table 16.3 Clinical features of allergic contact dermatitis.

Age of onset	Over 1 year old. Rare in dogs less than 1 year because at least 6 months induction period is usual
Cause	Many substances have been incriminated (see text)
Lesions	Erythema, macules and papules (acute) Hyperpigmentation and lichenification (chronic)
Lesion sites	Ventral abdomen, feet, (scrotum, chin, neck and pinnae)

Food allergy

There is some controversy regarding the incidence of food allergy in dogs. Some authorities state that it is common, while others regard it as rare.

Proven cases have been found to be primarily caused by meat protein, milk or wheat. The immunological mechanisms are not completely understood and skin changes are variable. Pruritus and self-inflicted trauma are the main signs.

A diagnosis can only be made by feeding a restricted "hypo-allergenic diet" of a protein source unfamiliar to the dog (commonly lamb), with rice for 2 weeks. Improvement in that time suggests food allergy. Specific protein sources may then be introduced into the diet on a weekly basis. Relapse followed by remission, when the offending allergen is removed from the diet, enables a diagnosis to be made.

Note that allergy skin testing is of no use in the diagnosis of food allergy, nor is changing from one commercial diet to another, since the offending allergen will commonly be present in both diets.

Food allergy is usually poorly responsive to glucocorticoids. The only effective cure is to identify the allergen and remove it from the animal's diet.

PYODERMA

It is probably true to say that most superficial and deep pyodermas are secondary, and the essential goal in treatment is to find the underlying cause and treat it. This is frequently difficult in practice, and inappropriate therapy results. As a result pyodermas may be considered to be the most difficult of the common skin conditions to diagnose and treat.

It is now recognized that the important pathogen of the skin is *Staphylococcus intermedius*. Also there has been a recent more useful classification according to the depth of infection, thus we may consider pyodermas to be surface, superficial or deep.

Surface pyodermas

These are infections of the outermost layers of the skin, with minimal bacterial involvement. Examples are acute moist dermatitis and fold pyodermas. Underlying causes include flea allergy, impacted anal sacs, or anatomical defects in the case of the fold pyodermas. In general the surface pyodermas are not difficult to diagnose and the underlying factors are more obvious than is the case with the deeper infections.

Superficial pyodermas

Superficial pyodermas are defined as infections in or at the level of the intact hair follicle. Two common types of superficial pyoderma discussed in this article are impetigo and folliculitis.

Impetigo

Impetigo is a subcorneal infection seen frequently in young dogs 1–3 months old, and occasionally in older dogs. The lesions are restricted to the non-hairy (glabrous) skin of the ventral abdomen. Impetigo is normally a relatively benign condition and only occasionally pruritic.

Folliculitis

Folliculitis is a more serious superficial pyoderma which may be difficult to recognize. The lesions are quite variable, from short-lived pustules to circular crusts, focal alopecia, papules and hive-like eruptions. Pruritus may or may not be present. The groin is the most frequent site of occurrence, often extending down the thighs and flanks if not treated early. In some cases, pruritus is severe and these have been described by some authorities as bacterial hypersensitivity (although the precise immunology has not been established), pruritic superficial pyoderma or inflammatory pyoderma.

Deep pyoderma

Deep pyodermas are infections deeper than the level of the hair follicle, and follicle rupture is common.

In general deep pyodermas are less difficult to recognize than superficial pyodermas, but the depth of infection necessitates prolonged therapy. Furunculosis and cellulitis are examples of deep pyoderma, and other types are classified according to site. For example, nasal pyoderma, callus pyoderma and anal furunculosis.

Management of pyoderma

The principal features to consider in the management of pyoderma are the possible underlying factors (Table 16.4), and appropriate antibiotic therapy.

Antibiotic therapy is the cornerstone of therapy in superficial and deep pyodermas. First line antibiotics commonly used include erythromycin, lincomycin, trimethoprim/sulphadiazine, and clavulanic potentiated amoxicillin. In severe deep pyodermas cephalexin is an important, and sometimes life saving, drug. Penicillin, ampicillin, and tetracyclines are not usually effective. Antibiotic therapy should be given for adequate duration – usually 15–25 days in cases of superficial

Table 16.4 Some important underlying causes of pyoderma.

Surface	Superficial	Deep
Acute moist dermatitis	*Impetigo*	*Furunculosis/cellulitis*
Flea allergy	Poor nutrition	Demodex
Anal sac infection/blockage	Dirty environment	Hypothyroidism
	Ectoparasites	
	Distemper	Immunosuppression
	Folliculitis	
Dirty coat/poor grooming	Hypothyroidism	Dermatophytes
Otitis externa	Flea allergy	Hyperadrenocorticism
Superficial wounds	Food allergy	
Fold pyodermas		
Anatomical defects	Atopy	
	Seborrhoea	

pyodermas, and 20–40 days or longer in cases of deep pyoderma.

Glucocorticoids are contraindicated in the treatment of superficial and deep pyodermas. When these conditions are pruritic there is a strong temptation to use glucocorticoids. They give a false sense of security in the early stages of treatment since they reduce inflammation and therefore pruritus. However, the clinician cannot tell whether the improvement has resulted from proper antibiotic therapy or from the use of the glucocorticoids. There will also be reduced sebum production and reduction of an adequate inflammatory response, favouring the continuance of the infection. Frequently when the glucocorticoids are stopped, there is rebound reaction with worsening of the initial condition. Proper antibiotic therapy usually results in a marked reduction in pruritus within a week and, in some instances, complete resolution of the pruritus is complete within a 3-week period.

Failure to recognize bacterial lesions or to investigate underlying factors, inappropriate antibiotic therapy (wrong antibiotic/dose/inadequate length), and the incorrect use of glucocorticoids are all factors which contribute to the considerable problem which pyoderma causes in practice. There have been several useful articles which address themselves to these problems, and that by Ihrke (1983) is recommended as essential reading.

NEOPLASIA

Some neoplastic conditions – notably mastocytomas and cutaneous lymphocytomas may be pruritic. Diagnosis is made by biopsy and accurate interpretation by a veterinary pathologist. Treatment of pruritic generalized cutaneous neoplasia is best undertaken at a referral centre accustomed to such cases and is not discussed further in this text.

SUMMARY

Many of the problems associated with the pruritic dog arise from symptomatic treatment (particularly with glucocorticoids), without a specific diagnosis being made. In many instances, however, a diagnosis can be made given adequate time and a logical approach.

The role of bacteria as secondary initiators of pruritus continues to be a major problem, and a deeper understanding of the pyodermas will greatly increase therapeutic success in practice. Glucocorticoids, when used rationally, are of major importance in the control of pruritus, but they do not cure skin disease, and they are contraindicated when there is an unresolved superficial or deep pyoderma present.

Most veterinary dermatologists have repeatedly advised against the use of repositol glucocorticoids. In spite of this they continue to be widely used in veterinary practice. Glucocorticoids should be used in the smallest dose, using short-acting drugs such as prednisolone, and on alternate days if long-term use is required. Used in this way side effects from the use of glucocorticoids are minimized. Whenever possible long term use of glucocorticoids should be reserved for those cases in which an accurate diagnosis has been made, e.g. atopy and for which no other therapy is suitable.

REFERENCES AND FURTHER READING

Ihrke, P. J. (1983) In *Current Veterinary Therapy* **VIII** (ed. R. W. Kirk) p. 505. Eastbourne, W. B. Saunders.

Lloyd, D. H. (1985) *British Veterinary Journal* **141**, 463.

Scott, D. W. (1980) In *Current Veterinary Therapy* **VIII** (ed. R. W. Kirk) p. 988. Eastbourne, W. B. Saunders.

Thoday, K. L. (1981) *Veterinary Dermatology Newsletter* **6**, 53.

CHAPTER 17

Helminths of the Dog: Treatment and Control

DENNIS JACOBS

INTRODUCTION

Many species of helminths occur as parasitic inhabitants of dogs in the United Kindom (Table 17.1). Their treatment and control requires a knowledge of each worm's epidemiology and life cycle and an understanding of its susceptibility to the available anthelmintics.

ASCARIDS

Toxocara canis is the commonest helminth of the dog. It occurs in all types of canidae, from the fox to the most pampered pet. It should be assumed that virtually every litter of pups is affected to a greater or lesser degree.

T. canis usually causes little obvious clinical effect, but ill-thrift, pot belly, diarrhoea, vomiting and respiratory signs frequently accompany heavy infections in young pups, and there may be nervous signs and death. This is also the nematode that causes the greatest concern to the general public, because its zoonotic potential has received so much media coverage in recent times.

Table 17.1 Major internal parasites of dogs in the United Kingdom.

Type	Species	Site	Source
Ascarids	*Toxocara canis*	Small intestine	Transplacental/via colostrum and milk/embryonated eggs/paratenic hosts
	Toxascaris leonina	Small intestine	Embryonated eggs/paratenic host
Hookworm	*Uncinaria stenocephala*	Small intestine	Ingestion of infective larvae
Whipworm	*Trichuris vulpis*	Caecum/colon	Ingestion of embryonated egg
Lungworms	*Filaroides osleri*	Bifurcation of trachea	Transfer of larvae in sputum
	Angiostrongylus vasorum	Right ventricle/pulmonary artery	Eating mollusc intermediate host
Tapeworms	*Echinococcus granulosus*	Small intestine	Eating offal with hydatid cysts
	Taenia species	Small intestine	Eating offal or carcase with cysticercus (depending on species)
	Dipylidium caninum	Small intestine	Eating flea/louse with cysticercoid

The life cycle of *T. canis* is complex and the features most important to the understanding of the epidemiology of toxocariasis in the domestic dog are summarized in Fig. 17.1. The eggs are sticky, resistant to most disinfectants and can survive for many months (Figs 17.2 and 17.3).

Adult worms are spontaneously expelled from pups during the early months of life. However, small numbers of egg-laying worms are found in about 10% of adult dogs. Substantial numbers may be found in lactating bitches during the period of perinatal immunosuppression.

Somatic migration will occur if embryonated eggs are

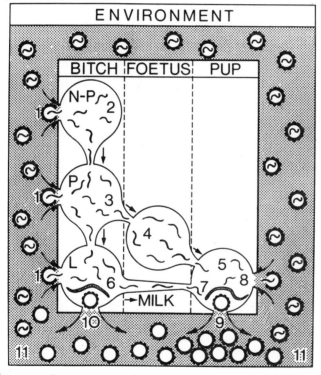

Fig. 17.1 A simplified view of the epidemiology of *Toxocara canis* infections in breeding kennels. NP, non pregnant; P, pregnant; L, lactating. 1. Bitch ingests embryonated eggs from environment. 2. Larvae accumulate in somatic tissues of non pregnant bitch. 3. During pregnancy many larvae cross placenta. 4. In the fetus larvae start migration through liver and lungs. 5. After pup is born larvae continue migration to intestine. 6. In lactating bitch some larvae enter mammary glands. 7. Pup reinfected by larvae in dam's milk. 8. Pup reinfected by embryonated eggs from environment. 9. Adult worms in pup's intestine produce many eggs which are passed into the environment. 10. Some adult worms also establish in intestine of lactating bitch. 11. Epidemiological cycle complete when eggs embryonate after period of weeks.

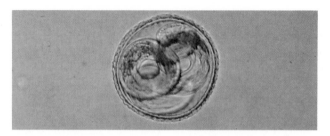

Fig. 17.2
Embryonated *T. canis*
egg: the toxocara
egg is not infective
until it contains a fully
formed larva.

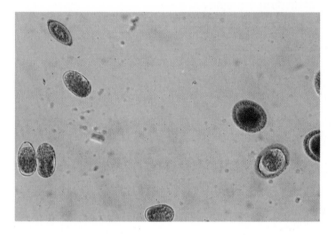

Fig. 17.3
The four types of
nematode egg
commonly seen in
dog faeces: top left
Trichuris species;
bottom left *Uncinaria*
species; centre right
Toxocara species;
bottom right
Toxascaris species.

ingested by man. Normally, human infections are apparently asymptomatic but disease can occur if massive numbers of larvae invade the body (visceral larva migrans) or if one larva comes to rest in the eye (ocular larva migrans).

The former mostly affects children under the age of 3 years and is usually associated with pica, while ocular larva migrans is seen in older children and sometimes adults. Figures (still awaiting official verification) indicate that 30 cases of toxocariasis were reported to the British medical authorities in 1989. However, it is not a notifiable disease and unreported or undiagnosed cases may also have occurred.

In statistical terms the incidence of human disease is very low. Nevertheless it is clearly the responsibility of the veterinary profession to promote worm control as an integral part of responsible pet ownership. This will ensure that the zoonotic risk is kept to an absolute minimum.

The development of *Toxascaris leonina* in the dog or cat is confined to the wall and lumen of the gastrointestinal tract and so there can be no prenatal or transmammary transmission. Infections tend, therefore, to be acquired later in life than in the case of *T. canis* with the highest prevalence occurring in the 6–12-month-old age group.

Migration of *T. leonina* larvae to the body tissues does occur in animals other than the dog or cat (or their feral relatives) following the ingestion of embryonated eggs. There is as yet no evidence to implicate *T. leonina* as a cause of visceral larva migrans.

HOOKWORM

The native hookworm of British dogs is *Uncinaria stenocephala*. The tropical hookworm, *Ancylostoma caninum*, may be found in imported dogs and, rarely, in indigenous animals. Both live in the small intestine and produce typical "strongyle" eggs (Fig. 17.3), those of *U. stenocephala* being marginally longer than those of *A. caninum*. The pathogenesis and epidemiology of the two is quite different.

The tropical hookworm is an avid bloodsucker that can cause a severe anaemia. It is transmitted from bitch to pups via the milk. Infections can also be established by skin penetration or ingestion of larvae.

U. stenocephala does not feed on blood. It does, however, produce diarrhoea and a leakage of protein into the gastrointestinal tract. These effects can retard the growth rate of young dogs. Patent infections are usually only established when the infective larvae are swallowed but skin penetration can provoke a dermatitis, particularly between the toes. Infection is common in sheepdogs, greyhounds and hunt kennels but is rarely seen in household pets.

WHIPWORM

Trichuris vulpis is found principally in the caecum where it lies with its long narrow neck buried in the superficial mucosa.

Infections are often tolerated without apparent ill effect, but weight loss and intermittent diarrhoea may occur.

The double-plugged brown eggs (Fig. 17.3) are easily recognized but are not always present in the faeces of even heavily infected dogs. Embryonation occurs very slowly under British conditions but the eggs can persist in soil for several years. Trichuriasis is usually associated with dogs from kennels which have grass exercise runs.

LUNGWORMS

Filaroides osleri, also known as *Oslerus osleri*, is a slender nematode growing to over 1 cm in length. Tangled groups of worms are found in fibrous nodules projecting into the trachea and bronchi at or near the bifurcation of the trachea. The females intermittently produce embryonated eggs which quickly hatch releasing sluggish larvae which have an "S" shaped tail into the tracheal mucus. The larvae are immediately infective but have a very short life span.

There is little evidence of horizontal transmission taking place between kennel mates. It is thought that the primary route of infection is by the transfer of sputum from bitch to pups during grooming.

Some dogs have no clinical signs of infection. Others develop a persistent non-productive cough with or without weight loss. Sometimes there is severe respiratory distress and death.

Parasitic tracheobronchitis is mainly associated with dogs bred in kennels where *F. osleri* is endemic. It is particularly widespread in greyhounds. Diagnosis poses problems as the larvae are not easy to see in the faeces and are not always present in sputum. Direct visualization by bronchoscopy gives the most reliable diagnosis.

ANGIOSTRONGYLUS

Angiostrongylus vasorum is longer and wider than *F. osleri* and lives in the right ventricle of the heart and in the pulmonary arteries. The eggs are transported to the lungs where the larvae hatch and ascend the respiratory tree. The larvae are more slender, more active and more numerous than those of *F. osleri* and are easily found in faecal samples.

The life cycle will proceed only if the larvae are eaten by a slug (the intermediate host) which is, in turn, consumed by a dog or fox.

The eggs and larvae in the lungs cause a foreign body pneumonia. In addition, the adult worms interfere with the blood clotting mechanism so that severely affected dogs are prone to bruising and haemorrhage. *A. vasorum* is endemic in Ireland and parts of Cornwall but appears to occur only sporadically in other parts of the United Kingdom.

TAPEWORM

ECHINOCOCCUS

Echinococcus granulosus is the tapeworm responsible for hydatidosis in man, the horse and meat animals. It is only a few millimetres long and penetrates deeply into the villi of the small intestine (Fig. 17.4). There may be hundreds or thousands in an affected dog, all releasing gravid segments which are passed with the faeces.

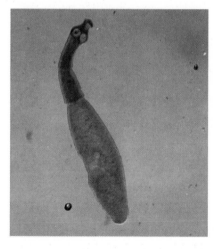

Fig. 17.4
Adult *Echinococcus* species: it is difficult to see at post-mortem examination as it is only a few millimetres long.

The eggs are indistinguishable from those of *Taenia* species. At present the only means of diagnosing infection in a living dog is by sieving the faeces produced by an arecoline purge, but hopefully more sophisticated immunodiagnostic techniques will soon become available. Strict hygiene precautions are necessary when handling possibly infected dogs or faecal material.

Tapeworm eggs are immediately infective and if ingested by a susceptible intermediate host will develop into a hydatid cyst. A fertile cyst will eventually contain thousands of protoscolices, each capable of becoming an adult tapeworm if swallowed by a dog.

There are two strains of *E. granulosus* in the UK, the horse strain which is widely distributed and the sheep strain which is mainly found in parts of Wales, the Pennines and the Western Isles. Circumstantial evidence suggests that the horse strain does not infect man.

TAENIA

Taenia species are large tapeworms which grow to lengths of 0·5–1 m or more. Five species occur in British dogs. Three are acquired by scavenging sheep carcasses or by being fed uncooked or undercooked sheep heads (*T. multiceps*), offal (*T. hydatigena*) or meat (*T. ovis*).

Sheep become infected while grazing pasture contaminated by dog faeces. *T. multiceps* is the cause of acute coenuriasis and classical gid, while the others are responsible for financial losses at the abattoir through tissue condemnations.

The larval form of *T. pisiformis* and *T. serialis* occur in rabbits and other small mammals. The likelihood of a dog acquiring a taenia infection and the species involved thus depends on its diet and how the food is prepared.

DIPYLIDIUM

Dipylidium caninum is the commonest tapeworm of dogs and is easily differentiated from *Taenia* species because the segments, which are often motile when passed, are oval rather than rectangular (Fig. 17.5). If microscopic confirmation is necessary, the eggs of *D. caninum* are always clustered in discrete "packets" (Fig. 17.6), while those of taenia are all separate. *D. caninum* eggs will develop if eaten by a flea larva or, less commonly, the biting louse of the dog. The life cycle is completed when the intermediate host is swallowed.

The adult tapeworm grows up to 50 cm in length and there can be dozens present in the small intestine of a single dog. A *D. caninum* infection can be established in man but this is a rare event.

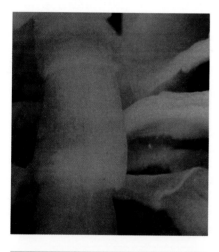

Fig. 17.5
Mature proglottids of taenia: the segments have a rectangular appearance.

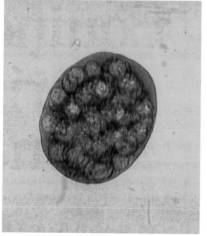

Fig. 17.6
Dipylidium species eggs within an egg capsule teased from a gravid segment.

HEARTWORM

Dirofilaria immitis does not occur in British dogs but may be found in animals imported from warmer regions such as the eastern United States (especially Florida), parts of southern Europe and eastern Australia (especially Queensland).

The presence of these long (up to 30 cm) worms in the heart and pulmonary artery produces progressive cardiovascular disease which often becomes clinically apparent as exercise intolerance. Because of the slow onset of the condition and the prolonged prepatent period of the parasite, infections may not be detected during the statutory quarantine period.

The presence of worms in the anterior vena cava can precipitate an acute syndrome with haemoglobinuria, jaundice and shock. Clinical suspicion of heartworm disease may be confirmed by the demonstration of circulating microfilariae (which have to be differentiated from those of the relatively harmless *Dipetalonema* species) but often supportive radiographic and biochemical evidence is required. The appropriate literature should be consulted for details. A review by Carlisle (1980) provides a very useful introduction to heartworm disease, its control and prophylaxis. A wide range of mosquitoes can act as vector for this parasite.

TREATMENT AND CONTROL

ANTHELMINTICS

The anthelmintics available at the time of writing for use by the veterinary surgeon are listed in Table 17.2. They may be categorized as "broad spectrum" or "narrow spectrum" (Table 17.3).

The former, which include fenbendazole, mebendazole, nitroscanate and oxfendazole, as well as combination products such as that containing febantel, pyrantel and praziquantel, are used where multiple parasitisms are known or suspected to occur. They also have application where the owner gives an ambiguous description of a worm seen to have been passed by the dog. However it should be recognized that none is

Table 17.2 Products currently available for the control of worms in dogs.

Trade name	Presentation	Legal status	Source/supplier	Active principle
Bandit	Suspension	P	Pitman-Moore	oxfendazole
Bayverm	Granules	PML	Bayer	febantel
Coopers Head-to-tail Veterinary Tapeworm Tablets	Tablets	PML	Pitman-Moore	bunamidine
Droncit	Table or injectable	GSL POM	Bayer	praziquantel
Drontal Plus	Tablet	PML	Bayer	febantel/pyrantel/praziquantel
Lopatol	Film-coated tablet	POM	Ciba-Geigy	nitroscanate
Panacur	Suspension, powder or granule	PML	Hoechst	fenbendazole
Strongid for dogs	Paste or suspension	PML	Pfizer	pyrantel
Telmin KH	Tablet	PML	Janssen	mebendazole
Various	Tablet	GSL	various	dichlorophen
Various	Tablet	GSL	various	piperazine
Yomesan	Tablet	PML	Bayer	niclosamide

Table 17.3 Dog wormers: Spectrum of activity claimed by manufacturer.

Product	Tapeworms			Ascarids	Hookworm	Whipworm
	Echinococcus	Taenia	Dipylidium	Toxocara/Toxascaris	Uncinaria/Ancylostoma	Trichuris
dichlorophen	0	+	+	0	0	0
febantel	0	0	0	++	++	++
fenbendazole	0	++	0	++	++	++
mebendazole	+	++	0	++	++	++
niclosamide	0	+	+	0	0	0
nitroscanate	+	++	++	++	++	0
oxfendazole	0	++	++	++	++	++
piperazine	0	0	0	+	1.5 X normal dose	0
praziquantel	++	++	++	0	0	0
pyrantel	0	0	0	++	++	0

Activity rating: ++ excellent, + very good, 0 erratic, poor or ineffective.

effective against all the parasites discussed.

Use of the narrow spectrum products is restricted to situations where a specific diagnosis is made on the basis of the clinical history or a parasitological investigation.

OBJECTIVES

Anthelmintics kill the worms present in the animal at the time of administration. Whether their effect is transient or lasting depends on factors such as opportunities for reinfection and the immune status of the treated dog. Control is therefore a wider concept than treatment and the reason for undertaking chemotherapy must be clearly defined if correct advice is to be given. In general, dogs are dosed for four main purposes:

(1)   To effect a clinical cure when an animal is suffering from parasitic disease. This is the simplest situation implying an accurate diagnosis and the correct choice of therapeutic agent.

(2)   To satisfy the aesthetic requirements of the owner. Consideration of the health of the dog in this case is secondary to the owner's revulsion at the thought of his or her pet having worms. This understandable emotion is sometimes exaggerated to the point of being a psychosis. The veterinary surgeon has to assume an educational and counselling role as well as providing the appropriate form of treatment for the dog.

(3)   To prevent the onset of clinical disease. This approach obviously requires a sound knowledge of the epidemiology of the parasitic infection in question as well as the attributes and limitations of the available anthelmintics.

(4)   To minimize or eliminate the risk of human infection. Depending on circumstances, this may involve the voluntary cooperation of individual owners on an *ad hoc* basis, e.g. for toxocariasis, or a carefully coordinated campaign as in the case of some hydatid control programmes. Again, education is an essential component of the treatment package.

TOXOCARIASIS

Therapeutic treatment

It should be noted that the products listed, when used at the normal dose rate, are effective only against those ascarids lying in the gastrointestinal tract. They do not kill somatic larvae in the tissues of the bitch. Pre-whelping treatments therefore do nothing to hinder transplacental infection of the fetuses.

Similarly, there is no control of larvae migrating through the liver and lungs of puppies. The early appearance of worms after dosing does not necessarily imply that the anthelmintic has not worked but indicates immediate recolonization of the intestine with migrating larvae.

Short-term conventional prophylaxis

Inspection of the life cycle shows that the puppy is exposed to infection from three main sources: transplacental, via the colostrum or milk, and by ingesting embryonated eggs from the environment. If the bitch and litter are kept in contaminated premises or have access to contaminated areas, conventional therapy cannot prevent any of these forms of transmission taking place.

A single dose of anthelmintic will therefore have only transient effect on the intestinal worm burden of the pups and repeat dosing will often be necessary to keep the litter healthy. The frequency and interval of dosing will depend upon the degree of challenge to which the pups are exposed.

Long-term conventional prophylaxis

The life cycle also shows that the ultimate source of infection for both bitch and pups is the embryonated egg. To achieve longer term control with conventional anthelmintic therapy, a clean environment must be created by combining a high standard of hygiene with regular dosing to suppress egg output.

Ideally, treatments should start when the puppies are 2

weeks of age as the first prenatally transmitted worms start producing eggs soon thereafter. Fortnightly dosing is required until only a small risk remains of new patent infections establishing, i.e. around 3 months of age in the majority of dogs.

Treatment at 6 months of age and at yearly intervals thereafter is advisable to deal with the small numbers of adult toxocara that sometimes appear in older dogs.

Recent work at the Cambridge veterinary school has demonstrated that the immunity of the bitch is suppressed during the periparturient period and that it is particularly prone to developing patent infections at this time. This emphasizes the recommendation that bitches should be dosed during lactation to prevent them becoming an additional source of toxocara eggs.

It is recognized that it would in many circumstances be impractical to employ this prophylactic programme in its entirety. Very often a compromise schedule has to be adopted which takes consideration of cost, ease of application of the chosen medicament (especially in smaller breeds) and the commitment of the owner.

It should also be noted that while this form of prophylaxis can reduce worm burdens substantially, it is rare for complete eradication to be achieved. The complexities of the life cycle and the practical problems mentioned above make it difficult to suppress egg production completely. The adhesive coating on the long-lived eggs means that only exceptionally vigorous hygiene can be guaranteed to produce a clean environment.

New methods of prophylaxis

By far the most important source of infection for puppies is the dam. Killing the somatic larvae in the bitch would reduce the worm burden of the pups very substantially. Until recently such an approach was not possible as conventional anthelmintic therapy was ineffective. However, it is now known that fenbendazole given orally at a dose rate of 50 mg/kg per day from day 45–50 or earlier of pregnancy (22–27 days before whelping) to 12–18 days post whelping does have the desired effect. At present this dosage schedule is rather cumbersome but more convenient treatments are likely to be developed in the near future.

This new approach does not obviate the need for good hygiene as reinfection with embryonated eggs has still to be avoided.

OTHER NEMATODES

Effective anthelmintics are available for the treatment of adult hookworm and whipworm infections (Figs 17.7 and 17.8).The latter is, however, notoriously obstinate and a second treatment

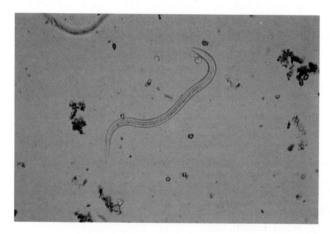

Fig. 17.7
Infective *Uncinaria* species larva from a grass paddock.

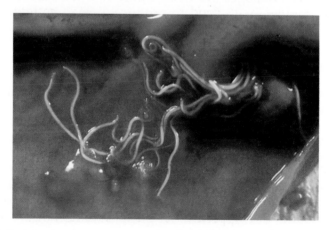

Fig. 17.8 *T. vulpis* adults with their anterior ends buried in the caecal wall.

is sometimes necessary to achieve satisfactory results. If repeat dosing fails to reduce egg counts, it is worthwhile to check that the eggs are in fact those of the whipworm and not those of *Capillaria aerophila*, a parasite of foxes that occasionally becomes endemic in kennels, the eggs of which are very similar in appearance.

It is difficult to prevent reinfection as the main reservoirs of infection for both the hookworm and whipworm are grass exercise paddocks or other often-frequented patches of herbage. Such areas are very difficult to keep clean and a horticultural flame thrower is the only feasible means of destroying the infective stages. An alternative but expensive approach is to provide concrete runs which can be hosed down and scrubbed regularly.

The chemotherapy of parasitic tracheobronchitis must be regarded as still being in the experimental stage. Treatments so far evaluated have either given inconsistent results or have been used on too few animals for recommendations to be given with confidence. Progress to date has been summarized by Clayton (1983) who lists the following materials, none of which has a product licence for use in the dog:

(1)   Levamisole per os at 7.5 mg/kg/day for 10–30 days (this preparation has a low therapeutic index in dogs and has a bitter taste which can be disguised by mixing with a honey base or diluting with dextrose).
(2)   Thiabendazole per os at 64 mg/kg/day divided into two doses and given with food for 23 days (this treatment may cause vomiting).
(3)   Albendazole per os at 25 mg/kg twice daily for 5 days, repeated after a 2-week interval (this compound is not currently recommended for use at this dosage rate in pregnant bitches).
(4)   Fenbendazole per os at 50 mg/kg daily for 7 days, repeated if necessary after 1 week.

The main obstacle to the control of *F. osleri* within a breeding colony is the presence of asymptomatic carriers. Theoretically, it should be possible to identify these by means of bronchoscopy but the author knows of no case in which this principle has been applied in practice. Ethical considerations may preclude this approach in many situations until more reliable treatments are available.

Fortunately the treatment of clinical angiostrongylosis is more straightforward as the condition usually responds to levamisole given subcutaneously on three consecutive days at a dose rate of 10 mg/kg.

TAPEWORMS

Of the several products available for tapeworm control the narrow spectrum compound praziquantel is generally acknowledged to have unsurpassed activity, especially when echinococcus is present.

Bunamidine is also highly effective against the adult *E. granulosus* but activity against the immature forms is incomplete. The prepatent period of *E. granulosus* is about 47 days and so a 6-weekly dosing regimen is required in intensive hydatid control programmes.

Such campaigns are usually based on the following general principles:

(1)   Collection of background information to define local epidemiological patterns and to provide a baseline for assessing progress.

(2)   Registration of all working, hunting and pet dogs in the district.

(3)   Routine treatment of dogs with an appropriate anthelmintic.

(4)   Regular assessment of the level of infection to monitor progress and identify sources of infection.

(5)   An intensive education programme.

(6)   Legislation to ensure that untreated offal is not fed to dogs.

Control of other tapeworms involves chemotherapy followed by strict dietary control in the case of *Taenia* species and the elimination of the flea intermediate host in the case of *Dipylidium* species.

HEARTWORM

Treatment of canine heartworm is complicated and potentially hazardous. Before treatment is attempted, the reader is advised to seek more detailed guidance than can be given in this brief review. Chemotherapy of the condition is divided into four phases:

(1) Symptomatic therapy. This is used to improve the bodily condition of the patient before administration of the potentially toxic anthelmintics.

(2) Destruction of the adult worms. It is desirable that this objective should not be achieved too suddenly as the dead worms are swept into the branches of the pulmonary arteries where they may cause severe lung pathology.

Thiacetarsamide sodium has been widely used to kill adult worms but it is difficult to obtain in the UK. It has to be given with great care and the patient should be hospitalized for the duration of the treatment. Accurate dosage is essential and leakage into surrounding tissues must not occur during intravenous injection. Thiacetarsamide sodium is hepatotoxic and nephrotoxic.

An alternative is the use of levamisole. There appears to be controversy over its reliability for this purpose but Australian workers claim good results with a dosage of 10 mg/kg per os twice daily for 2 weeks. Attention is again drawn to the narrow safety margin associated with this compound in the dog.

(3) Elimination of microfilariae. This objective can be achieved by the use of dithiazanine iodide, but this is unnecessary if levamisole has been used as an adulticide since this treatment also kills the microfilariae.

(4) Prophylaxis. This is unnecessary in the UK but infection or reinfection can be prevented when a patient is transported into an endemic area by the administration of diethylcarbamazine at 5·5 mg/kg every other day throughout the mosquito season. It is important to check that the dog is not microfilaraemic before commencing prophylactic therapy, otherwise a severe allergic reaction can occur. Alternatively, ivermectin can be used at monthly intervals at a dose rate of 6 μg/kg.

ACKNOWLEDGEMENTS

The author thanks Dr M. T. Fox and Mr D. Gunn for their assistance with the design of the life cycle illustration and Dr M. J. Walker for providing most of the colour photographs.

FURTHER READING

Boreham, P. F. L. & Atwell, R. B. (1988) *Dirofilariasis*. Boca Raton, Florida, CRC Press.

Clayton, H. M. (1983) The management and treatment of respiratory infections in small animals. In: Grunsell, C. S. G. & Hill, F. W. G. (eds), *Veterinary Annual*, 23rd edn, p. 254. Bristol, John Wright.

Lloyd, S. (1985) *Toxocara canis*: infection, treatment and control. In Grunsell, C. S. G., Hill, F. W. G. & Rae, M. (eds), *Veterinary Annual*, 25th edn, p. 368. Bristol, John Wright.

CHAPTER 18

Autoimmune Disease

DAVID BENNETT

INTRODUCTION

It was early in the 1900s that a German microbiologist, Paul Ehrlich, introduced the concept of "horror autotoxicus" to express the underlying biological principle that an animal generally does not respond to the chemical groupings in its own body.

Ehrlich speculated that if it did, the body's immune system would injure its own tissues, causing autoimmune disease. It is now known that autoimmunity is a primary cause or a secondary contributor in many well recognized diseases.

Autoimmune disease is characterized by the presence in the blood and, or, tissues, of autoantibodies or autoreactive cells. Autoantibodies are capable of reacting against self components. Autoreactive cells are immunocytes capable of also reacting against self. For a disease to be truly autoimmune, these autoantibodies and autoreactive cells must be involved in the pathogenesis.

THEORIES OF AUTOIMMUNITY

Various suggestions have been made to explain the concept of autoimmune disease. It is probable that there is no one complete explanation and that several mechanisms may operate together in any one particular disease.

SEQUESTERED ANTIGENS

The body's recognition of "self" depends on the establishment of immunological tolerance in the embryo and neonate. The immune system encounters body components at a stage when it is unable to mount an immune response against them and then on subsequent occasions it recognizes these as body constituents and continues not to mount an immune response. However, if these components are sequestered or "hidden" from the immune system in the immature animal (e.g. lens, myelin), or if they develop later in life (e.g. spermatozoa), they would behave as antigens to the competent immune system.

MODIFICATION OF BODY COMPONENTS

Alteration of a body component could result in the establishment of new material foreign to the body or in the unmasking of material hitherto "hidden" from the body. Such modification may result from chemical, physical or biological processes. Examples include drug interactions (by direct haptenic mechanisms or by the formation of immune complexes which adhere to cell membranes), microbial infections, especially the incorporation of viral antigens into cell membranes, and neoplastic changes, causing tumour antigens to appear in the cell surface.

CROSS-REACTIONS

Antigenic determinants on an exogenous antigen may be identical or very similar to those of a body component.

Antibodies produced against the exogenous antigen will cross-react with the body component to produce disease. Encephalitis following rabies vaccination may result from such a reaction initiated by heterologous nervous tissue in the vaccine. Certain drugs may be involved in cross-reactions.

ABNORMAL LYMPHORETICULAR SYSTEM

A spontaneous change in the normal immune system occurs such that the system reacts against self components. This might occur through random mutation leading to the development of harmful clones of immunocytes or by infection or neoplasia of the lymphoid system.

DEFICIENT SUPPRESSOR CELL FUNCTION

Most interest at present is centred on the role of suppressor T-cells in autoimmune disease. Suppressor T-cells are important in controlling the immune system, helping to "switch off" an immune response as required. A deficiency of suppressor cell function could allow an autoimmune response to occur; inherent in this theory is the supposition that autoimmunity is a normal immune response which is always present but kept in check by means of powerful inhibition from suppressor T-cells.

Some support for this theory has been gained by the study of experimental autoimmune encephalomyelitis in laboratory animals. There seem to be two important regions of the myelin protein in explaining the establishment of an autoimmune response.

One of these (the encephalitogenic determinant), when purified and injected into an experimental animal, causes autoimmune disease. The other (the tolerogenic determinant), when injected before the encephalitogenic determinant, will protect the animal against the autoimmune disease, i.e. it creates a state of tolerance to the myelin by stimulating suppressor T-cell function.

Such a scheme may operate in the normal animal i.e. natural self tolerance to myelin being maintained by the release of small amounts of the tolerogenic fraction of the myelin protein, during the normal turnover of myelin. This harmonious state could suddenly be destroyed by the intervention of a triggering agent such as a virus which could mimic the effect of an adjuvant and make the encephalitogenic determinant a powerful antigen, readily able to evoke an autoimmune response overcoming any T-cell suppression.

GENETIC FACTORS

It is thought that animals have a genetic susceptibility to at least certain types of autoimmune disease. Studies in man suggest that people of certain tissue types, i.e. possessing certain histocompatibility antigens are more likely to suffer certain forms of autoimmune disease. Interestingly, the genes which control the histocompatibility antigens are closely related to those which govern the immune system.

HORMONAL FACTORS

Certainly in humans, autoimmune disease appears to be more common in females.

AUTOIMMUNE HAEMOLYTIC ANAEMIA

Autoimmune haemolytic anaemia is a rapidly progressive anaemia associated with autoantibodies against red blood cells and is the commonest cause of haemolytic anaemia in the dog. It may occur in a primary form, the commoner, or secondary to a number of infective, neoplastic or other autoimmune disorders. The disease can occur in either sex (but predominates in females) and in any breed, although the cocker spaniel, poodle, whippet, collie, and Münsterländer breeds seem over-represented. Most are immature dogs or young adults.

There are different forms of autoimmune haemolytic anaemia based on different autoantibody characteristics, as shown in Table 18.1. The autoantibody may be optimally pathogenic at body temperature or at varying temperatures below body heat – the warm antibody and cold antibody types, respectively.

CLINICAL FEATURES

The clinical features vary according to which type of autoantibody is present. The *in vivo* haemolysin and in-saline autoagglutinating forms of autoimmune haemolytic anaemia are the most fulminating: the extravascular destruction or incomplete antibody type is the commonest.

The animals are presented with lethargy and weakness; pale, sometimes jaundiced mucous membranes are obvious. Pyrexia, inappetence, polydipsia, hyperpnoea, tachycardia, vomiting and cardiac murmur are other, less consistent features.

The anaemia of cold non-agglutinating disease is generally seen in cold weather but is usually not an acute or severe problem. The animal may show haemoglobulinuria and icterus in addition to the anaemia. The anaemia of cold haemaggluti-

Table 18.1 Classification of autoimmune haemolytic anaemia in the dog according to antibody type.

Type of disease	Some important characteristics of autoantibody
Intravascular haemolysis (*in vivo* haemolysin)	Warm type; complement activation. Destruction of red blood cells within circulation
Extravascular destruction (incomplete antibody)	Warm type; no or incomplete complement activation. Red blood cells have reduced life span: removed from circulation by spleen, bone marrow and liver
In-saline autoagglutinating	Warm type; causes agglutination of red blood cells *in vitro*
Cold haemagglutinating	Cold type; red blood cells agglutinated in peripheral extremities causing ischaemia of skin
Cold non-agglutinating	Cold type disease classically seen in cold weather

nin disease is similarly seen in cold weather although a more important clinical feature of this disease is skin involvement. The autoantibodies, when activated by a lowered temperature, cause agglutination of red cells within skin capillaries; blood flow is impeded and the skin becomes ischaemic and necrotic. The latter shows as ulcerative, scaly lesions on the extremities, where the temperature is lower, e.g. tips of the ears, tail and feet (Fig. 18.1).

DIFFERENTIAL DIAGNOSIS

The differential diagnosis of autoimmune haemolytic anaemia must include all cases of anaemia in the dog: haemorrhagic, haemolytic and dyshaemopoietic. The anaemia is invariably of a fairly rapid onset which excludes most causes of chronic anaemia. The absence of obvious haemorrhage is a useful aid (see immune-mediated thrombocytopenia).

The presence of a haemolytic anaemia can usually be confirmed by biochemical testing of the blood or by demonstrating haemoglobulinuria and autoimmune haemolytic anaemia is the commonest cause of haemolytic anaemia in the dog.

Certain bacterial infections can cause an acute haemolytic anaemia but are rare. Systemic lupus erythematosus must also be included in the differential diagnosis (see below).

Antibody and complement deposits on red blood cells are

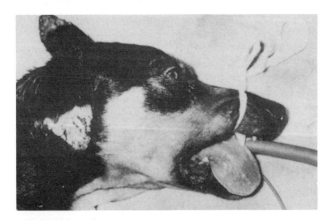

Fig. 18.1
Cold haemagglutinin disease (autoimmune haemolytic anaemia) showing necrosis of the ear tips.

found in a number of disease states, e.g. infections, neoplasia, and in most cases are of little significance. Occasionally they are associated with a secondary autoimmune haemolytic anaemia. Such cases must be identified, since the underlying disease process must be treated.

In the case of skin disease produced by the cold haemagglutinin form of autoimmune haemolytic anaemia, the differential diagnosis includes several skin disorders. Parasitic conditions, especially when the ear tips only are affected, should be eliminated. Cryoglobulinaemia can be associated with similar lesions; these abnormal immunoglobulins "gel" when the temperature is lowered and cause sludging of the capillary blood flow. Cryoglobulinaemia may occur in other immune based diseases, e.g. systemic lupus erythematosus, myeloma. Cutaneous vasculitis of unknown aetiology is another differential diagnosis.

LABORATORY FEATURES

Haematological examination will confirm the anaemia, associated with an erythropenia. The blood smear may show spherocytosis. Leucocytosis is often present although leucopenia is also reported. A degree of thrombocytopenia may be present. Blood bilirubin levels may be increased, particularly the unconjugated type. Bilirubinuria and haemoglobulinuria may be other features. The presence of increased numbers of reticulocytes in the blood is a good prognostic sign, although some cases fail to show red cell regeneration. Blood urea, blood enzymes and blood globulins are often elevated.

Confirmation of the diagnosis depends on showing the presence of red cell autoantibodies and, in some cases complement, on the surface of the patient's erythrocytes. In the case of the in-saline autoagglutination type, a drop of blood on a slide can be observed macroscopically or microscopically for agglutination.

Autoagglutination can be distinguished from rouleaux formation by adding a drop of isotonic saline solution – this will disperse rouleaux formation.

Similarly, cold haemagglutinin disease can be diagnosed by observing autoagglutination on cooling a drop of blood in the refrigerator.

The *in vivo* haemolysin and incomplete antibody types are diagnosed by performing the Coombs' direct antiglobulin test, i.e. producing agglutination of the patient's red cells by the addition of an anti-immunoglobulin G (IgG), anti-IgM and anti-C3 reagent (Fig. 18.2). A commercial Coombs' reagent is available for use in the practice laboratory (Miles Laboratories, Stoke Poges, Slough). The cold non-agglutinin disease can be diagnosed with Coombs' reagent if the test is performed at 4°C.

The indirect Coombs' test, using the patient's serum and red cells from a normal dog, is not totally reliable.

TREATMENT

Large doses of corticosteroids, e.g. prednisolone at a dose rate of 2–4 mg/kg, are indicated; the dose is gradually reduced once clinical improvement has occurred and been maintained for 3–4 weeks. Cyclophosphamide can be used, especially in severe cases.

Blood transfusions should be avoided if possible but if the packed cell volume falls below 0·10 litres/litre, they should be tried. Splenectomy is also advocated in some cases, particularly those that periodically relapse.

Ovariectomy may be done if relapses are related to oestrus. The mortality rate is approximately 1–2%; the majority of cases recover completely although a few will show relapses.

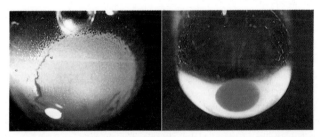

Fig. 18.2 A positive (left) and negative (right) Coombs' test for red cell autoantibodies. The positive tube shows agglutination of red cells, the negative shows a sedimentation "button".

IMMUNE-MEDIATED THROMBOCYTOPENIA

This rare disease is characterized by low numbers of circulating platelets causing a haemorrhagic anaemia. The exact pathogenesis is uncertain. It seems likely that the reticuloendothelial system is responsible for the removal of antibody-coated platelets although complement-mediated lysis is a possibility.

Immune-mediated thrombocytopenia may coexist with autoimmune haemolytic anaemia (Evans's syndrome), and in such cases the thrombocytopenia may not be sufficiently severe to cause clinical signs.

CLINICAL FEATURES

The onset may be sudden and acute resulting from massive haemorrhage, or more chronic associated with ecchymoses or petechial haemorrhages. Epistaxis, melaena, haematuria, easy bruising and subcutaneous haematoma formation may be seen, together with pale mucous membranes (Fig. 18.3). Cocker spaniels seem to have a predisposition to this condition.

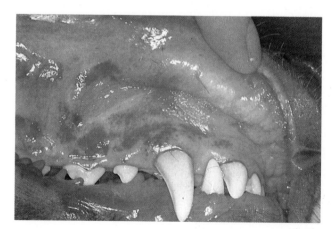

Fig. 18.3
Immune-mediated
thrombocytopenia.
Note the small
haemorrages within
the oral mucous
membrane.

DIFFERENTIAL DIAGNOSIS

The differential diagnosis includes other causes of anaemia (see above), in particular haemorrhagic anaemia. Warfarin poisoning is one of the more important differential diagnoses and often the history is useful in confirming this diagnosis.

However, cases of immune-mediated thrombocytopenia are often diagnosed initially as warfarin poisoning but fail to respond to vitamin K therapy. Haemorrhage associated with surgical or acquired trauma is usually obvious although some cases of immune-mediated thrombocytopenia only become apparent at the time of routine surgery when excessive bleeding is a problem.

Haemorrhage associated with neoplasia, e.g. splenic haemangiosarcomas is another differential diagnosis. Haemophilia in a young dog and haemorrhagic enteritis are others. Certain bacterial infections and toxaemia can cause petechiae and ecchymoses. Systemic lupus erythematosus (see below) should also be considered.

LABORATORY FEATURES

Haematological examination will reveal reduced numbers of platelets. Levels below $2 \times 10^5/mm^3$ are thought to be abnormal in the dog although levels as low as $4 \times 10^4/mm^3$ can be associated with normal clotting. Anaemia can be confirmed, but is variable. A prolonged clot retraction and bleeding time, but with a normal clotting time, also characterize this disease.

The presence of platelet autoantibodies is shown by the PF-3 test; it depends on the acceleration of clotting of plasma caused by the release of PF-3 (platelet factor 3) from damaged platelets. The test is laborious to set up and not completely reliable in the dog. Other tests are available for man but as yet have not been evaluated in the dog.

TREATMENT

Prednisolone is the drug of choice. In severe or refractory cases, vincristine may be given intravenously once a week (dose 1 mg/m^2 of body surface). Transfusions of platelet-rich plasma may be of benefit and splenectomy has been suggested.

SYSTEMIC LUPUS ERYTHEMATOSUS

Systemic lupus erythematosus is a multisystem disease associated with the presence of antinuclear antibodies in the blood. The pathogenesis involves autoimmunity and immune complex hypersensitivity. Autoantibodies against red blood cells, white blood cells and platelets can be present accompanied by the deposition of complexes of nuclear antigen and antinuclear antibody in tissues such as skin, kidney, joints (Fig. 18.4).

Antinuclear antibodies themselves may also have a direct pathogenetic effect. There is some evidence that in systemic lupus erythematosus in the dog there is an underlying viral infection.

The satisfactory diagnosis of this disease is difficult because of the plethora of clinical signs. Three diagnostic criteria are used: (a) there should be involvement of more than one body system; (b) antinuclear antibody should be demonstrated in the blood; (c) the immunopathological features consistent with the clinical involvement should be demonstrable (see Table 8.2). Criteria (a) and (b) should always be satisfied.

Antinuclear antibodies are not present at all stages at significant levels. Repeated laboratory tests are necessary, preferably during the active phase of the disease.

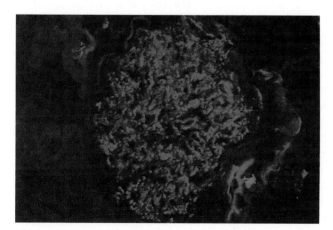

Fig. 18.4
Fluorescence within a glomerulus of the kidney indicating the presence of antibody (antinuclear antibody) in systemic lupus erythematosus. Direct immunofluorescence test, anti-dog IgG, fluorescein isothiocyanate.

Table 18.2 Diagnostic criteria for systemic lupus erythematosus.

Criterion 1	Multisystem involvement, i.e. there should be clinical signs referable to two or more of the following manifestations: polyarthritis, autoimmune haemolytic anaemia, immune-mediated thrombocytopenia, leucopenia, glomerulonephritis, skin disease, central nervous system disease, polymyositis, pyrexia, pleuritis, gastrointestinal disease
Criterion 2	Antinuclear antibodies in the blood
Criterion 3	Immunopathological features consistent with clinical involvement, e.g. autoantibodies against red blood cells, platelets, white blood cells in autoimmune haemolytic anaemia, immune-mediated thrombocytopenia and leucopenia, immunoglobulin and complement deposits in synovium, skin and renal glomeruli with polyarthritis, dermatitis, glomerulonephritis

Criteria 1 and 2 must always be satisfied. All 3 satisfied – definite systemic lupus erythematosus; 1 and 2 only – probable systemic lupus erythematosus.

CLINICAL FEATURES

The most consistent presenting feature is lameness associated with a bilaterally symmetrical polyarthritis. The animal may show just stiffness or be so severely affected that ambulation is impossible. Joints are usually obviously swollen and painful.

Skin lesions are not uncommon but are very variable; they include crusting and scaling with alopecia, generalized pruritus with erythema and eruptions at the mucocutaneous junctions.

Anaemia may be present associated with autoimmune haemolytic anaemia and there may be signs referable to immune-mediated thrombocytopenia. Glomerulonephritis is another possible manifestation of systemic lupus erythematosus and will show clinically as a loss of condition, fluid retention and eventually renal failure and death.

Polymyositis is another feature and is characterized by stiffness and pain. Respiratory signs may be associated with pleuritis. Central nervous system involvement can produce a variety of neurological signs, e.g. ataxia, epilepsy or personality change. Cyclical fever and peripheral lymphadenopathy are other signs. When presented, dogs with systemic lupus erythematosus will often show a combination of clinical signs depending on which manifestations of the disease are present;

more than one body system has to be affected to diagnose systemic lupus erythematosus, although multisystem involvement may occur only over a period of time.

Various breeds can be affected, although the German shepherd and Irish setter seem to predominate. Bitches are more often affected.

DIFFERENTIAL DIAGNOSIS

Since the manifestations of systemic lupus erythematosus are so variable and the clinical features so diverse, the differential diagnosis is extensive. Whenever a dog is presented with disease of more than one body system, systemic lupus erythematosus should be considered, although coincidental, non-related diseases of multiple body systems are always possible.

The commonest cause of polyarthritis in the dog is of the idiopathic (non-autoimmune) type and because most of these appear to be mediated by immune complex hypersensitivity reactions, other body systems can be involved and thus clinically the dogs can look very similar to systemic lupus erythematosus cases.

They differ in the absence of circulating antinuclear antibodies. Bacterial endocarditis can be associated with a polyarthritis and multisystem involvement and its recognition is difficult; such cases are likely to have a heart murmur and may give a positive blood culture.

Degenerative joint disease can affect multiple joints in a single individual but this is not common and radiography and synovial fluid analysis will generally distinguish degenerative and inflammatory joint disease.

LABORATORY FEATURES

If autoimmune haemolytic anaemia or immune-mediated thrombocytopenia are present, the haematological features will be similar to those already described. The Coombs' test and PF-3 test are used for diagnosis. Leucopenia may be present and this can be associated with autoantibodies against white cells. These autoantibodies can be shown by the antiglobulin consumption test.

Blood globulin levels are usually elevated and blood levels of muscle enzymes (creatinine phosphokinase and aldolase) may be increased in cases showing polymyositis. Proteinuria is present in cases with glomerulonephritis and, depending on the severity of renal involvement, blood biochemical examination will reveal impaired renal function.

Synovial fluid analysis from inflamed joints shows elevated white cells (average $3 \times 10^4/mm^3$), the predominant cell of which is usually the polymorph. The fluid is usually discoloured, turbid and of low viscosity with a poor mucin clot. Occasionally lupus erythematosus cells may be found in the fluid.

The identification of antinuclear antibodies in the patient's serum is important. The most useful method is the indirect immunofluorescence test using frozen sections of rat liver as the substrate for nuclear antigens. A titre of 1 : 32 or greater is abnormal in the author's laboratory. The test does give false positive results since antinuclear antibodies are released in many other diseases, especially infections.

Radioimmunoassay techniques, used to detect anti-DNA antibodies (the most specific for systemic lupus erythematosus) are available for the human patient but are not applicable to the dog because of non-specific DNA binding proteins in dogs' sera. The 'LE-cell' test can be used in the dog but is very insensitive. Commercial latex agglutination tests for antinuclear antibody estimations in man are again unsatisfactory for the dog.

Histopathological and immunopathological examinations of biopsies taken from affected tissues are helpful aids to diagnosis. Histological changes may be seen in the skin, glomeruli and synovial membrane. The direct immuno-fluorescence examination of frozen sections of these tissues may show immunoglobulin and complement deposits (representing immune complexes of nuclear antigens, antinuclear antibodies and complement) in the glomeruli, along the basement membrane of the skin and in the synovium. The deposits in the skin may be found in both normal and diseased tissue.

RADIOGRAPHY

Radiography of affected joints will show soft tissue thickening around joints and increased soft tissue density within joints and distension of joint capsules (Fig. 18.5). Obvious destructive changes are absent. Periosteal new bone and secondary osteoarthritic changes are rare. Abdominal and thoracic radiographs may be helpful in certain cases.

TREATMENT

High doses of prednisolone are again indicated. The dose can be gradually reduced once clinical improvement has occurred. Long term maintenance is often required but this can usually be achieved by alternate day therapy. Combinations of prednisolone and cytotoxic drugs (cyclophosphamide or azathioprine) can also be tried.

Removal of circulating immune complexes by a plasmapheresis/immunoadsorption technique has also been documented. The prognosis with systemic lupus erythematosus is

Fig. 18.5
Radiograph of an elbow joint of a Pekingese dog with rheumatoid arthritis. Note the obvious destruction of bone in the humerus and proximal radius (arrows).

guarded since relapses are common and constant medication is often necessary.

DISCOID LUPUS ERYTHEMATOSUS

Lesions in discoid lupus erythematosus are confined to the skin. They are symmetrical and involve the nose, face and ears. Pigment loss, erythema, alopecia and crusting are typical. The lesions are exacerbated by sunlight.

This disease is one of the common causes of so-called 'collie-nose'. The direct immunofluorescence examination of a skin biopsy shows immunoglobulin and complement deposits at the basement membrane (epidermal/dermal junction). A small number of dogs may show circulating antinuclear antibodies. Systemic and local corticosteroids are used in treating this disease and high doses of vitamin E (20 iu/kg, twice a day), have also been advocated. Avoidance of sunlight and the use of ultraviolet screen creams can help.

RHEUMATOID ARTHRITIS

The aetiology of rheumatoid arthritis is unknown although the pathogenesis would seem to involve an immune complex hypersensitivity state in the synovium. These complexes probably involve rheumatoid factor, which is an autoantibody against the dog's own immunoglobulin (IgG).

Rheumatoid arthritis is a chronic progressive inflammatory polyarthropathy which differs from the arthritis seen in systemic lupus erythematosus in that it is a destructive, erosive arthritis. Certain criteria are considered when diagnosing rheumatoid arthritis:

(1)   Morning stiffness
(2)   Pain or tenderness on motion of at least one joint
(3)   Swelling of at least one joint
(4)   Swelling of one other joint within a three month period
(5)   Symmetrical joint swelling
(6)   Subcutaneous nodules

(7) Typical radiographical changes
(8) Rheumatoid factor in the blood
(9) Abnormal synovial fluid
(10) Characteristic histological changes in synovial membrane biopsies
(11) Characteristic histological changes in subcutaneous nodule biopsies.

In order to diagnose 'classical' rheumatoid arthritis, seven of these criteria should be satisfied, and for a 'definite' diagnosis, five should be met. Criteria 1 to 5 should be present for at least six weeks. Of criteria 7, 8 and 10, the three most typical of the disease, two should be present.

CLINICAL FEATURES

Rheumatoid arthritis occurs in a variety of breeds of either sex. The age at onset is variable, with an average of four to six years. Lameness is the main presenting sign although a third of cases also show fever, inappetence and lethargy. The degree of lameness is variable, some dogs being so seriously affected that ambulation is impossible while others show only a generalised stiffness or lameness in a single limb. Joints are generally swollen with some pain and bilateral symmetrical involvement is consistently seen. Ligaments become weakened leading to rupture and joint instability. The latter, together with cartilage and bone destruction, can lead to joint deformity.

DIFFERENTIAL DIAGNOSIS

The differential diagnosis of rheumatoid arthritis includes all other types of polyarthritis (see systemic lupus erythematosus). Rheumatoid arthritis is the commonest cause of a destructive, erosive multiple arthritis. Infective arthritis causes bony destruction but multiple joint involvement, particularly in a bilaterally symmetrical fashion, is exceedingly rare.

D. Bennett

LABORATORY FEATURES

Elevation of the erythrocyte sedimentation rate is common. A mild anaemia is often present and some cases show a leucocytosis. Serum globulin is often elevated and various blood enzyme levels are sometimes increased.

Synovial fluid samples are increased in quantity, turbid and have a poor mucin clot. The viscosity is low and the white cell counts elevated (average $2.6 \times 10^4/\text{mm}^3$), the majority of which are polymorphs. The sample often clots on exposure to air. Ragocytes, i.e. white cells containing cytoplasmic inclusions, thought to be altered globulin, are sometimes seen in the smear.

Rheumatoid factor is detected in the dog's blood by a modified Rose-Waaler test. The reagent is prepared as required, by coating sheep red blood cells with dog antibody of the IgG class. The patient's serum is then mixed with the reagent and if rheumatoid factor is present, it attaches itself to the IgG on the red cells and causes them to agglutinate. The latter can be visualized macroscopically (Fig. 18.6).

The test is quantitated by reacting different dilutions of the serum with the reagent. A titre of 1 : 20 or greater is regarded as abnormal. Rheumatoid factor occurs in almost 80 per cent of dogs with rheumatoid arthritis; however, it also occurs in

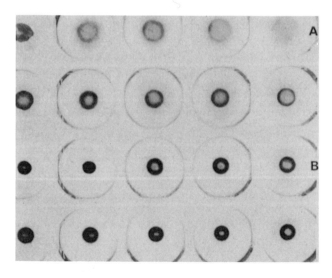

Fig. 18.6
Agglutination plate showing positive (A) and negative (B) results in a modified Rose-Waaler test for the detection of rheumatoid factor in rheumatoid arthritis. The positive result shows agglutination of red cells, the negative shows sedimentation of red cells at all dilutions.

a number of other disease states. Routine hospital tests used for detecting rheumatoid factor in man are not applicable to the dog.

The histopathological features of a synovial membrane biopsy are helpful in the diagnosis of rheumatoid arthritis. Classically the synovium shows villous hypertrophy, proliferation of superficial synovial lining cells, a marked infiltration of chronic inflammatory cells, especially lymphocytes and plasma cells, foci of cell necrosis and the deposition of fibrin (Figs 18.7, 18.8). The direct immunofluorescence examination of a biopsy can show immunoglobulin with antiglobulin activity. Subcutaneous nodules are very rare in canine rheumatoid arthritis but if present can be surgically excised and histologically examined.

RADIOGRAPHIC FEATURES

The classic feature is an erosive destruction of bone. This however, may not be present in early cases, so follow-up X-rays may be required. Other features may be present, such as soft tissue swelling, synovial fluid effusion, luxation/subluxation, deformity, periosteal new bone and secondary osteoarthritic change.

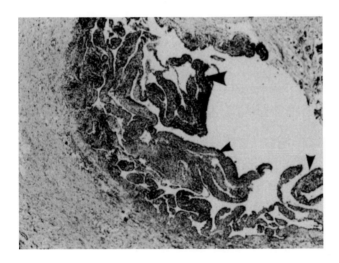

Fig. 18.7
Synovial membrane biopsy from a dog with rheumatoid arthritis. There is villous hypertrophy of the synovium with an obvious inflammatory infiltrate (arrows). Haematoxylin and eosin × 23.

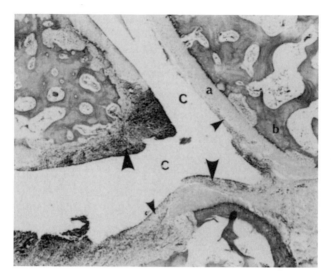

Fig. 18.8
Joint from a dog with rheumatoid arthritis. Note the large areas of articular cartilage which have become replaced with an inflammatory granulation tissue (arrows). a Articular cartilage; b subchondral bone; C joint cavity. Haematoxylin and eosin × 21.

TREATMENT

Treatment is difficult and in most cases may only give slight improvement. Prednisolone gives most relief but constant medication is usually necessary and often the dose has to be increased with time.

Various non-steroidal anti-inflammatory drugs have been used, e.g. aspirin, phenylbutazone, meclofenamic acid and mefenamic acid, but seldom with any real benefit.

Weekly intramuscular injections of gold salts (sodium auro-thiomalate, Myocrisin; May & Baker), sometimes help, particularly if combined with steroid therapy. Such injections are given once a week for six weeks (5 mg to 40 mg, depending on the dog's size); the course can be repeated later.

Levamisole has been used, in an attempt to stimulate suppressor T-cell function, but without success.

Surgical therapy may be indicated in some cases, especially if one joint is considerably more affected than others. Synovectomy, ligament repair, arthrodesis, patellectomy and excision arthroplasty have all been done with limited success.

BULLOUS AUTOIMMUNE SKIN DISEASE

There are several different types of bullous skin disease. They are characterised by the development of bullae and erosions of the skin and, or, mucous membranes and by the presence of circulating and, or, fixed autoantibodies against particular skin components (Table 18.3).

There are two main types of disease: pemphigus, of which there are several different sub-types (vulgaris, foliaceus, vegetans and erythematosus) and bullous pemphigoid. The classic bullae or blisters are seldom seen clinically probably because of the thin epidermis of the dog which rapidly ruptures leaving erosions, ulcerations and crusts.

CLINICAL FEATURES

It can be difficult to distinguish different types of bullous skin disease just by the clinical features, although some signs are more likely with certain of the diseases.

Table 18.3 Diagnostic features of the bullous autoimmune skin diseases.

Disease	Position of bullae	Deposition of immunoglobulin and complement	Antinuclear antibodies in blood
Pemphigus vulgaris	Intraepithelial	Intercellular	Negative
Pemphigus foliaceus	Subcorneal	Intercellular	Negative
Pemphigus erythematosus	Subcorneal	Intercellular Basement membrane	Occasional
Pemphigus vegetans	Intraepithelial	Intercellular	Negative
Bullous pemphigoid	Subepithelial	Basement membrane	Negative

Systemic lupus erythematosus cases show immunoglobulin and complement deposits along basement membrane in normal and diseased skin with antinuclear antibodies in blood

Discoid lupus erythematosus show immunoglobulin and complement deposits along basement membrane in diseased skin, occasionally with antinuclear antibodies in blood

Pemphigus vulgaris

This mainly produces lesions of the oral mucous membranes and the mucocutaneous junctions, especially those of the lips (Fig. 18.9). The nares and skin may be affected. Ulceration and sloughing of the foot pads has been reported and paronychia is another feature. Systemic illness sometimes occurs.

Pemphigus foliaceus

This affects the skin, usually that of the face and ears initially, but can become generalised. Involvement of mucous membranes is not seen and lesions of the mucocutaneous junctions are very rare.

Pemphigus vegetans

This disease is characterised by pustules on the skin of the body and extremities. The pustules rupture and coalesce to form verrucous vegetations. Lesions of the mucosae and

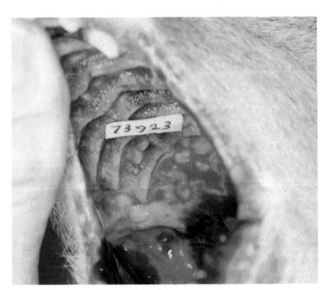

Fig. 18.9
Pemphigus vulgaris.
Note the ulceration of
the palate and the
encrusting of the
mucocutaneous
junction of the lips.

mucocutaneous junctions have not been recorded. Alopecia and pruritus are usual.

Pemphigus erythematosus (Senear-Usher syndrome)

Crusting and exudative lesions occur on the face. The nose is most often affected although lesions can spread to around the eyes or to the ears (Fig. 18.10). This disease can look similar to discoid lupus erythematosus and, indeed, is another cause of 'collie nose'. Leucoderma can occur, resulting in photodermatitis.

Bullous pemphigoid

In the acute form, this disease is very similar to pemphigus vulgaris. There is ulceration, crusting and scarring of the oral mucosae, the mucocutaneous junctions and the skin especially

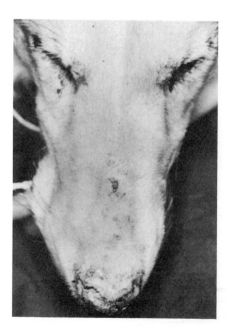

Fig. 18.10
Pemphigus erythematosus in the dog. Note the crusty lesions over the bridge of the nose.

of the face, neck, ears and tail (Fig. 18.11). Animals may be
pyrexic, inappetent and dull and a lymphadenopathy may be
present. Chronic forms are encountered in which the ulceration
is restricted to small areas only.

DIFFERENTIAL DIAGNOSIS

The differential diagnosis of the bullous autoimmune skin
diseases can be difficult especially if it is a type not showing
the more characteristic involvement of the mucocutaneous
junctions and oral mucous membranes.

Parasitic and fungal infections need to be eliminated.
Allergic dermatitis including contact and inhalant allergic
disease and drug eruptions, pyoderma and neoplasia should
be included in the differential list.

Other causes of immune based skin disease should be
included, e.g. systemic lupus erythematosus, discoid lupus
erythematosus, dermatitis herpetiformis and the Vogt-Koyanaghi-Harada syndrome. Subcorneal pustular dermatosis,
impetigo and toxic epidermal necrolysis are possibilities and
epidermolysis bullosa has been reported in young collies.
Other differential diagnoses for cases showing nasal dermatitis
include nasal solar dermatitis, trauma, depigmentation, hyper-

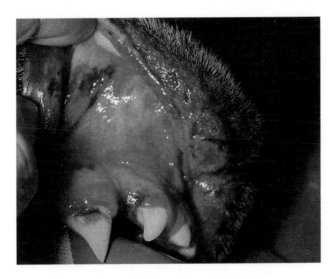

Fig. 18.11
Bullous pemphigoid.
Note the ulceration
and scarring of the
oral mucous
membranes and
involvement of the
lips.

keratosis, zinc-responsive dermatitis and idiopathic nasal dermatitis.

Other causes of oral ulceration should also be considered, e.g. bacterial and mycotic infections, trauma, caustic chemicals, dental disease, chronic uraemia, vitamin deficiencies, neoplasia and idiopathic (necroulcerative) stomatitis.

LABORATORY FEATURES

Confirmation of the diagnosis of bullous autoimmune skin disease and its categorisation depends on the histopathological and immunopathological features of a skin and, or, mucous membrane biopsy (Fig. 18.12). Several biopsies should always be taken, especially of recent lesions, so as to have a good chance of finding the pathognomonic features.

Histologically, the pathologist is searching for areas of separation (cleft formation or blister formation), either within the epithelium (epidermis) or between the epithelium and underlying connective tissue (dermis). With pemphigus vulgaris, the separation occurs low in the epidermis, at the prickle cell/basal cell interface. With pemphigus foliaceus and erythematosus, the separation occurs high, beneath the stratum corneum. With bullous pemphigoid the blister or cleft formation occurs between the epithelium and connective tissue. Intraepidermal abscesses composed almost entirely of eosinophils characterise pemphigus vegetans.

Frozen sections of the skin or mucosal biopsy are examined

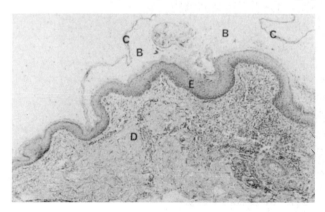

Fig. 18.12
Skin biopsy showing a subcorneal blister (B) as seen in pemphigus foliaceus and erythematosus. C Stratum corneum; D dermis; E epidermis. Haematoxylin and eosin × 34.

D. Bennett

by the direct immunofluorescence test in order to detect immunoglobulin (autoantibody) and complement deposits (Fig. 18.13). Circulating autoantibodies can be detected by the indirect immunofluorescence test but such antibodies seem to occur at very low titres in the dog and are thus difficult to detect. Antibodies occur against the intercellular space material of the epithelium in pemphigus vegetans, foliaceus and vulgaris.

The antibodies are against the basement membrane in bullous pemphigoid (Fig. 18.14). In pemphigus erythematosus there are antibodies against both the intercellular material and

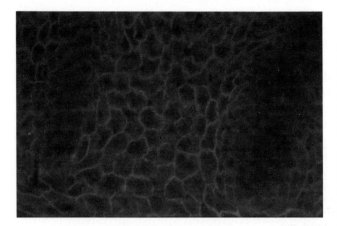

Fig. 18.13
Skin biopsy showing fluorescence of the epithelial intercellular material indicating the presence of skin autoantibodies as found in pemphigus vulgaris, foliaceus and erythematosus. Direct immuno-fluorescence test, anti-dog IgG fluorescein isothiocyanate.

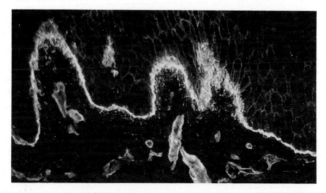

Fig. 18.14 Mucosal biopsy showing fluoresence of the basement membrane indicating the presence of skin autoantibodies as found in bullous pemphigoid and pemphigus erythematosus. Direct immunofluoresence test, anti-dog IgG fluorescein isothiocyanate.

the basement membrane. In addition, some cases also have circulating antinuclear antibodies.

TREATMENT

Large doses of corticosteroids should be given; the dose can be lowered as clinical improvement occurs. However, most animals require constant medication, and some cases are only controlled with very high doses.

A combination of azathioprine (1.5 mg/kg) and prednisolone gives better results. Other cytotoxic drugs have also been used.

Weekly gold injections (1 mg/kg) for two to three months have been used with some success in pemphigus foliaceus. Avoidance of sunlight and, or, the use of topical sun screens or even tattooing may be necessary in dogs with pemphigus erythematosus. The prognosis with these diseases is always guarded; some dogs have died, presumably because of an overwhelming toxaemia.

NODULAR PANNICULITIS

This is a condition characterised by an inflammatory reaction in the subcutaneous fat, producing nodules which liquefy and burst. Although the aetiology is unknown, there is a possibility of an autoimmune reaction against fat. In man, the syndrome is of multiple aetiology. The author has seen the disease in collies and Cairn terriers (Fig. 18.15); dachshunds are said to be prone to the disease.

The animals are presented with subcutaneous nodules and, or, areas of furunculosis or even sloughing of the skin. The lumbar flank area of the body is most often affected. Secondary infection of the skin is common. Combinations of corticosteroids and antibiotics are necessary for treatment. Permanent cure is rare.

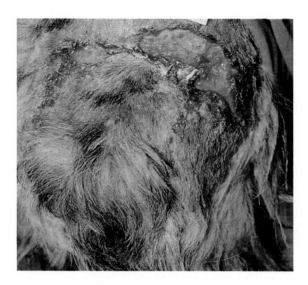

Fig. 18.15
Nodular panniculitis
in a Cairn terrier.
Note the large area
of skin which has
ulcerated.

AUTOIMMUNE THYROIDITIS

Hypothyroidism is commonly diagnosed in veterinary medicine and recently antibodies to thyroglobulin have been demonstrated in some cases. Classically, the thyroid gland shows destruction and infiltration by plasma cells and lymphocytes. Therapy is usually directed at relieving the endocrine deficiency by supplementation with thyroid hormones.

AUTOIMMUNE NEUROLOGICAL DISEASES

A role for autoimmunity has been postulated for a variety of neurological diseases.

DISTEMPER DEMYELINATING ENCEPHALOMYELITIS

The presence of autoantibodies against myelin in cases of distemper demyelination raises the possibility of an autoimmune response, presumably initiated by the distemper virus attack. A variety of neurological signs may be seen. Immuno-suppressive therapy may be of benefit in such cases.

MYASTHENIA GRAVIS

This disease, characterised by excessive muscular weakness and fatiguability is the result of a defect in neuromuscular transmission. Some cases are associated with circulating autoantibodies against acetylcholine receptors. The disease can also be produced experimentally in certain laboratory animals by the injection of purified acetylcholine receptor.

Treatment is mainly with anticholinesterase drugs although thymectomy and immunosuppressive drugs are also used.

CAUDA EQUINA NEURITIS SYNDROME

Antibodies to myeline protein P2 have been shown in some cases of cauda equina neuritis in the horse, but similar studies in two dogs with the syndrome have not shown such antibodies.

PERIPHERAL DEMYELINATING NEUROPATHIES

Some cases have been associated with autoantibodies and autoreactive cells against peripheral myelin.

AUTOIMMUNE OCULAR DISEASES

Sjøgren's syndrome, which is characterised in man by kerato-conjunctivitis sicca ('dry eye') and xerostomia ('dry mouth') and is associated usually with rheumatoid arthritis or systemic lupus erythematosus, has been described in the dog. Autoanti-bodies against salivary and lacrimal tissue are usually present.

Chronic superficial keratitis (corneal pannus) of the German shepherd dog has been associated with autoreactive cells, sensitised to corneal proteins. Some cases of uveitis in the dog have been associated with autoimmunity and a syndrome of severe uveitis and generalised skin depigmentation has been described in Siberian huskies and akitas where there is some evidence of autoreactive cells to melanin (Vogt-Koyanaghi-Harada's syndrome). Autoimmune mechanisms may play a role in the dissolution of lenticular tissue following lens trauma.

OTHER AUTOIMMUNE DISEASES

Nephrotoxic glomerulonephritis, characterised by antibodies against the glomerular basement membrane, has been described in the dog but is very rare. Leucopenia associated with autoantibodies, but not part of the systemic lupus erythematosus complex, has been reported in the dog. Demyelinating encephalomyelitis following rabies vaccination may be caused by an immune reaction against heterologous nervous tissue. Diabetes, Addison's disease (hypoadrenocorticism), pancreatitis, ulcerative colitis, endocardiosis, chronic active hepatitis and polyarteritis) have all been reported in the dog and the role of autoimmunity suggested.

CONCLUSIONS

In recent years, there has been an apparent increase in the incidence of autoimmune disease in the dog. It is difficult to know whether this represents a true increased incidence or just an increased awareness of these diseases coupled with the availability of improved diagnostic tests. The laboratory diagnosis often involves specialised techniques which are only available at certain university departments where a research interest is present. Testing by local hospitals is not recommended since most of the tests used on human patients need considerable modification for veterinary species and indeed some tests are not applicable.

REFERENCES

Bennett, D. (1980) *Physiological Basis of Small Animal Medicine*, Eds A. T. Yoxall and J. F. R. Hird, Blackwell Scientific Publications, Oxford. Chapter 11.

Bennett, D. (1984) *Canine Medicine and Therapeutics*, 2nd edition. Ed E. A. Chandler, Blackwell Scientific Publications, Oxford. Chapter 7.

Bennett, D. (1984) *The Veterinary Annual*, 24th issue. Scientechnia, Bristol.

Halliwell, R. E. W. (1978) *Advances in Veterinary Science and Comparative Medicine* **22**, 221.

CHAPTER 19

Inheritable Defects

MIKE STOCKMAN

INTRODUCTION

Although there has been a considerable expansion of our
knowledge of the inheritance patterns of many canine defects
of recent years, there are still large gaps and research is
necessary before the profession can give breeders the help
they request. In addition, methods by which such defects can
be diagnosed with certainty in the puppy stage are needed
in order that animals can be culled from the breeding plan
before they have reached sexual maturity. Some conditions
are not only inheritable but also congenital, while some
congenital conditions are due solely to accidents during
development and cannot be passed on to successive gener-
ations. Fortunately, many of the defects which are in fact
congenital are either lethal or prevent the sufferer from
breeding. This chapter will deal only with those conditions
which are either known to be inherited or which strongly
suggest that such is the case.

CONDITIONS INVOLVING THE SKELETAL SYSTEM

It is often difficult to draw a distinct line between specific body shapes which appear abnormal but are accepted within breed standards and true skeletal abnormalities. Conditions such as achondroplasia, where the head becomes large but the limbs remain stunted, acromegaly, the excessive enlargement of the extremities, and brachycephalicism, in which the skull is enlarged while the nasal bones and upper jaw are underdeveloped, often resulting in protrusion of the lower jaw, are all seen in dogs which are considered typical of their particular breeds. Breed standards are descriptions of the desirable and breeders and judges must interpret them sensibly. It is the avoidance of excesses which is most important and the stress laid on minor points such as ear-length at the expense of fundamentals such as soundness of movement or temperament serves only to produce dogs which are far removed from the type envisaged by those who composed the original standard.

CERVICAL SPONDYLOPATHY

It is generally accepted that some breeds have cervical vertebrae which possess a greater freedom of movement in relation to each other than normal. As a result the anterior part of one vertebral body tilts dorsally and produces a 'kink' in the spinal cord leading to ataxia.

The condition is most common in the dobermann but has been reported in the great dane and basset hound (Fig. 19.1). Treatment is usually by fixation of the vertebrae concerned by screws driven through one vertebral body into the next (Denny, 1980). More research is required by veterinary surgeons and breed clubs to establish the true picture of inheritance of the condition.

INTERVERTEBRAL DISC PROTRUSION

It is obvious that certain breeds are more prone to protrusion of the discs than others. Denny (1980) refers to the fact that

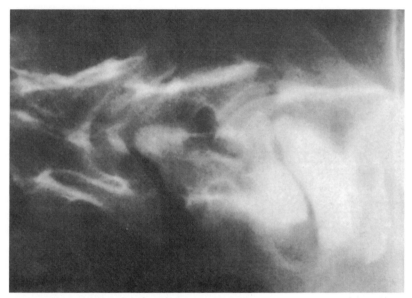

Fig. 19.1 Radiograph showing cervical spondylopathy in a five-year-old great dane.

changes in the composition of the disc are more rapid in the dachshund and the pekingese, and this may well be the reason for the greater incidence of disc protrusion in these breeds (see Fig. 19.2). Treatment, either by conservative methods such as enforced rest and pain relief, or by surgical interference (fenestration) leads in a high percentage of cases to at least acceptable levels of recovery. However, the control of a condition which does not normally manifest itself until well after the breeding life will have been started, is not simple. Breeders must be advised to study the history of those animals which they intend to employ in breeding programmes and avoid those whose close relatives show a high incidence. This is easier said than done as few breeders are keen to advertise the fact that a dog which has been successful in the show ring and at stud has later suffered from any form of paralysis.

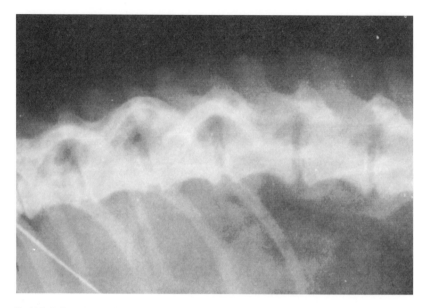

Fig. 19.2 Multiple disc calcifications and prolapse at T12/13 and T13/L1 in a six-year-old dachshund.

ELBOW DYSPLASIA

Of recent years the condition of ununited anconeal process has been reported in several breeds. Denny (1980) records cases in the German shepherd dog and the basset hound, while Corley and others (1968) suggest that the condition is due to the presence of three dominant genes. Hutt (1979) considers however that the condition is polygenic and makes the point that, since surgical correction is apparently relatively simple and effective, breeders must be on their guard against the use of animals that have been physically cured. In view of the fact that there has been an increasing number of reports of the condition in the Irish wolfhound (Fig. 19.3), this warning should be heeded by those who have the veterinary care of kennels concerned with the breed.

HIP DYSPLASIA

As a subject this condition must have been the cause of more papers than any other concerned with inherited disease of the

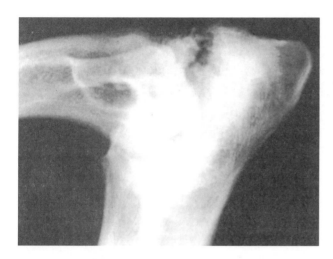

Fig. 19.3
Ununited anconeal
process in a 10-
month-old Irish
wolfhound.

dog. Fortunately, however great the degree of disagreement
on minutiae, all the recognised authorities are in agreement
over the hereditability of the condition. The consensus of
opinion is that while excessive exercise in the immature
puppy is to be avoided and that over-enthusiastic nutrition
is liable to lead to all too rapid weight gain, the basic factor
is inheritable.

For the best part of three decades the BVA and the Kennel
Club have combined in running a scheme to assist breeders
to recognise those of their breeding stock which show radiographic evidence of defects in the structure of the hip. In
those breeds where the problem was only slight it was simple
for breeders to eschew the use of any animal which was even
marginally affected but where there was a grave lack of
breeding stock capable of achieving a 'pass', it was inevitable
that the cognoscenti should demand some indication as to the
degree of 'failure'. It was in this situation that the members
of the German Shepherd Dog League Foundation through the
good offices of Dr Malcolm Willis approached the BVA with
the request that a scheme should be set up with a view to
sponsoring a method of assessing hip structure in such a
fashion that breeders would be able to determine the degree of
abnormality in hip radiography (phenotype) of any specimen
which they were considering using in a breeding programme.
The present scheme, based on a 'score' derived from the

measurements of nine individual factors within the hip joints
is termed the scoring scheme and has produced useful
information. It is employed for all breeds and it is hoped that
it will, with the benefit of veterinary/genetic advice, lead to
a gradual improvement as breeders select against badly
affected (i.e. high-scoring) dogs and bitches. As in the case
of many conditions of inherited origin, the vital decision lies
in the hands of the breeders. Practitioners must recognise the
fact that hip structure is not the only factor on which breeding
policy is to be based and should proffer their advice in such
terms as may be most helpful to their clients on a 'whole-dog'
basis.

OVERSHOT/UNDERSHOT JAW

It is a debatable point whether jaw structure comes within
the remit of a review of inheritable abnormalities of the dog.
The history of those dogs which by fashion now have upper
and lower jaws which are of dissimilar length is based on
requirements which are today no longer applicable. There is
no breed whose breed standard requires that its upper jaw
be longer than its lower, i.e. overshot. There are, however, a
number which suggests some degree of 'undershotness', that
is that the lower jaw should protrude beyond the upper. These
include the bulldog . . . . 'the lower jaw should project
considerably in front of the upper and turn up', the Boston
terrier . . . . 'bite even, or sufficiently undershot to square
muzzle', the French bulldog . . . . 'lower jaw . . . . slightly
undershot and well turned up', the lhasa apso . . . . 'a reverse
scissor bite', the shih tzu . . . . 'mouth level or slightly
underhung', griffon bruxellois . . . . 'mouth slightly undershot
with regular teeth'. The pity is that the wording of such
standards along with that of the boxer . . . . 'is normally
undershot' . . . . appear reasonably moderate whereas, in fact,
show fashion dictates that exaggeration is acceptable.

As a result the dentition of many specimens of the breeds
enumerated leaves a great deal to be desired. The bulldog,
which was designed by selection to be able to breathe
satisfactorily while hanging on to the bull which it was
attacking, was less undershot in its working days than it is
at present; breeders have chosen to stress by selection the

very factors which militate against its chances of survival if it was left to its own devices and not attended by veterinary surgeons capable of coping with the problems of respiratory embarrassment and dystocia peculiar to the breed. The practitioner is faced with the choice of failing to honour the oath which he takes on qualification to act to protect animals within his care from suffering, while realising that his skills may allow the unreputable breeder to maintain undesirable characteristics in his breeding stud.

PATELLAR LUXATION

It is possible to find luxation of the patellar in any breed of dog but cases in the medium and large sizes are usually the result of trauma. The causes of inherited patellar luxation in small breeds such as the miniature poodle, yorkshire terrier, griffon and many others, are several. They include malposition of the anterior tibial tuberosity, insufficient depth of the femoral trochlear groove, and malalignment of the force of contraction of the quadriceps femoris. Treatment is commonly surgical using a variety of techniques to counteract the causal abnormality. Both Hutt (1979) and Foley and others (1979) suggest a polygenic pattern of inheritance and counsel selection against it by avoiding the use of parents of affected dogs, their litter-mates, or any animals where the condition has been surgically corrected.

PATENT MOLERA (FONTANELLE)

The breed standard of the chihuahua talks in terms of a well-rounded skull, 'with or without molera'. In other words the concept of the fetal gap in the bony case surrounding the brain remaining in the adult dog is considered acceptable. Obviously this can result in traumatic damage and should not be encouraged. Those specimens which exhibit the condition should not be used in the breeding programme.

TARSAL SUBLUXATION

Campbell and others (1976) reported on 44 cases of intertarsal subluxation and eight cases of tarso-metatarsal subluxation. Of the former, 22 were in the Shetland sheepdog and 10 in collies and collie crosses. In most of the cases involving Shetland sheepdogs there was no history of trauma and the majority were larger than the breed standard specifies (Fig. 19.4). The authors suggest that high bodyweight combined with thin limb bones may be an important factor in the development of intertarsal subluxation. Most practitioners are accustomed to so-called Shetland sheepdogs being considerably in excess of the breed standard which has a top limit of 15½ inches and it is evident that breeders have difficulty in keeping the breed within this limit.

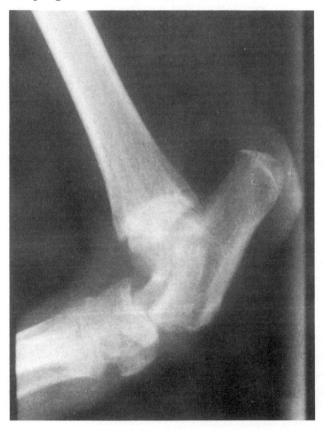

Fig. 19.4
A stressed radiographic view of a fibular/tibular tarsal subluxation in a seven-year-old Shetland sheepdog.

VON PERTHES DISEASE

Von Perthes disease (Legge-Perthe's disease) which is the result of ischaemic necrosis of the femoral head, is seen specifically in smaller breeds such as the West Highland white terrier, and the miniature and toy poodles (Fig. 19.5). In spite of extensive research into the condition including studies in depth of relevant pedigrees, the best that can be said is that there is considerable evidence of a familial predisposition to the condition in such breeds. The advice therefore to breeders must be to avoid known affected animals and their near relatives (Webbon, 1978).

OSTEOCHONDRITIS DISSECANS

This condition is included here simply because veterinary surgeons are seeing more and more cases of osteochondritis dissecans in the larger breeds. The joints affected are the shoulder and elbow and, less frequently, the stifle and hock

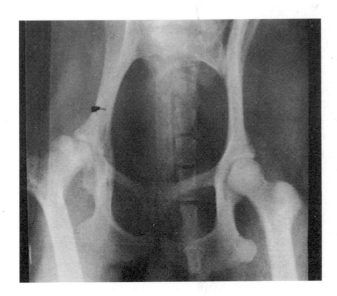

Fig. 19.5
A radiograph to show Von Perthe's disease in the right hip of a nine-month-old Yorkshire terrier.

(Fig. 19.6). The majority of cases occur in animals between four and 10 months of age, (Denny, 1980) but there is no satisfactory evidence to suggest that there is a hereditary component to the aetiology. It is usually seen in well-nourished animals and this has led to the theory that dogs which are growing rapidly and allowed to engage in violent activity including jumping before maturity is achieved, may be subject to traumatic forces which their osseous and cartilaginous tissues are not yet able to withstand. However, many ortho-paedic experts are today tending towards the view that there

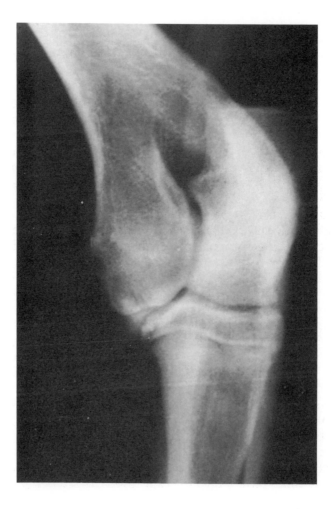

Fig. 19.6
Radiograph of a
seven-month-old
labrador with
osteochondrosis of
the elbow.

is an hereditary element involved and advising against using affected dogs or bitches in a breeding programme.

THE NEURO-MUSCULAR SYSTEM

CHRONIC DEGENERATIVE RADICULOMYELOPATHY

Chronic degenerative radiculomyelopathy (CDRM) is seen reasonably frequently in large breeds with a particularly high incidence in the German shepherd dog.

Affected animals show varying degrees of ataxia and weakness of the hindlegs; they are often presented because the owners have noted a tendency to sway the hindquarters when standing still.

Questioning will reveal that the condition has been in existence for some weeks or months, appears to cause no pain and only interferes in that the dog slips occasionally and finds some difficulty in rising, or in climbing stairs.

Examination will usually show that the dog has difficulty in recovering balance if pushed sharply on one hip or the other from the side. Placing one foot on a sheet of paper and drawing the sheet away to the side causes the dog to 'do the splits', being unable to lift the foot in the normal fashion in order to replace it alongside its pair.

Radiography reveals nothing, although spondylosis deformans or hip dysplasia may be concurrently present in the same animal. Gradual worsening of the signs such as walking on the knuckle of the hind feet, excoriation of the skin on the upper side of the toes and eventual paraplegia with incontinence is inevitable.

Treatment is ineffective although keeping the dog in as light condition as feasible may prolong the period during which it can be kept alive.

CDRM is caused by degeneration of long cord tracts and, although the cause is unknown, the prevalence of the condition in the German shepherd suggests that there is a familial linkage.

GIANT AXONAL NEUROPATHY

Giant axonal neuropathy has been reported in German shepherd dogs on several occasions. Four cases have been reported in dogs which were from two matings of the same parents.

The earliest signs were seen at around 14 months and consisted of slight dragging of the hind toes. Ataxia worsened over the next few months and occasional vomiting of bile and gastric juices was seen. Eventually faecal incontinence, loss or diminution of bark, and megaoesophagous leading to inhalation pneumonia was reported.

The lesion is characterised as multifocal axonal swellings at the ends of motor and sensory tracts in the central nervous system as well as the distal tibial nerve. There is obviously some similarity in the appearance of the disease condition with that seen in CDRM, but the age group affected is greatly different. It is suggested that the condition is inherited as an autosomal recessive trait.

PROGRESSIVE AXONOPATHY

As far as is known at present progressive axonopathy is only seen in the boxer. There is progressive loss of nerve control of the hindlimbs in the three to six month age group and this leads to unsteady gait and a tendency for the hindlimbs to cross when turning.

The lesion is seen in the nerve axon and its medullary sheath, producing a reduction in the number of myelinated fibres and a narrowing of the medullary sheath. This, in turn, leads to degeneration of the fibres. The mode of inheritance is that of a simple recessive gene.

The UK boxer breed council has agreed guidelines for the control of the condition which is widespread throughout the country, although only about 30 cases have been reported to date. The council has issued a pamphlet giving details of the condition, its clinical signs and diagnosis, as well as naming five veterinary surgeons to whom the general practitioner can refer a suspect case for further examination.

The pamphlet also lists dogs and family lines which have been incriminated in the ancestry of clinical cases and gives recommendations to assist breeders in combating the disease.

SCOTTIE CRAMP

Scottie cramp is seen almost exclusively in the Scottish terrier, often as young as two months of age. Certainly, most cases occur in the first 18 months. The onset is precipitated by excitement and exercise and affected animals show stretching of the forelegs and superflexion of the hindlegs. The pathology is unknown. Treatment with diazepam is recommended. The inheritance is generally considered to be an autosomal recessive.

EPILEPSY

The incidence of epilepsy in certain breeds of pedigree dogs has led, at times, to suggestions that there is a definite inherited tendency, and indeed some geneticists have come down in favour of the condition being controlled by an autosomal recessive gene.

It is generally agreed that any animal can suffer an epileptic fit provided the stimulus or insult is sufficient to exceed the threshold. It is reasonable to assume that some dogs have lower threshold values than others and that it is this factor which may be the common thread in a high breed incidence.

The use of the electroencephalograph is of great assistance in arriving at a more accurate diagnosis but a 16 year survey of large numbers of keeshond dogs and bitches which were intended as future breeding stock by breeders in the UK demonstrated that electroencephalographic readings as used in that study had little or no relation to the occurrence of fits and no genetic justification has been found for the segregation of animals with positive and negative readings.

The best advice that can be given in the light of present knowledge of the inherited pattern is that known epileptics should not be used in a breeding programme and the mating responsible should not be repeated.

CEREBELLAR CORTICAL AND EXTRAPYRAMIDAL NUCLEAR ABIOTROPHY

This condition, which leads to a progressive ataxia in young puppies in the Kerry blue terrier, commences by affecting the hindlimb movement but progresses into the forelimbs and eventually affects head movement.

The condition is thought to be one of autosomal recessive inheritance and must be tackled in the same manner as any other recessive condition.

FUCIDOSIS

Fucidosis in the English Springer Spaniel causes a progressive gait abnormality together with mental deterioration. The affected animal becomes progressively more incoordinate. Swallowing, eyesight and hearing may all be affected and the dog may lose weight. The disease is caused by an autosomal recessive gene, but control is made easier for breeders because the "carrier" state can be diagnosed through a blood-test. In the UK, this test is available through Kings College in London and details are obtainable through the English Springer Spaniel Club. The Club is doing its best to carry out its most important function of ensuring the good of the breed.

HAEMOPOIETIC SYSTEM

ABNORMALITIES OF CLOTTING

Several conditions can result in coagulation defects. They can be divided into those which are inherited as sex-linked recessives (haemophilia A and haemophilia B, deficiencies of factors VIII and IX respectively) and those which are autosomal dominants (factor VII deficiency, factor XI deficiency, factor X deficiency, von Willebrand's disease, fibrinogen deficiency, and various platelet function deficiencies).

In the case of the sex-linked recessive conditions, dogs which show the defect should not be used for breeding, while the carrier state could be detected by test-matings. Removal of affected animals from the breeding pool should be all that is required where the trait is dominant or incompletely dominant. In some conditions the heterozygous state can be detected by blood-sampling.

CANINE CYCLIC NEUTROPENIA

Canine cyclic neutropenia has been seen in grey collies and is characterised by a periodic failure of neutrophil production which is normally rapidly fatal in early life, although a few puppies may last to six months or more. The cause is a simple autosomal recessive gene.

CONGENITAL HAEMOLYTIC ANAEMIA

Inherited as an autosomal recessive gene, congenital haemolytic anaemia occurs in the basenji breed. The condition results from pyruvate kinase deficiency and is a severe and progressive anaemia seen in dogs from one to three years of age. Control is aided by the fact that carriers can be detected by the estimation of pyruvate kinase in blood samples.

A second form of congenital haemolytic anaemia is found in the Alaskan malamute but in this breed the condition is characterised by changes in the morphology of the erythrocytes. It is associated with chondrodysplasia and dwarfism reported from the USA by various authors. Again the defect is expressed as an autosomal recessive but there is some evidence to suggest that blood tests may be of assistance in detecting the carrier state.

CARDIOVASCULAR SYSTEM

A number of cardiovascular defects are reported in the dog and several are considered to be congenital. The evidence for any hereditary pattern is somewhat more vague. Certain breeds are considered to have a higher than average incidence with regard to individual defects.

Poodles sampled at random from a survey carried out by the University of Pennsylvania's school of veterinary medicine in 1968 showed an incidence of just over 1 % of patent ductus arteriosus. When affected animals were mated together the incidence in the progeny rose to 82.9 %.

Similar work using affected sires and dams produced a 10-fold increase in the incidence of persistent right aortic arch in German shepherd dogs. It would appear that these two defects and others such as pulmonic stenosis and the tetralogy of Fallot which are all reported in American work, are by no means as common in this country. Certainly the incidence in some strains of American keeshond of the tetralogy of Fallot is a matter for concern but the condition has not been recorded here.

As the conditions listed all cause some degree of cyanosis, dyspnoea and fatigue, their existence would tend to be suspected early in life. Whether the genetic explanation is one of polygenes or not, the use of afflicted dogs and their close relatives for breeding should be avoided.

UROGENITAL SYSTEM

CRYPTORCHIDISM

Total absence of one or both testicles is very rare in the dog but failure of descent from the abdominal cavity into the scrotum is by no means uncommon.

All Kennel Club standards now end with the following clause: 'Note – Male animals should have two apparently normal testicles fully descended into the scrotum'. There was a period during which show regulations forbade the exhibition of unilateral or bilateral cryptorchids but this was altered so that it is now the responsibility of the judge to decide what significance should be attributed to the defect.

Whether or not this should be considered a retrograde step is a subject for discussion; in the United States of America the ban is still in force. The Kennel Club bases its attitude on the fact that while geneticists are generally agreed that there is a genetic nature to the condition there is still doubt as to whether one gene is involved or more.

Willis (1963) considered that banning cryptorchids from the ring merely prevented their exhibition, not their use. If the ban was logical then it should be followed by a ban on the registration of cryptorchid sires. It would seem that the best advice the profession can offer to breeders is that the use of unilateral cryptorchid sires involves an unnecessary risk. It may be as well to avoid using a dog which has sired a cryptorchid.

The necessity for good and extensive record keeping by breed clubs would be of considerable assistance, but it is not a subject which breeders usually discuss enthusiastically when it occurs in their own kennels.

RENAL CORTICAL HYPOPLASIA

A chronic progressive renal disease characterised by the usual classic symptoms of polyuria, polydipsia, vomiting and weight loss has been reported in several breeds such as the elkhound and the English cocker in dogs between three and 18 months of age. Workers at the Small Animal Centre of the Animal Health Trust has been carrying out surveys in collaboration with breeders of cocker spaniels and it is hoped that this work will elucidate some of the answers with regard to the pattern of inheritance.

RENAL DYSPLASIA

A condition has been reported in the soft-coated wheaten terrier for some 20 years. The breed club has worked in conjunction with Dr Nash of Glasgow University and Dr Cattanach. Diagnosis is made from urine and blood samples but the post-mortem examination of the animal's kidneys is highly desirable in order that the actual dysplasia may be determined. Kidneys should preferably be sent to Dr Nash and such examination will be carried out free in arrangement with the Club. It is possible that the condition in the wheaten may be the same as that in renal cortical hypoplasia in the dachshund and the elkhound.

HIGH URIC ACID EXCRETION

It is a well recorded fact that the dalmatian excretes uric acid in excess in its urine. The cause appears to be an autosomal recessive and as the condition occurs in almost all members of the breed, no advice is likely to reduce its incidence.

THE DIGESTIVE TRACT

CLEFT PALATE

Cleft palate has been recorded in a great variety of dogs but is considered in the Bernese mountain dog to be the result of a dominant factor. In most other breeds where the incidence is above average, such as those which are brachycephalic, there must be some suspicion of an hereditary factor but it would be unwise to assume that a recessive gene was the cause.

The defect varies enormously in its degree and in the number of affected pups from any one bitch. The use of lines in which the condition is regularly and extensively observed should be avoided but it would be wrong to discard any bitch which has produced one defective puppy in a single litter.

GINGIVAL HYPERPLASIA

Gingival hyperplasia has been recorded in related boxers but it would be unwise to draw any conclusions from a relatively small number of cases. The breed undoubtedly does have the problem but it is unlikely that any constructive steps could be taken to limit its appearance.

INTESTINAL MALABSORPTION

Most common in German shepherd dogs, intestinal malabsorption has been recorded in several breeds. Some degree of familial tendency is suggested, but there is little evidence available and research work currently in progress may elucidate useful information.

OESOPHAGEAL ACHALASIA

A condition characterised by dilation of the oesophagus has been termed oesophageal achalasia and various authors have assumed that inheritance plays some part in the incidence on the grounds that several related animals have been affected. There is little proof for such an attitude but if a number of cases appeared in an individual kennel or strain, the advice given should be tempered with caution.

COPPER TOXICOSIS

This condition may occur in the Bedlington terrier. Affected animals do not utilise copper correctly and too much builds up in the liver. As a result the dog is poisoned by the metal. The condition is another autosomal recessive and a high proportion of the Bedlington terriers in the UK are either affected or carriers. Diagnosis can be made from estimation of SGPT (Serum glutamic pyruvic transaminase) but in the early stages the SGPT may be normal; it is therefore commonly advised that in order to obtain an early diagnosis to enable decisions about breeding to be made liver biopsy should be undertaken.

The Bedlington Terrier Association produces a most helpful leaflet which is available to all Bedlington owners. This gives information about the condition and deals with the best way to find a puppy which comes from the best stock.

DIABETES MELLITUS

Diabetes mellitus is an endocrine deficiency but with a close metabolic connection with the digestive system.

The fact that the condition is hereditary in man has led to a presumption that the situation is similar in the dog. If this is the case, the pattern of inheritance is far from proven, although a recurring incidence in a particular strain within any breed would, no doubt, lead to a counsel of care.

TRYPSIN DEFICIENCY

One condition affecting the pancreas leads to consideration of another. The excessive incidence of trypsin deficiency as reported in the German shepherd dog may well suggest an hereditary problem but there appears to be little hard fact which can assist veterinary advice to breeders.

PITUITARY DWARFISM

While considering endocrine problems it would seem appropriate to record the occasional appearance of an inherited inability of the anterior lobe of the pituitary gland to secrete a hormone necessary for growth in the German shepherd dog.

Pituitary dwarfism is a rare disease in which animals fail to grow satisfactorily after the first few weeks of life. Apart from a marked failure to grow, affected animals show a puppy-like coat-type along with some signs of symmetrical hair loss. The pattern of inheritance has some evidence for an autosomal recessive gene and avoidance of close relatives of affected animals should help to limit the incidence to a handful of cases as in the present situation.

SENSORY ORGANS

DEAFNESS

There is a considerably increased tendency towards deafness in certain breeds such as the bull terrier, the dalmatian and the sealyham.

In all these there appears to be a connection with lack of pigment, i.e. white or predominantly white.

In these breeds it has been suggested that a recessive gene is involved but the evidence is by no means conclusive and the advice is that affected dogs, including those which are only partially deaf, should not be bred from.

The blue merle gene (affecting coat colour) in such breeds as the Shetland sheepdog, the collie, the dappled dachshund and the harlequin great dane when homozygous appears to be connected with the same tendency.

EAR SHAPE

It may be felt that ear shape should not be included in a list of inherited abnormalities but it is undoubtedly true that the heavily feathered ear flaps of the cocker spaniel, the long leathers of the basset hound and the hairiness of the external canal of the poodle, for example, lead to a high percentage of the ear problems investigated and treated by the average veterinary surgeon in practice because of the poor circulation of air and the retention of wax which results from these structure extremes.

The descriptions within the breed standards which dictate the shape, type and positioning of the pinnae has led to exaggerations as in the case of the basset which requires a flap 'at least' as long as the muzzle; in other words it lays down a minimum without indicating a moderate maximum.

The profession has a duty to urge breeders to consider such factors not only when selecting breeding stock but also when discussing the excellence of individual breed standards.

CATARACT

Although cataract formation in the dog can result from nutritional defects, diabetes mellitus or trauma, or may be congenital in origin, a high proportion of cataracts are hereditary.

K. C. Barnett (personal communication) lists the following breeds as having cases of primary hereditary cataract – Boston terrier, Staffordshire bull terrier, miniature schnauzer, golden retriever, labrador retriever, American cocker, Welsh springer, Afghan, old English sheepdog and German shepherd dog.

There is considerable debate between different authorities as to whether the mode of inheritance is dominant or recessive and, indeed, both types are found.

Secondary cataract is often found in dogs which have already shown generalized progressive retinal atrophy as in miniature and toy poodles. The BVA/KC schemes which have been in existence for many years have helped a great number of breeders in reducing the incidence of hereditary cataract. Unfortunately, it is not possible to give a permanent certificate of clearance from the condition until after the normal age for commencing breeding operations. Nevertheless the scheme remains the most effective method of control and conscientious breeders have made much use of it.

COLLIE EYE ANOMALY

The condition of collie eye anomaly is seen in rough and smooth collies, Shetland sheepdogs and, more recently, the border collie. The lesions are so varied that there has been some difficulty in arriving at consistent agreement over diagnosis among the acknowledged experts.

The condition is both inherited and congenital; it can be diagnosed at a very early age which means the evidence will be detectable before the normal time for selling. The examination of those retained for breeding can be repeated later as a safeguard.

It is widely considered that the genetic influence is an autosomal recessive but Hutt (1979) does not entirely accept this view. He suggests that the expression of the defect is typical of polygenic inheritance and cites work of K. C. Barnett which points, in the sheltie, to a connection between the change in head shape in the breed to the narrower skull of the rough collie and the emergence of collie eye anomaly in the breed. Certainly, the incidence in both collies and shelties is alarmingly high and avoidance of affected dogs in breeding lines in almost all strains is extremely difficult.

CORNEAL DERMOID

Corneal dermoid condition has been reported most often in the German shepherd dog but little is known about its inheritance pattern if, indeed, it is hereditary.

CORNEAL DYSTROPHY (CORNEAL LIPIDOSIS)

Seen most frequently in the rough collie, the shelties, the golden retriever, the German shepherd and the Afghan, corneal dystrophy is usually non-progressive and at times self-eliminating; as such its inherited nature, if any, is of little significance.

DISTICHIASIS

The presence of extra hairs sprouting from the margin of the eye lid in such a way as to cause irritation of the cornea with excess lacrimation is reported by Barnett (loc cit) to be the most common hereditary eye abnormality. He records it particularly in the sheltie, cocker, pekingese, poodle (miniature and toy) and miniature long-haired dachshund, but it can occur in a great variety of breeds.

Foley and others (1979) state that the cause has been reported as an autosomal dominant gene with incomplete penetrance but appear unconvinced. They do, however, suggest selecting against dogs showing the trait.

ENTROPION

Entropion, the turning in of the eyelid, is common in a great number of breeds but particularly in the chow chow, the cocker, and the golden and labrador retrievers. It has been suggested that the genetic pattern is that of an autosomal dominant.

In some breeds, looseness of the skin on the head (chow, St Bernard and bloodhound) probably plays a part and the wording of some standards appears to encourage this.

While surgical correction of the condition is both simple and successful many dogs, whose appearance has been altered, are seen in the show ring in spite of the Kennel Club's regulations about exhibition of dogs so treated.

The practitioner is placed in a difficult position as it is his duty to relieve suffering which must include that caused by entropion and yet he knows that many dogs so corrected will be exhibited.

It is undoubtedly time that the Kennel Club made definite pronouncements in order to counteract this unsatisfactory state of affairs. There will be little or no improvement in, for instance, chow circles until the nettle is firmly grasped.

ECTROPION

The turned out lower lid, ectropion, is commonly seen in the basset hound, the St Bernard, the bloodhound and several other breeds. As it usually results in inflammation of the lower conjunctival sac it is a defect which should, if possible, be eliminated but where breed standards encourage a certain amount of 'haw' to be visible it is difficult to discourage breeders from conforming to the 'blue-print'. Once again the worst affected should be avoided as breeding stock.

EVERSION OF MEMBRANA NICTITANS

Breeds such as the German shepherd tend on occasion to suffer from a defect in which the third eyelid curls forward like a scroll. It may be advisable to avoid breeding from such dogs.

GLAUCOMA

Barnett (personal communication) lists among those breeds which show primary glaucoma the American cocker, the cocker, the springers, the beagle and the basset along with the smaller types of poodle.

It would appear that the hereditary pattern is not clear but, presumably, affected animals and their close relatives should not be bred from.

HEMERALOPIA

The Alaskan malamute is the unanimous choice of all authorities when describing hemeralopia (day blindess) which results in blindness in bright light, although vision is retained in dim light. The miniature poodle has also been incriminated. In the malamute the cause is reported as an autosomal recessive gene and the appropriate action requires to be taken in affected strains.

LENS LUXATION

Spontaneous luxation of the lens occurs primarily in certain terrier breeds. The wire-haired fox terriers, its smooth counterpart, the sealyham, the Tibetan terrier and the Jack Russell are all more than normally susceptible.

Although earlier authors have not been definite as to the hereditary pattern, Willis and others (1979) consider that the evidence within the Tibetan terrier breed, which has taken great pains to evaluate its knowledge of the condition, overwhelmingly indicates a simple autosomal recessive gene.

Unfortunately, the condition does not usually manifest itself until after breeding age has been reached. The Tibetan Terrier Association provides its members with a booklet on the subject with recommendations to avoid known affected and carrier dogs and bitches, a sentiment for which they should be praised.

MICROPHTHALMIA

Double merle (affecting coat colour) matings in the Shetland sheepdog which can lead to white puppies appears to produce an occasional microphthalmic puppy. As merle to merle matings are not usually encouraged in any of the appropriate breeds, the event should not happen.

PERSISTENT PUPILLARY MEMBRANE

Reported universally in the basenji by various authors, persistent pupillary membrane is a failure of regression of a structure present in the fetal eye. It rarely causes serious eye defects, as far as vision goes.

Barnett records the condition in the Welsh corgi (Pembroke), long-haired miniature dachshund and the cocker. Hutt (1979) mentions that it probably has a genetic origin, Foley and others (1979) report a suggestion that a dominant gene is incriminated, as does Startup (1969).

PROGRESSIVE RETINAL ATROPHY

Progressive retinal atrophy (PRA) must be the best known of all inheritable canine defects as a result of the work carried out by W. Rasbridge and the late S. J. F. Hodgman in the Irish setter. As a result of persistent campaigning on Rasbridge's part, the Kennel Club was persuaded to refuse the registration of Irish setters unless the parents had been test-mated to eliminate any possibility of the carrier state.

The work is an example to all breeders faced with any form of inherited problem. The early diagnosis which was possible, though, made the technique easier than is the case in many inherited conditions of the dog.

Two forms of PRA occur – generalised and central. Generalised PRA occurs in the Irish setter, the miniature and toy poodles, the Tibetan terrier, the cocker, the miniature long-haired dachshund and the elkhound.

The central type is found in the labrador and golden retrievers, the border collie and the briard. Early diagnosis with the aid of an electroretinogram has made control considerably easier of recent years.

Some forms of central PRA are considered to be controlled by a dominant gene and this presumably makes the control easier. However, most breeds show a recessive gene and, therefore, while elimination of affected dogs will reduce the incidence of the condition considerably, nothing short of ruthless test-mating has any true prospect of total elimination.

The briard breeders are making a massive effort in a survey aided by Dr Peter Bedford of the Royal Veterinary College.

RETINAL DYSPLASIA

Retinal dysplasia usually involves complete detachment of the retina and is seen in the labrador, the sealyham and the Bedlington terrier.

Of recent years, Barnett has reported it in the English springer spaniel and attempts by mass survey are being made to control the condition. Once again the condition is reported as a recessive gene.

TRICHIASIS

Facial hair, usually in the form of eyelashes arising from the normal area but growing in the wrong direction, may well interfere with and irritate the cornea. The condition is seen most frequently in the pekingese and constitutes yet another good reason for breeders to attempt to avoid some of the structural excesses which have for decades bedevilled the breed. Grossly afflicted dogs should be removed from the breeding pool.

THE SKIN

CUTANEOUS ASTHENIA

Some breeds of dog suffer on occasion from an abnormally fragile skin which tears easily, resulting in large wounds. Affected breeds are reported as including the springer, the beagle and the Manchester terrier. The hereditary factor is said to be an autosomal dominant and the control should be relatively straightforward.

DERMOID SINUS

The Rhodesian ridgeback earns its name from the curious distinguishing formation of a ridge of hairs on the back which grow in the opposite direction to the rest of the hair.

The dermoid sinuses or cysts occur either just in front of or behind the ridge and not in the ridge itself. Since the sinuses tend, eventually, to become infected they are usually removed surgically.

The genetic basis is by no means clear; different authorities have suggested dominance with incomplete penetrance and alternatively polygenes.

Refraining from the use of affected dogs in a breeding programme reduces the incidence considerably but only test-mating will reveal the symptomless carrier.

SEBORRHOEA

Some breeds of dog appear to have a higher than average tendency to chronic attacks of seborrhoea; these appear to include the English setter and the West Highland terrier. While there is presumably a familial tendency, there is no true evidence to support a genetic basis and any control measures must be left in the hands of the breeder and his veterinary adviser.

In common with other such disadvantageous characteristics, a breed's popularity can be adversely affected and it is good commonsense to try to eliminate those strains which produce the worst affected specimens if such can be reliably identified. This may be far from easy to accomplish.

VARIOUS CONDITIONS

UMBILICAL AND INGUINAL HERNIAS

Many strains in several breeds have been reported as showing a high incidence of both types of hernia. In the case of the umbilical variety, it is common to find small hernias containing only a minimal amount of omental fat soon after birth; many of these either shrivel and disappear with maturity or remain small and insignificant throughout adulthood.

Unless a number of larger hernias are found in a particular strain, it is probably unnecessary to take any action in order to reduce the incidence. Inguinal hernias tend to be larger and therefore of greater significance. Animals with either such hernias themselves or those which have produced herniated offspring would be best eliminated from the breeding pool.

PITUITARY DWARFISM

The German shepherd dog demonstrates an inherited inability to produce in the anterior pituitary a growth promoting hormone. Affected dogs are stunted to differing degrees but all are patently greatly undersized. The evidence suggests that the basis is that of an autosomal recessive and the appropriate steps should be taken to achieve control.

LARYNGEAL PARALYSIS

A form of laryngeal paralysis has been reported in Afghan hounds and suggestions have been made to the effect that too great a concentration of the blood of one particularly eminent sire was responsible for the appearance of the defect in several dogs some years ago. Recently the incidence seems to have fallen dramatically but it would be wise to be on the look-out for the defect in the breed.

TEMPERAMENT

The whole question of breed temperament is extremely difficult. Obviously it would be unreasonable to expect the same type of behavioural patterns in such diverse breeds as the Siberian husky, the pekingese, the labrador retriever and the Welsh corgi.

In an era in which the great majority of pups of any breed will end up as pets, it is essential that the aggressive or treacherous tendencies are stamped out as soon and as completely as possible.

It may well be debatable whether some of the recently imported working guard and sheepdogs from Europe are suited to modern housing and exercise facilities; possibly the devotees of such breeds should reconsider the number of litters which they produce in view of the size of those litters and the inevitable surplus which will be seeking homes on the pet market.

There is evidence that there is an element of inheritance in temperament but it would be unwise to ignore the influence of environment in the form of handling of varying standards.

The veterinary surgeon has a responsibility for counselling his breeder clientele on all matters of policy which may affect adversely the standard of progeny produced. This applies, not least, in pointing out the dangers of using as brood bitches and stud dogs animals which cannot be trusted to behave in a civilised manner.

Even those who breed purely for the guard dog market have a duty to supply animals which can be controlled effectively and the ravaging savage which is sometimes used has no place in their kennels.

Equally, the fact that some of the smaller breeds do not inflict serious wounds when they bite is no excuse for some of the highly doubtful temperaments seen in some toy breeds.

Whether or not the subject of temperament has a true place in an article such as this, it nevertheless remains a fact that the veterinary surgeon should be as concerned with this area as in dealing with the avoidance of physical abnormality.

ACKNOWLEDGEMENTS

All the radiographs printed in this chapter were kindly supplied by Dr Gary Clayton Jones of the Royal Veterinary College, London.

REFERENCES AND FURTHER READING

AHT Publications (1983) *Hereditary Eye Abnormalities in the Dog*. Newmarket, Animal Health Trust.

Campbell, J. R., Bennett, D. & Lee, R. (1976) *Journal of Small Animal Practice* **17**, 427.

Corley, E. A., Sutherland, G. & Carlson, W. D. (1968) *Journal of the American Veterinary Medical Association* **153**, 543.

Denny, H. (1980) *Guide to Canine Orthopaedic Surgery*. Oxford, Blackwells.

Foley, C. W., Lasler, J. F. & Osweiler, G. D. (1979) *Abnormalities of Companion Animals*. Iowa State University Press, USA.

Hodgman, F. F. J. (1963) *Journal of Small Animal Practice* **4**, 447.

Hutt, F. B. (1979) *Genetics for Dog Breeders*. W. H. Freeman and Co, London.

Startup, F. G. (1969) *Disease of the Canine Eye*. London, Baillière Tindall.

Webbon, P. M. (1978) *Journal of Small Animal Practice* **19**, 729.

Willis, M. B. (1963) *Journal of Small Animal Practice* **4**, 469.

Willis, M. B., Curtis, R., Barnett, K. C. & Tempest, W. N. (1979) *Veterinary Record* **104**, 409.

Index